Southern Black Women and Their Struggle for Freedom during the Civil War and Reconstruction

This rich and innovative collection explores the ways in which Black women, from diverse regions of the American South, employed various forms of resistance and survival strategies to navigate one of the most tumultuous periods in American history – the Civil War and Reconstruction era. The essays included shed new light on individual narratives and case studies of women in war and freedom, revealing that Black women recognized they had to make their own freedom, and illustrating how that influenced their postwar political, social, and economic lives. Black women and children are examined as self-liberators, as contributors to the family economy during the war, and as widows who relied on kinship and community solidarity. Expanding and deepening our understanding of the various ways Black women seized wartime opportunities and made powerful claims on citizenship, this volume highlights the complexity of their wartime and postwar experiences, and provides important insight into the contested spaces they occupied.

Karen Cook Bell is Professor of History and the Wilson H. Elkins Endowed Professor at Bowie State University, Maryland. Her book *Running from Bondage: Enslaved Women and Their Remarkable Fight for Freedom in Revolutionary America* won the Afro-American Historical and Genealogical Society International Book Award in 2022.

Southern Black Women and Their Struggle for Freedom during the Civil War and Reconstruction

Edited by

KAREN COOK BELL

Bowie State University

Shaftesbury Road, Cambridge CB2 8EA, United Kingdom

One Liberty Plaza, 20th Floor, New York, NY 10006, USA

477 Williamstown Road, Port Melbourne, VIC 3207, Australia

314–321, 3rd Floor, Plot 3, Splendor Forum, Jasola District Centre, New Delhi – 110025, India

103 Penang Road, #05–06/07, Visioncrest Commercial, Singapore 238467

Cambridge University Press is part of Cambridge University Press & Assessment, a department of the University of Cambridge.

We share the University's mission to contribute to society through the pursuit of education, learning and research at the highest international levels of excellence.

www.cambridge.org
Information on this title: www.cambridge.org/9781316514757
DOI: 10.1017/9781009090803

First published 2024

A catalogue record for this publication is available from the British Library

Library of Congress Cataloging-in-Publication Data
NAMES: Bell, Karen Cook, editor.
TITLE: Southern black women and their struggle for freedom during the Civil War and Reconstruction / edited by Karen Cook Bell.
DESCRIPTION: Cambridge, United Kingdom ; New York, NY : Cambridge University Press, 2024. | Includes bibliographical references and index.
IDENTIFIERS: LCCN 2023037163 | ISBN 9781316514757 (hardback) | ISBN 9781009090803 (ebook)
SUBJECTS: LCSH: African American women – Southern States – History – 19th century. | African American women – Southern States – Social conditions – 19th century. | African American women – Employment – Southern States – History – 19th century. | United States – History – Civil War, 1861–1865 – African Americans. | United States – History – Civil War, 1861–1865 – Women. | Reconstruction (U.S. history, 1865–1877) – Social aspects. | Southern States – Social conditions – 19th century.
CLASSIFICATION: LCC E185.86 .S678 2024 |
DDC 908.996/07307509034–dc23/eng/20230907
LC record available at https://lccn.loc.gov/2023037163

ISBN 978-1-316-51475-7 Hardback
ISBN 978-1-009-08745-2 Paperback

Dedicated to my mother Mable Thomas Cook

Contents

Figures

Tables

Contributors

Karen Cook Bell is Professor of History at Bowie State University in Bowie, Maryland. She is the University System of Maryland Wilson H. Elkins Professor. Her areas of specialization include slavery, the Civil War and Reconstruction, and women's history. Her scholarship has appeared in the *Journal of African American History; Georgia Historical Quarterly; Passport; U.S. West-Africa: Interaction and Relations* (2008); *Before Obama: A Reappraisal of Black Reconstruction Era* (2012); *Converging Identities: Blackness in the Contemporary Diaspora* (2013); and *Slavery and Freedom in Savannah* (2014). She has published *Claiming Freedom: Race, Kinship, and Land in Nineteenth Century Georgia* (University of South Carolina Press, 2018), which won the Georgia Board of Regents Excellence in Research Award; and *Running from Bondage: Enslaved Women and Their Remarkable Fight for Freedom in Revolutionary America* (Cambridge University Press, 2021), which received Honorable Mention for the ABWH Letitia Woods Brown Memorial Book Prize for Best Book in African American Women's History. She is a former AAUW Dissertation Fellow.

Brandi C. Brimmer is the Morehead-Cain Associate Professor of African, African American, and Diaspora Studies at the University of North Carolina, Chapel Hill. She is the author of *Claiming Union Widowhood: Race, Respectability, and Poverty in the Post-Emancipation South* (Duke University Press, 2020), which received Honorable Mention for the ABWH Letitia Woods Brown Memorial Book Prize for Best Book in African American Women's History. Prior to joining the faculty at UNCH-CH, she taught at Morgan State University and Spelman College.

Brimmer has received numerous awards and fellowships for her research. These include a research grant from the Institute of American Cultures at UCLA, an Archie K. Miller Fellowship from the North Caroliniana Society, a Mary Lily research grant from the Sallie Bingham Research Center at Duke University, and a postdoctoral fellowship from the Ford Foundation. Brimmer's articles have appeared in the *Journal of the Civil War Era and the Journal of Southern History*.

Katherine Chilton is Lecturer at San Jose State University. Her research focuses on urban slavery and emancipation in the District of Columbia, particularly the experience of women and their interactions with the Freedmen's Bureau. Her publications include "American Slavery and Gender," a chapter in the historiographic volume *Slavery: Interpreting American History* edited by Aaron Astor and Thomas Buchanan (Kent State University Press) and "Beyond Big Data: Teaching Introductory U.S. History in the Age of Student Success," an article coauthored with Bridget Jones, Christopher Endy, and Brad Jones, published in the *Journal of American History* in March 2020.

Kaisha Esty is Assistant Professor of History at Wesleyan College. She is a historian of slavery and its aftermath, sexuality, empire, and Black womanhood in the nineteenth century. Her current book project is titled "Weaponizing Virtue: Black Women and Intimate Resistance in the Age of U.S. Imperial Expansion." Her research has been supported by organizations including the Arts and Humanities Research Council, the Andrew Mellon Fund, the Warren and Beatrice Susman Fellowship, the American Historical Association, and the African American Intellectual History Society. Dr. Esty completed her BA and Masters in American Studies at the University of Nottingham. She holds a PhD in African American and Women's and Gender History from Rutgers University.

Crystal Feimster (PhD, Princeton University, 2000) is Associate Professor of African American Studies, History and American Studies at Yale University. Feimster's academic focus is racial and sexual violence; currently, she is completing a project on rape during the American Civil War. Her book *Southern Horrors: Women and the Politics of Rape and Lynching* focuses on two women journalists, Ida B. Wells, who campaigned against lynching, and Rebecca Latimer Felton, who urged White men to prove their manhood by lynching Black men accused of raping White women.

Hilary Green is the James B. Duke Professor of Africana Studies and History at Davidson College. She earned her Ph.D. in History from the

University of North Carolina at Chapel Hill in 2010. She is the author of *Educational Reconstruction: African American Schools in the Urban South, 1865–1890* (Fordham University Press, 2016). She has developed the Hallowed Grounds Tour and Project that explores slavery, the experiences of enslaved laborers and memory at the University of Alabama. She is currently developing a book manuscript on how everyday African Americans remembered and commemorated the Civil War and a document reader with Kevin Levin exploring the Confederate Monument debates.

Felicia Jamison is Assistant Professor of History at the University of Louisville. Her research focuses on the lives and experiences of nineteenth- and twentieth-century African Americans who lived in the rural South. She is currently working on a monograph that analyzes the strategies southern Black women used to accumulate property during slavery and purchase land during the late nineteenth and early twentieth centuries. Jamison received her PhD at the University of Massachusetts Amherst. Additionally, she was a President's Postdoctoral Fellow in the History Department at the University of Maryland College Park.

Kelly Houston Jones is Associate Professor of History at Arkansas Tech University. She is author of *A Weary Land: Slavery on the Ground in Arkansas* (2021) and several essays concerning slavery, women, and the Civil War era appearing in *Agricultural History*, the *Arkansas Historical Quarterly*, and *Arkansas Women: Their Lives and Times* (2018), among other volumes.

Arlisha R. Norwood is Assistant Professor of History at the University of Maryland–Eastern Shore. Her research examines the experiences of single African American women in Virginia in the Civil War and post–Civil War era. She has produced several publications on the topic including "A Father in My Affliction: African American Women and Their Wartime Letters to President Lincoln" featured in *Lincoln Lore* magazine, and "African American Widows in Post-emancipation Maryland," published by the Association of Black Women Historians. She is currently working on a manuscript tentatively titled "To Never Truck with No Man: Single Black Women during the Civil War and Reconstruction."

Acknowledgments

This book began as an idea nearly ten years ago and would not have been possible without the encouragement of Sharita Jacobs and Brandi Clay Brimmer. All of the contributors are indebted to the scholarship of Thavolia Glymph, whose groundbreaking research on women during the Civil War provided the foundation for this volume. Several of the papers were presented at the Association for the Study of African American Life and History (ASALH) and we owe a debt to this organization which has consistently provided a platform for new and emerging scholarship on the African American experience. I thank LaShawn Harris who chaired the panel at ASALH on "Black Women Struggles during the Civil War and Reconstruction." I also thank Jeffery Kerr-Ritchie at Howard University for his insightful feedback on the papers. A grant from Bowie State University's Career/Collaboration and Research Excellence for Scholars Program provided funding and release time to complete the manuscript.

During the early phase of this project, Randall Miller and Stanley Harrold read several chapters and provided incisive comments offering advice on how to shape the papers. They understood the vision for this book and offered guidance on ways to make it stronger. We also thank the anonymous peer reviewers who read the chapters and offered constructive feedback. We hope this book will be generative in leading to more studies on how southern Black women navigated the turmoil of the Civil War and Reconstruction. Freedom, as several studies have demonstrated, did not come quickly or with ease. Emancipation was an uneven, nonlinear process that impacted every region of the South differently. What is clear in the pages that follow is the determination of Black women to create a life in freedom while confronting power structures that hindered their progress and advancement. They paid the price on the battlefields of war and freedom.

Introduction

Black Women during the Civil War and Reconstruction

Karen Cook Bell

In February 1868, Emily Surall filed a complaint with the Freedmen's Bureau in Savannah, Georgia, against William Murphy. Murphy held Emily's three children as "bound laborers" against their will and without the consent of Emily in violation of the Thirteenth Amendment.[1] Murphy's actions along with Emily's protest and her complaint to the Freedmen's Bureau illustrate the complex environment of slavery's afterlife. Freedom was a contested process that created new relationships to state power and implied equity during and after emancipation. Black women and the labor of their children were central to the southern economy and southern households. Black women sought to redefine their relationship to the southern economy and the South by asserting their right to equality while contending with gendered and racialized violence. Freedom meant the right to marry and have self-sustaining homes; the right to secure property and acquire land through one's labor; the right to receive an education by attending school; the right to bodily autonomy for themselves and their children; and all of the benefits of citizenship. *Southern Black Women and Their Struggle for Freedom during the Civil War and Reconstruction* examines the ways in which Black women, from diverse regions of the American South, employed various forms of resistance and survival strategies to navigate one of the most tumultuous times in American history. This work highlights the complexity of Black women's wartime and postwar experiences, and provides important insight into the contested spaces they occupied.

The chapters in this volume represent an important contribution in the process of understanding how the Civil War and Reconstruction affected Black women in the US South. The recent culture wars on the role of slavery and race in our nation's historical discourse underscore how vital it is to understand what Eric Foner refers to as the "Second Founding" and its impact on newly emancipated women.[2] During slavery, southern Black women were valued for their productive and reproductive labor and faced sexual exploitation on a daily basis. Black women were also central to the slave family and the slave community as wives, mothers, caregivers, midwives, and in numerous other roles. Emancipation began the process of changing the legal status of Black women; and their labor, gender roles, and experience with gender violence were also transformed. In fact, they experienced conflicting notions of linear, seasonal, and "Revolutionary" time where emancipation did not bring the experience of one event leading to another logically. Their sense of space and geography were disrupted, and their homes were transformed.[3] As Black women began the process of emancipating themselves during the Civil War, they told themselves and others what was happening in disparate regions of the South and thus formulated stories of the war and freedom, which reflected race and gender.[4] At the same time, participants in the war and observers of the war advanced their perspectives of the changing landscape and the harsh realities of war, which sometimes included, but often excluded, the on-ground acts of Black women.[5] As Thavolia Glymph makes clear, "enslaved women waged war against individual slaveholders and the Confederate state in myriad ways. They fought as combatants and noncombatants, civilians and partisans."[6] When the war ended, Black women moved emancipation and freedom forward by disrupting the plantation regimen, taking former slave owners to court for unpaid wages, fighting for military pensions for their families, leading the movement for reparations for slavery, becoming landowners, and advancing themselves and their children through education. They did all of this in the midst of a second war being waged against them during Reconstruction and in the Jim Crow South.[7]

The central arguments presented in this collection are twofold. First, time and place shaped freedom and the lived experience of southern Black women. During the Civil War, Black women experienced emancipation differently from men as they struggled against sexual violence, re-enslavement, and the tensions inherent in the contests over the realization of freedom. Second, freedom's boundaries after the war were often contested and fluid as Black women's lived experience was characterized by ambiguity, the persistence of "unfreedoms," persisting racial and gender violence, and unequal citizenship. The essays in this collection, working from varied perspectives, help us to understand the complexity of Black women's struggle. Collectively, the chapters demonstrate how Black women defined and claimed the freedom promised after the official end of slavery and demanded rights as citizens in the Civil War and postwar period.

This volume builds on scholarship that has envisioned emancipation within the context of a long freedom movement in which Black women played a central role. This study goes further with individual narratives and case studies of women in war and freedom that show the ways in which Black women recognized that they would have to make their own freedom and how that influenced their postwar political, social and economic lives. It critically examines Black women and children as self-liberators, as contributors to the family economy during the war, and as widows who relied on kinship and community solidarity. *Southern Black Women* thereby both expands and deepens our understanding of the various ways Black women seized wartime opportunities and made powerful claims on citizenship. It captures the variability of that struggle through an examination of diverse geographical locations.

Two themes have emerged in the historiography of Black women and slave emancipation. The first centers on how Black women negotiated the transition to freedom under a variety of competing influences. The second centers on the violence that Black women experienced in their transition to freedom. Although numerous studies have been devoted to examining the impact of the Civil War and Reconstruction on former slaves, very few provide a comparative regional perspective of Black women's experiences. Thavolia Glymph's *The Women's Fight: The Civil War Battles for Home, Freedom, and Nation* (2020) is the most recent study to provide an analysis of what the war meant for Black and White women in the North and South. As with previous wars such as the Revolutionary War and the War of 1812, the Civil War forced many women from their homes and beyond the confines of the domestic sphere. Black women took to the roads fleeing armies or enslavers, made their way to battlefields as nurses and, in the case of Harriet Tubman, served as spy and scout and led soldiers in a campaign to liberate slaves. Black women also labored in army camps as seamstresses and laundresses. Glymph's work is part of a larger historiography that has attempted to move gender to the forefront of our understanding of the Civil War and Reconstruction period. Amy Murrell Taylor's *Embattled Freedom: Journeys through the Civil War's Slave Refugee Camps* (2020) also exemplifies this trajectory. Studies by Kidada Williams, *They Left Great Marks on Me* (2014) and *I Saw Death Coming: A History of Terror and Survival in the War against Reconstruction* (2023), and Hannah Rosen, *Terror in the Heart of Freedom* (2009), which examine gender and violence, have demonstrated that freedwomen laid claim to full and equal citizenship, to their own conceptions of womanhood, and to access to public spaces that had previously been denied them.[8] More recently, Carole Emberton's study of Priscilla Joyner's long emancipation underscores the paradigm of freedom as a process in which women navigated the boundaries of coercion in a new economic, political, and ideological moment.[9] *Southern Black Women* demonstrates how different geographical contexts can together underscore common experiences of struggle over feminine roles, war and postwar violence, family formation, household labor practices, and participation in the public sphere.

The contributors to this volume illuminate broad geographical contexts and categories. Part I, "Emancipation and Black Women's Labor," considers how emancipation impacted the labor of formerly enslaved women. Katherine Chilton's chapter explores the unique experience of women in the District of Columbia and argues that Black women drew on women's strong position in the urban economy to choose work that allowed them to help support their families and demand respect and reciprocal obligations from their husbands. The strategies practiced by African American women during and after emancipation reveal the continuities between the pre– and post–Civil War periods that made urban freedom in the District of Columbia different and distinct. Despite the dislocations of the Civil War and the Reconstruction and the attempts of agents of the Union Army and the Freedmen's Bureau to impose Republican ideals on Black women, emancipation ultimately served to reinforce prewar patterns of gendered behavior in former slave households. While Black men experienced great demand for their labor during the war, the resumption of a peacetime employment market meant that the majority of Black women would have to work in freedom.

Arlisha R. Norwood examines a special category of women, those who temporarily or permanently could be classified as "single" in Virginia. This chapter argues that this population which includes unmarried, divorced, widowed, abandoned, and separated women were the most economically vulnerable group during and after the war. Despite the unique obstacles they faced, single Black women asserted their needs, worked together to prevent destitution, and challenged the agendas of governmental agencies and private organizations whose well-meaning intentions often clashed with their own expectations. Their petitions for support and compensation altered the roles and responsibilities of federal and local agencies and made these women prominent characters in defining freedom, welfare, citizenship, and womanhood in the nineteenth and early twentieth centuries.

Felicia Jamison analyzes Black women in the Georgia Low Country during the Civil War who used the personal time afforded them after laboring on rice plantations to acquire property and pass on goods to their children. Using the testimonies of women in the records of the Southern Claims Commission, Jamison demonstrates how Black women secured property before the war, lost their valuable property as Union soldiers traversed the region and commandeered their goods, and petitioned the Commission for restitution to provide for themselves and their families after the war. Using the "politics of acquisition" as a framework, Jamison argues that women in Liberty County, Georgia, used property to enhance their lives and secure their freedom. She demonstrates that the loss of personal goods such as clothing, livestock, and bushels of agricultural products severely hampered Black women and their family's transition into freedom.

Part II, "War, Gender Violence, and the Courts," provides important context to the legal and violent dimensions of emancipation for Black women. Karen Cook Bell interrogates how Black women in Louisiana and Georgia used Freedmen's Bureau courts and their knowledge of the landscape "to make their own freedom." In both regions, low wages and legal battles placed formerly enslaved women at a disadvantage; however, their labor aided their families and communities. Through the "contract labor system" in Louisiana and access to abandoned lands in Georgia, these women were able to improve their conditions in the short term. While some freedpeople derived marginal economic benefits from wage labor in the immediate aftermath of the war, in Louisiana these newly emancipated women were persistent in their demands for full and fair compensation from the Bureau of Free Labor, which adjudicated a significant number of cases in their favor.

Crystal Feimster examines the Black soldiers of the 4th Regiment of the Native Guard (also known as the Corps d'Afrique) stationed at Fort Jackson, Louisiana, and the laundresses who served them and their White officers. Both Black soldiers and laundresses were formerly enslaved people who had seized their freedom by joining and aiding the Union cause. Over the course of six weeks, in December 1863 and January 1864, they engaged in open munity to protest racial and sexual violence inflicted by White Union officers. In so doing they made visible the violent terms of interracial interaction that informed the meaning of wartime freedom and Black labor (terms that were still very much rooted in the prisms and discourses of enslavement). More importantly, as free labor Black women began to negotiate a deeply abusive racial and sexual terrain.

Kaisha Esty demonstrates that during the American Civil War, laboring African American women and girls in Union-occupied territory embarked on their own war over the use of their bodies. As fugitives, "contraband," and refugees, displaced Black women and girls of liminal status confronted gender violence in conditions that often resembled the systemic sexual violence of slavery. As this chapter argues, central to this gender violence was the assumption that Black women were always willing to negotiate sex as part of their (nonsexual) labor. The introduction of wartime legislation protecting women from sexual assault was pivotal. In race-neutral terms, such legislation created a powerful avenue for refugee Black women and girls not only to seek sexual justice but also to challenge and redefine existing cultural and legal understandings of sexual consent. Analysis of testimonies to wartime sexual violence in Tennessee and South Carolina uncovers how formerly enslaved African American women and girls located their violation in relation to their sense of virtue, respectability, and sexual sovereignty. These testimonies mark a significant period of Black women's vocalization as liminal and stateless actors, prompting a reframing of histories of dissemblance, respectability, labor, and gender violence.

"Emancipation, the Black Family, and Education" composes Part III. Family and education were the sinew of the Black community. Kelly Houston Jones explores this dimension of emancipation, illuminating the intersection of several processes in wartime and the postwar decades such as Black women's social and family networks and their struggle to claim their rights in connection to the service of their men. Using the records connected to the 54th United States Colored Infantry (the *other* 54th – not the 54th Massachusetts of "Glory" fame), Jones reconstructs the geography of USCT women's family, work, and society in the post–Civil War years, paying closest attention to the twenty-five years after the war. Emphasizing Black women's political placemaking during and after the war's refugee crisis, Jones argues that Black women provided support for their soldiers and the US Army presence overall, but they also constituted part of the occupation force of Arkansas's capital. They formed the backbone of Unionist Little Rock and forged alliances with White progressive allies. They fought for rootedness, gaining unprecedented control over their domestic lives, and claimed privileges via their association with Black soldiers.

Brandi Clay Brimmer follows the story of Fanny Whitney, an enslaved woman, who belonged to a community of men and women that was bound together by extended ties of kinship and other connections in Union-occupied areas of eastern North Carolina. Brimmer's essay pieces together the historical trajectory of widowhood for Black women in post–Civil War America. Using the case files of Fanny Whitney and other southern Black women who applied for survivors' benefits after 1866, the year the federal government recognized "slave marriage" in pension law, this chapter asks what happened to the women and children Black soldiers depended on, left behind in freedmen's camps, and reunited with after the war. Black women who were widows, she contends, pieced together their existence on a daily basis. Evidence from the pension files of Black Union widows in eastern North Carolina deepens our understanding of Black women's lives and labors and sheds light on the ways they struggled to define widowhood for themselves. Brimmer expands the discourse regarding widowed Black women who used community and kinship networks to shape freedom.

Black women have been central to efforts to educate African Americans. Hilary Green examines this aspect of freedom by considering Emerson Normal School and institution building in the postwar era and the important role of education in the lives of formerly enslaved women in Mobile, Alabama. Green posits that Emerson Normal was instrumental in permitting former slaves as well as the children born after the end of slavery to become teachers, administrators, and, most important, leaders within their communities. Emerson Normal represented the expansion and refinement of the educational partnership between Black Mobilians and the American Missionary Association after the creation of state-funded public schools. This partnership played a critical role in creating the corps of teachers required for the new public school system. Outside the classroom, graduates employed their preparation for middle-class leadership by actively participating in racial uplift organizations and campaigns. Never viewing their service as limited to the classroom, Emerson Normal graduates became an essential asset for Black Mobilians and their slow, arduous struggle for African American public education and racial equality in Mobile.

Southern Black Women and Their Struggle for Freedom during the Civil War and Reconstruction demonstrates that only through case studies can we witness the ways in which Black women directed definitions of freedom to meet specific demands. Through this wide lens, national patterns in realizing emancipation become visible. The essays herein, though diverse, ultimately offer a broad though not exhaustive survey of emancipation's meanings and an examination of the challenges of and the contests over the realization of freedom. Ultimately, Black women fashioned a distinct worldview that aided them as they negotiated their new lives during and after the Civil War. They confronted the power structures with the tools available to them and did so with both measured and phenomenal success. In order to understand the influence of race, gender, and class, historians must be willing to rethink important questions of the Civil War and Reconstruction era: how did Black women live their daily lives? How did they view themselves and their role in the Black community? What did they believe and what was their worldview? What liberation strategies did they embrace and why? The pages that follow bring Black women's voices into the core of analysis in answering these questions.

PART I

EMANCIPATION AND BLACK
WOMEN'S LABOR

"The Proceeds of My Own Labor"

Black Working Women in the District of Columbia during the Civil War

Katherine Chilton

As the home of the "first freed," the nearly 3,000 enslaved men, women, and children liberated by Congress April 1862 in the District of Columbia represented a unique site for women struggling for emancipation during the Civil War and Reconstruction. Eight and a half months before the Emancipation Proclamation, the District of Columbia Emancipation Act freed Black women in the District of Columbia and paid compensation to the White men and women who claimed them as property. As the Civil War progressed, these women were quickly outnumbered by runaway enslaved men and women entering the city and the Union camps that formed a protective barrier around the capital. This influx forced the Union Army, and later the Freedmen's Bureau, to determine how to define dependency when it came to Black women and for a time transformed the city into a "laboratory of social policy."[1] Although willing to utilize the benefits and programs provided by the government when it helped them, Black women in the District of Columbia understood that they could also look to the city's existing free community of color for guidance. Like other southern cities, the urban economy in Washington had long offered opportunities to women. Freedwomen, both those who gained their freedom in the city and those who arrived during and after the war, turned to existing resources in the form of strategies long practiced by free women of color as well as asserting their right to the new resources of the Union Army and Freedmen's Bureau as they made their transition to freedom.

Black women's experiences in the District of Columbia suggest the need to take a more expansive view of the struggle for freedom that also includes the free community of color. The recognition that freedpeople's ambitions were founded in their experiences of enslavement has led scholars to look back implicitly and explicitly in their work to connect slavery, the Civil War, and Reconstruction. As Steven Hahn suggests, it seems "increasingly apparent that slavery was not mere background or prologue; it was formative and foundational." Scholarship on the rural South has shown how the reconstruction of free labor in rural areas built on the customary practices and privileges of slavery that were sometimes called the "internal economy" as former slaves, plantation owners and government representatives negotiated the transition from enslaved to free labor. Yet, in urban areas, free men and women of color's experiences and strategies were also foundational to freedpeople's ambitions and their abilities to achieve them, as historians Letitia Woods Brown and Elizabeth Clark Lewis have demonstrated in their studies of the District of Columbia.[2]

During the antebellum period, free women of color left rural Maryland and Virginia in pursuit of a more meaningful freedom in the District of Columbia, seeking to reunite their families, work independently for themselves, and to find security and community within thriving Black institutions.[3] As a result, women were overrepresented in the Black populations of Upper South cities like Washington and Baltimore. In the District of Columbia, there were seven women to every five men by 1840, and this discrepancy was most pronounced among young working-age adults. Unlike in cities in the lower South, where the higher numbers of free women of color in the population were often caused by their greater manumission rates, in Upper South cities like the District of Columbia, the sexual difference in the free population was caused by women's higher migration rate in response to economic opportunities in the city.[4]

The limited employment opportunities for Black men in a city with little industry meant that women's labor was often critical to family survival and success, but free people of color's household economies in the 1850s and 1860s suggest that Black households tried to control the extent of women's participation in wage labor.[5] While few free women of color could afford to avoid work altogether, many families tried to limit women's work outside the household.[6] By far the most popular occupation for women was washing and taking in laundry, which could be performed in their own homes rather than entering White households as full-time servants. For example, Cassandra Adams and her sister-in-law Martha Adams were both listed as washerwomen in the 1860 census, and as they lived next door to one another, they may have pooled their resources to get the washing done or received help from Martha's fifteen-year-old daughter Sarah. Both women had young children in their households, so they likely valued washing work they could perform from their own homes.[7]

In addition to washing, free women of color demonstrated their preference for other employment forms that prevented direct White supervision and allowed them to remain in their own home, such as sewing as seamstresses or marketing food, produce, or other goods at the District's weekend markets. Elizabeth Keckley, the city's most famous Black resident, earned her freedom as a seamstress before becoming Mary Todd Lincoln's personal dressmaker and close confidant.[8] Free women of color also took in boarders to their homes to provide additional income without resorting to outside employment. In households headed by a married couple, boarders, either related or unrelated, were more likely to be present when the wife did not work outside the home, suggesting that Black families preferred this financial strategy to outside employment for women.[9] Families created a domestic economy that adapted to allow women to take advantage of the demand for their labor but under their own terms. Whenever possible, women sought to work from within their own households; both protecting them from direct White supervision and its attendant consequences and enabling them to care for their children. Freedwomen's ambitions after emancipation drew on these precedents and strategies.

The Civil War brought considerable change and challenge to the District of Columbia, the capital of the Union and the headquarters of the Union Army. During the war, 3,000 slaves in the District were emancipated by Congress and tens of thousands of fugitive slaves fled to the safety of the city and the surrounding army camps. As a result of this migration, Black men outnumbered Black women for the first time in the city. Women navigated this early rehearsal for Reconstruction in ways that drew on established strategies by free communities of color in the city as well as taking advantage of new resources created by the war. The mass migration of Black women to the District of Columbia pushed the government to provide for women even as the Union Army resisted defining them as dependents worthy of support.

Formerly enslaved women freed through the abolition of slavery in the District of Columbia sought to emulate strategies established by free women of color and remove themselves from White households as much as possible. Abolition in the District represented a compromise between the Republican Party's radical and conservative wings, as while it made a statement by ending slavery in the one territory unequivocally controlled

by Congress, it also included provisions for compensating slave owners and encouraging the colonization of the freed population. Slave
owners' compensation petitions cross-referenced with records from the
United States Census offer clues to how women made decisions about
their future.[10] Some women chose to remain with the family who had
owned them as slave property and had even been compensated for the
loss of their labor. For example, Martha Ann Blaxton had been born the
property of James Riordan and remained with him after emancipation.
Riordan claimed in his petition for compensation that Blaxton "does
not associate with people of her own color ... accompanies her mistress
to the communion table, loves my children, and is entrusted with the
keys to my desk." At twenty-eight, Blaxton was not too old to consider
starting afresh, but she instead chose to continue as a domestic servant
living in the Riordan household. After her enslaver's death, perhaps
Blaxton was persuaded to remain and help the family, and as a conces-
sion, a young girl was hired to aid her in her duties.[11] Those women who
remained with their previous enslavers often negotiated for recognition
of their skills or for specific duties within the household. Lucy Lancaster
remained in Noble Young's household, although her children who had
also been enslaved chose to leave and find new employment. Young listed
Lancaster in his petition in 1862 as a domestic slave, but by the 1870
census her occupation was listed as a cook.[12] After emancipation, Black
women who had been general domestic servants negotiated to take on
specific responsibilities and jealously guarded their new positions, often
threatening or exercising their new right to quit if they were required to
perform other duties.[13]

For many former slaves, the ability to change employers was one of
their most precious new rights, and domestic servants exercised this
right as they sought the best employment terms and the most agreeable
employers. Young single women particularly demonstrated the most
mobility. Yet, women who changed employers almost all remained as
domestic servants for White families, demonstrating that while freedom
brought some opportunities for change to Black women the employment opportunities open to them remained circumscribed. For example,
Elsie Curtis had worked as a domestic while enslaved to Ann Bisco of
Washington, and as a free woman she continued to work as a domestic servant for George S. Bright, a sailor in the US Navy.[14] The limited
employment opportunities available to women and the increasing cost
of living in Washington during the war contributed to the involvement
of Black women in the sex and leisure economy.[15] After emancipation,

some women who left their former enslavers did not seek employment, if they had husbands or children who could help to support their households. Women tried above all to control their own labor, and by withdrawing from the workforce they could avoid the supervision of a jealous wife or predatory husband. This option, however, was only available to those who could rely on other kinds of household income. Mary Lee had worked as a lady's maid to a White Washington family, but after emancipation she remained at home in the new household she formed with her husband John Lee and their children. Caroline Gray did not have a husband present in her household after emancipation, but her children's labor might have allowed her to stay at home after a lifetime spent caring for Joseph Fearson's family.[16]

Despite the symbolic significance of slavery's abolition in the District of Columbia in 1862, the path to freedom of most women who made their way to the city was less dramatic and less clear cut. Once General Butler established the policy at Fortress Monroe, Virginia, in May 1861, of accepting Black male laborers as "contraband of war" the numbers of fugitives fleeing to the capital increased dramatically, drawn by the promise of freedom. However, as military policy focused on offering Black men freedom in exchange for their service, the position of women and children remained uncertain and contingent throughout the war. Enslaved women who fled to the city faced an uncertain situation throughout the war and their path to freedom was often dependent on their marital status. The First Confiscation Act did not provide any protection for women, and the 1862 Militia Act only offered freedom to the female dependents of Black men who served the Union. Women whose enslavers claimed loyalty to the Union were not covered by this policy, which would have excluded many women from nearby Maryland. These women could not claim freedom until February 1865, when the Enlistment Act freed the wives of Union soldiers from loyal states, although Maryland had abolished slavery by this time.[17]

Some women who came to the city and nearby army camps as fugitive slaves were able to find employment as cooks and laundresses serving the troops. Once White women nurses claimed the treatment of the sick as their proper purview, Black women began to be employed at army hospitals doing washing for the surgeons and the wounded soldiers. Even though enslaved women had performed field labor alongside men, the army maintained its traditional gender distinction, only employing men as laborers and women at traditionally female and lower-paid occupations such as cooking and cleaning.[18] The flood of Black men who came to the city to supply the intense demand for labor pushed the Union Army and the Republican government to ensure their freedom in exchange for their service. Yet, it was the Black women who migrated to the city following their husbands or in search of their own freedom who put tremendous strain on the resources of the army, benevolent societies, and government officials charged with their care. The initially reluctant military government soon assumed unprecedented responsibility for Black women in the District of Columbia.[19]

Many of these women made their transition to freedom, at least temporarily, in the contraband camps established by the army and staffed by philanthropic organizations like the American Missionary Association. Although Black women did not experience the same intense demand for their labor from the army as did Black men, many single women found a ready market for their labor as domestic servants in the city, particularly after the abolition of slavery in the District. Single women were more likely to be offered live-in positions, and because few employers wanted to feed and clothe children many married women remained at the contraband camps indefinitely. Others were trapped at the camps waiting for wages that had been promised to husbands serving in the military or as laborers for the quartermaster's department.[20] For most women who had fled to the city, domestic service represented a major change in labor for former field hands from rural counties in Maryland and Virginia, but some women were able to benefit from skills learned in slavery as they adapted to the urban employment market. As a teacher at the contraband camps commented, many women knew "more about sewing than anything else having been obliged to sew their own clothes while in slavery."

Despite wartime privations, demand in the District of Columbia for domestic servants remained high throughout the war. When slaves from the city left their former enslavers, White residents rushed to the employment offices established within the camps in search of new servants. Former slave and prominent abolitionist Harriet Jacobs visited the contraband camps at Duff Green's Row and observed that the office of the superintendent "was thronged by the day by persons who came to hire the poor creatures." Those without children were most able to take advantage of the demand for their labor and find work in the city as servants, washerwomen, and cooks. Jacobs commented on how "single women hire at four dollars a month, a woman with one child two and a half or three dollars a month."[21] Despite the continued demand, the oversupply of potential servants from the migrant population clearly suppressed wages for Black women during this period. Before the war, slave owners reported hiring out their female property as domestic servants at wages almost double those during the war, at eight to ten dollars a month.[22] This made subsisting in the city particularly difficult for women with children, who depended on the rations and assistance available at the camps even when employed.

The operation of employment offices to find work for women living in the contraband camps in the city reveals the contradictions inherent in the military government and army's policies towards Black women in the District of Columbia. At first, the demand for male labor led army officers to welcome Black soldiers and army workers' dependents to the city and offer them freedom and protection, including food and shelter at the hastily established contraband camps. By 1862, however, the rising number of Black women, children, and the elderly in the District of Columbia spurred the government to introduce a new policy that taxed the wages of Black men working for the army to fund the contraband camps. Secretary of War Edwin Stanton ordered that

in view of the fact that the Government is supporting several hundred women and children of the same class, who are unable to find employment, and also furnish medical care, support, and attendance to the sick and helpless; the Secretary directs that you cause five dollars per month to be deducted from the pay of the said colored teamsters and laborers in the quartermaster department.[23]

The government aimed to ensure that all Black women and children would be provided for through Black men's wages, regardless of their relationship. Although army officials argued that "these are rid of such a responsibility very cheaply, at a cost of only one fifth or less of their monthly pay, and few white laborers are so favorably circumstanced," they did not acknowledge that White laborers were only responsible for their own relatives' support.[24]

Despite this tax, officials and civilians at the contraband camps still stressed the necessity of formerly enslaved women, whether married or single, finding work in the city to support themselves. Even though Black men were responsible for supporting all destitute formerly enslaved migrants in the city, Black women were considered unworthy to be dependent on the government. Weekly reports from Camp Barker listed the number of "able-bodied females over 14 fit for duty," and these women and girls were encouraged to find employment with local residents or the army. Women with children, whose husbands were away with the army, missing, or dead, found it much more difficult to find enough work to support their families and more frequently had to remain in the camps and become dependent on government relief. When freedmen's aid societies sought to find shelter for the soldiers' wives, army officials replied that they would take responsibility for destitute children, but that women should be self-supporting. While very young children deserved charity, officials made it clear that Black women without other support would be expected to work. If necessary, they could place their children in the camp's orphanage to take employment.[25] By insisting that Black women should continue to work if they were able, army officials revealed the contradictions in free labor ideology regarding race and gender that would continue to be evident in the freedwomen's relationship with their successor in the city, the Freedmen's Bureau.

After the end of the Civil War and the mustering out of Union Army troops, the demand for labor in the city quickly returned to its prewar status. Black women were soon outnumbered two to one by men at the Freedmen's Bureau employment offices once the demand for male soldiers and laborers concluded. In part, this reflected the greater employment opportunities available to women without children as domestic servants. However, it could also have reflected married women's attempts to avoid waged labor and use the opportunities afforded by the city to devote their energies to their own households wherever possible. Tracing the households established by a sample of former slaves from the District of Columbia and those who migrated there during the war reveals that a high number of freedwomen listed no occupation in the 1870 United States Census. Yet, in the District of Columbia, there is little evidence of a panic about women withdrawing from the labor force. Even before the war, residents in Washington regularly lamented the difficulty in getting good help due to servants' efforts to control their own labor by "doing just what they please and going away just when they please."[26] In rural areas, similar behavior by freedwomen led planter employers to complain that Black women were trying to "play the lady." In fact, women were attempting to reduce the hours they spent laboring for White employers in favor of directing their labor towards their own families, taking care of children and garden plots. In urban areas, where labor relationships had always been more fluid and White employers were accustomed to making temporary arrangements with free people of color and hired slaves, permanent contracts were less common and if the Bureau ever attempted to enforce them, they appear to have quickly given up and instead focused on the employment offices.[27] Black women's struggles to support themselves and their families demonstrated the continuities of household strategies.

In 1870, nearly 70 percent of married women sampled who lived in two-parent households in the District of Columbia listed their occupation as "keeping house." Even in female-headed households, 44 percent remained out of the workforce, usually reflecting families with an older mother and adult working children. While this might have been striking in rural areas of the South, in 1860, 58 percent of married free women of color in Washington sampled had also declared themselves to have no occupation.[28] Freedwomen tried to support their family through their own domestic labor whenever possible, rather than working for another family for wages. Just as free women of color had attempted to separate themselves from slavery by avoiding live-in domestic service, after emancipation women who had already experienced domestic service while enslaved in the District of Columbia sought to avoid the drudgery of service and White supervision and intrusion into their lives. Those who had been separated from their husbands and their children's fathers during slavery sought to establish themselves as in control of their own households rather than another woman's servant. While enslaved, Mary Lee had served as a lady's maid to Margaret Loughborough, but upon her emancipation she reunited with her husband, John Lee, to create a household for their six children in Georgetown. By 1870, John Lee appeared to be supporting the family with his earnings as a laborer, allowing Mary to stay at home with their children.[29]

On the surface, these statistics suggest that Black married women were choosing to stay at home with their children, rather than take waged work in the city. However, just under half of the households in which married women were listed as "keeping house" contained boarders. In the urban economy, by taking in paying occupants of their houses Black women could engage in the same unseen and unwaged form of labor commonly practiced by free households during the antebellum period. Taking in boarders was not just a strategy to help support the household, but allowed many women avoid wage labor outside of their own household. Taking care of the house and perhaps making food for boarders or extended family members represented productive labor for urban women, yet this work was not recognized by the census takers or the Freedmen's Bureau. Gilbert Rich and his wife Hester, migrants from Stafford County, Virginia, shared their home with four boarders, none of whom were obviously related to the couple. They owned nine hundred dollars in real estate, so they may have used the house they owned to make additional household income that enabled the couple to support themselves on Gilbert's wages as a laborer.[30]

The urban economy also afforded Black women in the District of Columbia the opportunity to work for wages within their own households, by taking in laundry and ironing. The large numbers of government workers who lived in boarding houses or whose families lived in the city during the congressional session created a significant demand for washing workers. When married women had to work for wages, they appeared to prefer working as a laundress to domestic service outside the home. Laundresses and washerwomen most commonly did not live in with the families they served but collected clothing they washed and ironed in their homes or communities. This allowed them to keep an eye on their children and grandchildren and to take care of their own household needs at the same time as they earned money to contribute to those households. Crucially, it also enabled women to avoid the White mistresses' close supervision or White masters' unwanted advances.[31] Women who had worked as domestic servants while enslaved in the District of Columbia often possessed laundry and ironing skills from their former occupations that they were able to use as free laborers. For example, Lydia Sampson had been considered a valuable house servant by her mistress Sally T. Matthews, who was granted $350.40 in compensation for the loss of her services in 1862. Sampson, who went by her married name, Elizabeth Middleton, in the 1870 census, worked as a laundress, possibly while she cared for her two youngest daughters. Samuel, her husband, who was not listed as a member of the Matthews household, now worked as a laborer in the city.[32]

Demonstrating the reciprocity in gender relations created by the urban economy, women's ability to withdraw from domestic service positions was closely related to the ability of their husbands and families to find stable employment. Married women who worked as domestic servants were most likely to have husbands who were laborers or day laborers, the least skilled and least stable employment form in the city. Most single women without any male support had to find work in the waged economy, although those with older children were sometimes able to send their children to work instead. Salina Williams had been born into slavery in the District of Columbia and had borne into slavery six children and two grandchildren by the time she was emancipated at the age of fifty-one in 1862. Her family was valued at over $2,500 by the Commissioners of the Board of Emancipation of the District of Columbia, although Williams never saw any of the compensation paid to their former enslaver. By 1870, her family had established their own household in the Third Ward where Salina kept the house and cared for her grandchildren, while her sons and daughters worked in the city. Her daughter Lydia worked as a washer-woman, so Salina may have helped with this waged labor, but after her long years of bondage Salina was able to devote her labor predominately to her own family for the first time.[33] The majority of women who listed their occupation as live-in domestic servants appeared to be single, as none had children who lived with them in the White households. As in the antebellum period, it appeared that domestic service was younger women's preferred employment before they established a household of their own.

Freedwomen in the District of Columbia thus drew on established strategies as they reconstructed the relationships between gender and labor in their households. As in rural areas, they attempted wherever possible to control their own labor conditions and to focus their efforts on their own families rather than those of White employers. The urban economy, however, offered them greater opportunities and flexibility to conduct waged work from within their households, including washing or taking in boarders, such that married women's significant withdrawal from domestic service did not create a panic among White observers and the Freedmen's Bureau. Negotiating from a position of comparative strength, freedwomen nevertheless demonstrated their willingness to use government resources to ensure their support and survival in the city. While most freedwomen came to the city to find work and support their families in an environment free from White supervision, Bureau accounts reveal that they increasingly began to see government assistance as their right and part of their new privileges. Agents complained that "some person or persons have indirectly given the colored people to understand that the Government is obliged to support them, and ... relieve all their wants, real or imaginary." This "someone" may indeed have been philanthropic agent Josephine Griffing, a former abolitionist and suffragist, whose sympathies led her to believe that the freedpeople were entitled to government assistance in return for their years of unpaid service in bondage.[34] Although the Freedmen's Aid agents' opinions undoubtedly influenced the freedpeople to approach the Freedmen's Bureau for assistance, many former slaves arrived in the capital with expectations of assistance from the government. Superintendent John Vandenburgh indignantly reported the case of Lucy Hill, who despite having a husband and two daughters at work earning good wages, applied for relief as she "thought she could as well have her share as not." Freedwomen demonstrated that they believed that Bureau programs were supposed to operate for their benefit and that they would happily use Bureau assistance through programs such as food and clothing rations and subsidized housing to supplement their own earnings.[35]

Freedwomen saw no contradiction in using Bureau services that helped them, while rejecting Bureau programs or incentives that did not fit with their own goals for freedom. Although the Bureau in the District of Columbia made efforts to encourage freedwomen to leave the city for healthier country homes and employment, formerly enslaved women's general refusal to return to their former homes in Maryland and Virginia and their violent dislike of the government farms established around the city pushed Bureau agents to utilize their funds, and the freedmen's aid societies' resources to provide relief and social programs to women in the city. Seeking to break with their past labor in bondage, freedwomen told Bureau agents that "they would rather work for three dollars a month in Washington or Baltimore than to work for the traitors here for twelve."[36] Mindful of their mission to teach the former slaves the value of free labor and self-sufficiency, Bureau agents rapidly established employment agencies in the city. Freedpeople who had been used to obtaining work through the contraband camps established during the Civil War eagerly took advantage of the employment offices set up at various locations around the city. Although both men and women registered in large numbers, the resumption of prewar employment patterns offered fewer opportunities for Black men. Josephine Griffing reported in 1866 that "since the mustering out of colored troops, the dismantling of forts, and the closing up of warlike operations, the numbers of unemployed males, has exceeded that of females, and during the past six months, two thousand males and eight hundred females have applied for situations."[37]

Freedwomen looked to the Freedmen's Bureau not only for assistance in finding a job, but in adapting to the potential employers' demands. They eagerly attended the industrial schools established by various freedmen's aid societies, where they could learn needlework and sew suitable clothing to dress themselves for their attempts at finding new employment. During the industrial schools' first year of operation, women who had been "field hands" cut and sewed 300 pairs of pants, which in addition to clothing the needy of the District, trained the women in domestic skills. One woman reported that the sewing she had learned enabled her to earn three dollars a week "with her needle." Women who had worked long days in the fields eagerly took up the occupations that would enable them to find work and support their families in the city. After learning needlework skills at one of the industrial schools, a freedwoman spoke enthusiastically to the head of the school about her new employment conditions, remarking that "she prefers it to the shovel."[38]

As in their attempts to find employment, freedwomen could look to the Freedmen's Bureau in the District of Columbia for support as they tried to gather their families. However, freedwomen also resisted attempts by the Bureau to define family structure in a narrow way. Instead of the neat, nuclear families envisioned by the Freedmen's Bureau officials, Black households in the District of Columbia welcomed extended family, kin, and friends to provide mutual support and share labor and childcare burdens. Bureau agents' implicit assumption was that if Black families formed nuclear households headed by an able-bodied Black man, they would not become a charge on the government. Bureau officials saw the high rents that forced freedpeople to cram together in substandard housing as one of the greatest problems facing the city's Black population. One of the earliest acts of the Bureau was therefore the conversion of army barracks into tenement housing, at Duff's Green Row, Wisewell Barracks, and other locations across the city. The Bureau specifically sought to rent these rooms to Black nuclear families, stating that only one family would be allowed to occupy each room and that only couples who could prove their lawful marriage could become tenants. Despite this, as other agents working in the District realized, many households welcomed extended family and friends for personal as well as pragmatic reasons. Josephine Griffing commented that "the strong social nature of this Race, made doubly strong by the violations of domestic relations in slavery, offers great opposition to the separation of families and friends, reaching over three and four generations of those long separated in slavery, but now gathered together in freedom."[39]

Freedwomen's determination to use the resources of the Freedmen's Bureau to pursue their own ambitions for freedom continued to challenge the free labor ideology held by the majority of the Bureau agents in the city, and to reveal, as Mary Farmer Kaiser has suggested, that "when it came to freedwomen, the bureau's rigid policies just never seemed to translate simply into practice."[40] Debates over the meaning and appropriate response to female dependency between Bureau agents and the largely female group of philanthropic society agents who served the city illustrated the distinct ways that race and gender influenced Bureau policy. While the demand for their labor meant that single women were able to find employment in the city to help support themselves, women with children continued to find self-sufficiency a challenge in the postwar period. Soon becoming the most infamous freedmen's relief worker in the District, Josephine Griffing particularly battled with the local Bureau agents over her sympathy for women with children in need of assistance.

Bureau agents' chief commitment was to instill the values of free labor into their charges, which held that those who worked hard would be rewarded by moral virtue, social mobility, and independence. Agents feared that charitable provision would encourage the former slaves towards dependency rather than industry. The mainly female agents employed by the freedmen's relief societies active in the city, in contrast, were seen as too sympathetic to the freedwomen's plight and unable to objectively judge their claims' worth.[41] Captain Spurgin, the first Bureau Superintendent for Washington and Georgetown, complained that female agents "bend ear to their complaints, make no discrimination between those able to work and those unable and advise them to apply to the Bureau for assistance." Official Bureau policy dictated that those able to support themselves even if lacking the "conveniences of life" should be encouraged to work to supply their needs rather than apply for relief.[42]

Despite the demand for female labor in the city, women with children who had lost their husbands due to the dislocations of slavery and war or through desertion or death often found themselves living on the border between poverty and destitution, where sickness or misfortune could force them onto government charity. In many Bureau agents' minds, these women were destitute only because they were unwilling to give up their children and work to support themselves. If there was nothing physically wrong with Black women, then there was no reason why they should not be able to find employment. Although the Bureau aided women in retrieving their children from the countryside to help reunite families, when caring for children prevented women from working, agents frequently denied their role as mothers. Echoing his predecessors in the Union Army, Bureau agent J. V. W. Vandenburgh complained that if only "the women would send their children to homes where they could earn their own living and the smaller ones to the Orphans Home, the mothers could become self-supporting." Although he acknowledged that this did seem harsh, he believed that freedwomen in the city must be forced to see the reality of their situation, and "be governed by force of circumstances, as all poor people must do." Despite the suffering and family separations caused by slavery and illegal apprenticeships, Vandenburgh argued that the Black poor must learn that their poverty entitled them to no special treatment and that if they could not afford to support their children, they must give them up or send them out to work.[43] Whenever possible, however, Black women rejected any attempts to give up their children, and instead claimed their new position as dependents to force the Bureau to aid them.

The urban labor market's realities meant that few Black men could support families on their wages alone, so that women also contributed to the household economy through outside labor and domestic production. They aided their husbands to bring in money for the family when times were hard, but women were also willing to use the Freedmen's Bureau's resources to go after absconding husbands who refused to support them or their children. As Mary Farmer Kaiser has suggested, "they sought bureau involvement in domestic affairs on their terms, accepted its support when it was to their benefit, and rejected it when the wishes of the federal government differed from their own." Bringing their private concerns into the public realm, freedwomen claimed their role as a dependent to draw the Bureau agents' sympathies, who wished to see Black men, rather than the government, take responsibility for Black women and children.[44]

By asserting their position as dependents, Black women were able to use the Freedmen's Bureau's resources to achieve their independence in the city. For example, Catherine Stevenson asked the Bureau to compel her husband to support her and their children in Alexandria because he had left her and taken up with another woman in the city. In her letter to General C. H. Howard she did not ask the Bureau to make him return to her, only to provide for their family's needs. Rebecca Tolliver's husband traveled to Washington from Culpepper County, Virginia, in 1866, but when he failed to send her any money for their three children, she wrote to the Bureau asking that either her husband be sent back to help her raise the children or that he be made to "remit her funds for that purpose." In Sarah Ann Taylor's case, Bureau agents were unable to compel her husband to return to his family as he had legally married another woman during his four-year absence in Washington. Instead, they had him pay his wife thirty dollars to bring their children to the city, where he promised to "take them in charge" and provide for them. As they could not compel the man to support all his dependents, Superintendent Spurgin believed that "the arrangement for the Father to provide for the children was the best that could be affected."[45]

Women clearly used the Bureau's power to go after their husbands, indicating that they fully understood the precarious position of single women with children to support in the urban economy. On the other hand, the city offered a far greater opportunity for Black women to provide for themselves than did the rural countryside, where planters were reluctant to provide room and board to women with children in return for whatever agricultural labor they could undertake. In the city, women who had been deserted or whose husbands did not provide support could in many cases maintain their own households. Julia Jones found that she was able to take care of her own household because of the opportunities for women in the urban economy. When her husband, Henry Jones, sought to reunite with her after his desertion, she refused to return to him, stating that when they were married she had to support him, and further denigrated his masculine character by charging that "he is a lazy and abusive man." Although Jones clearly had no desire to return to her abusive husband, she also refused to return to a situation where she had to support him through her labor. Having found stable employment as a washerwoman in Washington, making five dollars a week to provide for herself and her six-year-old child, Jones felt little need to return to her husband. Investigating the case, Superintendent Vandenburgh concluded "she is undoubtedly self-supporting" so that from the Bureau's perspective there was no need to induce her to return to her husband.[46]

Women's ability to provide for their families could also cause disputes within the household. When men could not find work or regular employment in the city, the household support burden often fell on Black women. Women's ability to find domestic service positions in the city challenged the gender roles suggested by free labor ideology and prominent Black and White leaders. As the freedmen's political, legal and civil rights were based on their responsibilities as household head, many Black leaders stressed a patriarchal definition of the family that emphasized men's roles as providers and women's responsibility for making the home "a place of peace and comfort."[47] Men who struggled to fulfill their roles as household heads in the District had to learn to compromise and accept their wives' and children's earning potential or prepare to seek employment elsewhere either temporarily or permanently. For example, although the Lacy family moved to the District of Columbia in search of greater freedoms for their household, James Lacy soon found that the scarcity of skilled work or even regular employment for Black men frustrated his dreams of providing for his wife Mary and their young daughter Julia. In contrast, Mary appeared to flourish in the city. With her mother providing childcare for Julia, Mary was able to find work as a domestic servant for H. H. Hildreth. Her labor supplemented whatever James could earn and often provided the family's entire support. When James, frustrated with his inability to sustain his family in the city, wanted to return to his old enslaver Samuel Ricksay in Culpepper County, Mary refused to accompany him, saying "that she did not intend to come among the old secesh any more."[48]

Although a discouraged James was willing to return to his old enslaver for the promise of fifteen dollars a month and a house for his family, Mary was unwilling to give up her dreams of freedom. When James Lacy took Julia from her grandmother's house and returned to Culpepper County, Mary reported him to the Freedmen's Bureau for stealing their child. In his testimony, James invoked his masculine duties to claim that he had little choice but to take her away as he was unable to provide for his family in the city, and his wife refused to come with him. He told the Bureau that "as I could not make sufficient to support her and child in Washington DC, I was obliged to leave there as before stated," but that he had always supported his family to the best of his ability up until the day he left Washington. Mary, however, painted a different picture, asserting that "my husband has done nothing to assist in supporting me for the past two years, nor has he assisted in providing for the child." She claimed her own ability to support the family through her employment as a domestic servant and that she had "supported the child from the proceeds of my own labor."[49] The urban labor market could therefore empower Black women to claim equal respect and responsibilities as household providers.

Black women were able to draw on a variety of resources unique to the District of Columbia as they navigated their transition to freedom after emancipation. The established Black community provided relief to those in need, church fellowship, and schools for their children. The city's White population offered employment opportunities to those seeking domestic positions, washing work, or other service occupations. Perhaps most importantly, freedwomen could draw on the experiences of generations of Black women who had come to the city in search of freedom, rehearsing their own transition from enslaved to free labor. In addition, newly emancipated Black women could look first to the Union Army and later to an active Freedmen's Bureau for help and support finding their way in the city and becoming self-supporting. Seeking out Bureau agents when they wanted assistance but resisting Bureau attempts to define the conditions of their freedom, Black women further radicalized the Freedmen's Bureau in the District of Columbia. Urban employment conditions meant that few Black women could afford to withdraw from employment altogether, thus freedwomen in the city rarely were accused of "playing the lady." However, drawing on the same strategies practiced by free women of color for many years, formerly enslaved women during the Civil War and Reconstruction tried to control their own labor conditions wherever possible. By choosing work that could be done from their homes, such as washing or taking in boarders, many women in Washington were able to help support themselves and their families. Like Mary Lacy, they saw the Freedmen's Bureau as a potential ally in their struggle, but ultimately asserted their ability to define their freedom through "the proceeds of my own labor."

2

"Please Attend to It for Me"

Single Black Women in Civil War and Reconstruction Era Virginia

Arlisha R. Norwood

In 1865, Catherine Massey of Hampton, Virginia penned a poignant letter to Secretary of War Edwin M. Stanton. In her short appeal, Massey pleaded with Stanton to intercede on her behalf as she worked to procure money from her husband, who had left her in "detrimental circumstances." Massey communicated a rather dire situation and a complex relationship with her estranged husband. She stated, "I am his lawful wife, and he has neglected to treat me as a Husband should." As the wife of a United States Colored soldier, Massey was very transparent about her husband's faults in the marriage, labeling him as "spendthrift" and "slothful." Perhaps, to further gain support she ended the letter by drawing attention to her role in the marriage before the union deteriorated: "I think it no more than right that he should be made to do what he has never done and that is to help me to support myself as I helped yes not only helped but naturally did support him before he came in the army."[1]

Massey transmitted her feelings of betrayal and disappointment clearly. In her eyes, her status as his "lawful" wife positioned her to some means of support. Without assistance, Massey admitted she was "declining daily." Although short, this appeal reveals numerous ways Black women perceived the Union Army. Massey believed that Stanton could prevent destitution while her husband was serving, and she explicitly stated that if the army did not use their authority and power to "arrange" for her to receive compensation, she would remain unable to meet her "present wants." Her appeal not only conveyed her need for support, but she also called on the army to intercede and mediate on her behalf. She ended her letter with a desperate plea, asking Stanton to "please attend to it for me and my prayers to almighty God."[2]

Massey's urgent message reveals how single Black women fared during
the Civil War and Reconstruction. This chapter examines this special category of women, who temporarily or permanently could be classified as
"single in Civil War and Reconstruction era Virginia." This population
which included unmarried, divorced, widowed, abandoned, and separated women were the most economically vulnerable group during and
after the war. Despite the economic obstacles they faced, single Black
women asserted their needs and challenged the agendas of governmental agencies whose well-meaning intentions often clashed with their own
expectations. Ultimately, their petitions for support and compensation
altered the roles and responsibilities of federal and local agencies and
made these women prominent characters in defining freedom and welfare
in the nineteenth and early twentieth centuries.

One of the first consequential battles of the war occurred in Virginia.
On July 24, 1861, the *Richmond Dispatch* announced the defeat of the
Union Army in the First Battle of Manassas. The paper stated, "we have
the inexpressible satisfaction of announcing this morning another victory of our arms."[3] The editor went on to proclaim the victory as the
"most important battle ever fought on the American continent." As evidenced in the 122 battles that followed, Virginia would be an important
location in the Eastern theatre. For nearly four years, both Confederate
and Union armies would tear through the state, destroying the landscape
and permanently changing the social, economic, and political lives of
every resident.[4] Before the war started, Virginia was positioned as one
of the most important southern states. In the 1860 census, Virginia held
490,865 enslaved people, thus being the state with the most slaves in the
United States.[5,6]

On eve of the Civil War, Virginia planters produced 123,968,312
pounds of tobacco. The state was considered one of the brightest examples of agricultural progress in the country. Virginia planters were
frequently recognized for their success and profits. They owed their economic prosperity to the labor of enslaved men, women and children.[7]
Virginia's enslaved population carried the burden of sustaining the economy. Although enslaved Black Virginians endured life in the chattel slavery system, they also bluntly resisted the repression of the institution. In
1832, Nat Turner killed nearly fifty White Virginians while attempting to
start a full-scale rebellion. Turner's defiant act altered slavery in the Old
Dominion and throughout the country.

Early in the Civil War, Union forces occupied northern Virginia cities and counties located near Washington, DC. The presence of troops

created a unique environment. As enslaved laborers absconded from southern Virginia, the African American population in northern Virginia counties increased at an unprecedented rate. Throughout the war, southern coastal counties also encountered a heavy Union presence as Union forces gained control of counties in Virginia such as Fortress Monroe. African Americans in southeastern counties like York, Northampton and Gloucester found themselves consistently navigating the shifting boundaries of freedom and bondage, which changed based on the military presence. The tentacles of war touched every part of Virginia, even regions that were not economically tied to slavery. Before the Civil War, much of the enslaved population lived in eastern Virginia. The western part of the state, specifically the northwestern counties, had a smaller enslaved population. By the beginning of the Civil War, this dissimilarity between the two regions was exacerbated when Virginia seceded from the Union. In response to Virginia's secession in 1861, the northwestern counties established a new territory known as West Virginia, forever reshaping the state.

As soon as the war started, enslaved African Americans began to dismantle the institution of slavery. As early as 1861, African American women entered Union lines, declaring their freedom. The Union Army approached freedom-seeking women with ambivalence. Throughout 1861, army commanders ordered their camps closed to fugitive slaves and in some cases returned them to their owners under the Fugitive Slave Act, 1850. This did not dissuade African Americans from flooding into army lines. In May 1861, in Hampton, Virginia, three men enslaved by Colonel Charles Mallory, a commander in the Confederate army, sought refuge at Fortress Monroe. Once the men entered the lines of the Union Army, they requested to see General Benjamin Butler who decided to use them for labor until "better advised." Butler sent a letter to Colonel Mallory informing him that his enslaved laborers had been confiscated as "property." Butler designated freedom seekers as "contraband of war" who would not be emancipated or returned to their owners, but would work as laborers for the Union Army. Secretary of War Edwin Stanton endorsed this policy which was adopted by military leaders in the army and navy. "Butler's decision had far-reaching implications for local and federal policy. During the next few days, 'men, women and even whole families' arrived at Fortress Monroe eager to take advantage of the Union's new policy."[8] This policy was codified into law as the First Confiscation Act by Congress in August 1861. This departure from previous policy led to the construction of more than 100 refugee camps that lasted until the end of the war. These camps were created in river or coastal areas and functioned as short-lived cities. At the end of the war, the military authorities shut down most of the camps, with a few remaining that were operated by the Freedmen's Bureau.[9]

Even after Butler's pronouncement, the presence of freedom-seeking women perplexed the Union Army. Under the status of "contraband," African American women could work and receive compensation, but the opportunities for paid labor were diminishing with the influx of escaping women, men, and children. The Union Army's resources, which were already scant, were being stretched to assist those who could not find work. Additionally, by the end of the year, the population had swelled. With limited options, officials suggested that the large population be forcibly relocated. Postmaster General Montgomery Blair proclaimed, "I am in favor of sending them straight to Hayti.... We could support them better in Hayti than we can do so in Virginia." Longtime abolitionists like Lewis Tappan suggested "a removal of the refugees to the farms and workshops" in the North. Although General Butler listened to all advice, he declared he would continue to "receive and protect all of the negroes." Additionally, he pointed out that one population required most of the army's attention and resources, the "women and children."[10]

Single African American women entered Union lines for various reasons. Some women made the initial trek alone, headed to freedom to be with partners who escaped ahead of them. Other women came to contraband camps after threats of being sold on the auction block. Runaway ads reveal just how frequently Black women took their chances with the embattled freedom available in Union lines. In August 1861, Elizabeth Gibbs ran away from B.J. Vaughan's plantation. Two years later Vaughan placed an advertisement in the *Richmond Dispatch*, which read, "ranaway ... my negro women Liza, sometimes called Elizabeth Gibbs, half white, hair inclined to court, large Black eyes, tall and straight, a small spot on one side of her face, does not speak very quick when spoken to about 28 or 30-year-old."[11] Days later in the same newspaper, Robert Tarift placed a similar want ad for his "two negro women" who were believed to be "making their way to Fredericksburg, a city where Union soldiers were stationed."[12]

Black women who chose not to leave the plantation and remained within Confederate lines continued to wage an inconspicuous war from the inside.[13] Pro-Confederate newspapers frequently reported on the way that Black women sought to undermine their efforts. In 1862, two African American women were "administered lashes" for "feeding

Confederate soldiers dog meat mixed with pork."[14] Women on the home front also suffered through the Confederate and Union armies' mistreatment. Hannah Bailey remembered during the Battle of Manassas, the Confederate cavalry "took everything." Mollie Booker confirmed a similar encounter. She recalled, "what they did not take they burned."[15]

Freedom behind Union lines was precarious. Much of Virginia remained in turmoil for the entirety of the war, and the movement of Confederate and Union troops caused the status of enslaved African Americans to remain in flux. Moreover, rumors of re-enslavement remained rampant. Captain C. B Wilder, Superintendent of Freedmen at Fortress Monroe, confirmed this when he testified some of the "fugitive" slaves were returned to enslavement by Union soldiers.[16] Neither rumors nor the uncertainty of a precarious freedom could stop Black women from running away. They flooded into many eastern counties of Virginia. As a result, cities like Norfolk and Hampton experienced a significant influx of the African American population. In a "chain migration" pattern, whole communities absconded, some in small groups, others all together. Later, these sorts of familial relationships formed in the first months of freedom proved to be crucial in surviving the postwar years. With the passage of the Second Confiscation Act in July 1862, with freed slaves coming under federal control, the population of freedom seekers increased. The numbers swelled further with the passage of the Emancipation Proclamation on January 1, 1863. In the first census after the Proclamation, the Union Army recorded almost "10,000" newly arrived African Americans in the "four lower counties" in southeast Virginia.[17]

When Black women reached Union lines, they joined others and started constructing new lives and identities. Reunion with family members and kin relations were their primary concern. In freedom, the Union supported the formation of a nuclear family structure, which meant formal unions as husband and wife. The Union Army encouraged couples to join together through marriage ceremonies. The army's motivation for family reunification and marriage may have seemed well-meaning; however, internal correspondence reveals officials were primarily concerned with decreasing the number of single women.[18]

Early in the war, Union officials refused to use Black women as laborers. However, this policy changed as the war progressed, and their labor proved invaluable as cooks, laundresses, and nurses. By contrast, the army actively worked to recruit Black men as laborers. As the army moved, Black men constructed the infrastructure by digging ditches, and building bombardments and various other structures necessary to support large encampments. Union officials believed that Black women were unable to provide the crucial physical labor needed, and they were oftentimes viewed as a nuisance. The chaos of war and the constant movement of the Union Army made it impossible to take an accurate count of the number of single Black women.[19]

Throughout the war, the Union Army expressed concern regarding the number of single Black women who received assistance, and proposed solutions to remove them from army camps. Assistance came in many forms, but most of the women either received rations or shelter. A year after the Emancipation Proclamation, there were almost 4,000 women and children receiving government assistance.[20] Their presence forced officials to answer questions regarding their care: what should be done with women who could not find employment? how should they be properly cared for? and how long should the army provide rations, shelter, and clothing for them? Unfortunately, the army was unable to establish a uniform policy. This made for unstable economic lives for single Black women. A few officials believed the Union should relinquish responsibility and forcibly transport the women to the North. Until 1864, several officials stationed in Virginia corresponded with the Pennsylvania Abolition Society with the intention of sending Black women to "respectable families" for work. The plan was thwarted several times but not without the recommendation from a Union lieutenant to halt rations for the women who "refused to go." The army disregarded Black women's familial connections in their relocation plans. Despite objections, the army continued to float ideas about involuntary and voluntary migrations.[21] These plans included sending single Black women to designated contraband camps such as Craney Island in Portsmouth.[22]

Yet, single Black women often worked in critical positions during the war. They labored as cooks, nurses, laundresses and as general domestics, occupations that many had held during slavery. These occupations required culinary and organizational skills, paid between eight and ten dollars per month, and included rations. The army, however, was not consistent in paying Black women for their labor, so that women consistently complained about nonpayment of wages. In the transition to free labor, the army often served as the enforcer of labor contracts during the war in areas that came under the control of Union forces. In November 1864 in Accomack County, Virginia, nearly 130 Black women signed labor contracts to work as either domestics or as laborers on farms, receiving wages from one dollar to four dollars per month. As might be expected, domestics received higher wages than farm laborers. These arrangements typically included shelter, housing, and clothing. In some cases, single mothers like Amy Ashley and her three children did not receive wages, but clothing, food, and shelter for the year in an arrangement that resembled servitude.[23]

Some women worked in the underground economy. Eliza Reed saw the army as a viable market for her goods. In 1864, she was found guilty of "unlawfully selling intoxicating liquor." Other Black women joined the popular sex work industry during the war. Historian Michelle Krowl estimates the "Norfolk provost court sentenced approximately fifteen Black women for prostitution."[24] Some women turned to theft to survive. Sarah Chase, a volunteer stationed at Craney Island, recalled a case where "five or six women stole sheets from a box in the hall." Chase was assigned to the investigation, but she concluded the case would remain unsolved because "the poor women have been knocked about so long with the army, their honesty is frequently challenged."[25]

With or without employment, life under Union authority was a gamble for single Black women. Many reports revealed that Union soldiers were abusive and violent. In Richmond, one Black woman recalled she was assaulted by Union soldiers twice, stating, "I was in the field working, the Yankee soldiers was marching and about six of them stopped and took a razor blade and cut my hair." Another formerly enslaved woman recalled a time when she and her friends were cut by Union soldiers while walking along the road. The assaults were more violent and intrusive in other cases. In Richmond, Union private Charles Clark was convicted of raping Laura Ennis, a freedwoman. He was dishonorably discharged from the army. Similarly, another Black Virginia resident, Harriet Ann Foster, was sexually assaulted by Private Maurice Miller. As with Private Charles Clark, the army punished Miller with dishonorable discharge.[26]

Black women were overwhelmingly recipients of government aid during the war. This aid included monthly or weekly rations as well as housing and clothing. However, women continued to face economic hardships despite the assistance they received. Moreover, once granted help, the Union Army could withhold rations for numerous reasons. The army was notoriously unorganized and bureaucratic. There was a lack of response when freedwomen complained about the destitution they faced, and officials even admitted to the outright mismanagement of resources. This delay in assistance often put Black women in a dire situation. Several women from Yorktown, Virginia, complained to the Department of Negro Affairs about a Union soldier, Mr. Churchill. Churchill not only refused to "issue rations," but he also impressed the women's husbands. They testified, "their husbands were carried away to Washington, DC a year ago and which time they have not received any money or heard a word from them."[27] Aware they were unable to provide consistent help to those who were in need, the Union resorted to holding other African Americans accountable for the single Black women population. In a quasi-communal welfare system, a quartermaster in Alexandria demanded the army deduct money from the army laborers to support the "sick and helpless"; he elaborated that the helpless meant the "elderly, children and women without husbands."[28]

After the enlistment of African American men in the Union Army in 1863, officials were also forced to deal with the wives of soldiers. On December 5, 1863, General Order 46 stated, "to the family of each colored soldier so enlisted and mustered, so long as he shall remain in the service and behave well, shall be furnished suitable subsistence, under the direction of the Superintendents of Negro Affairs, or their Assistants."[29] Additionally, the order helped the family if the soldier was killed while serving. Although they were married, United States Colored Troops (USCT) wives were counted as single, due to the absence of their husbands. The wives of Black soldiers were supposed to receive their husband's pay, but they often had to prove their relationships and sometimes wait for the Union Army to approve their claims. Such was the case for Jane Fitchett, mother of six and wife to USCT soldier Andrew Fitchett. In March 1863, when she applied for benefits, her claim was denied. One month later, she submitted an appeal. The Union Army did not answer her until December 1863. This delay forced Fitchett and her family into destitution for a few months and even after she finally received her husband's allowance and rations; with six children, the rations were not sufficient. Fitchett eagerly waited for the war to end.[30]

In March 1865, the month before the surrender of General Robert E. Lee at Appomattox Court House in Virginia on April 12, Congress established a new federal agency, the Bureau of Refugees, Freedmen, and Abandoned Lands, referred to as the Freedmen's Bureau, to aid African Americans in their transition to freedom. Black women received a variety of aid from the Bureau and used the Bureau's unique postwar court to disentangle themselves from undesirable or harmful relationships. The Freedmen's Bureau was designed as a temporary organization from its inception. The Bureau negotiated labor contracts, legalized slave marriages, adjudicated court cases, established schools and hospitals, and operated Freedmen's Banks in nearly every southern city.[31] Early on, agents determined that single Black women were the population most in need. W. D Tidball, a Freedmen's Bureau agent stationed in Virginia, regularly reported the conditions of the free people in his district. His chief concern was the "large majority" of women, who had been "abandoned by their husbands."[32]

The agency was heavily involved in the lives of Black women without spouses. Much like the Union Army, Bureau agents perceived these women as undeserving of aid. Yet, the organization struggled to create a comprehensive policy. In their dealings with the Bureau, single Black women achieved two objectives: they remained on ration lists despite the Bureau's effort to stop assistance; they also used the Bureau courts to exercise new rights as freedwomen. Although they experienced some success with the agency, it came at a price.

The Bureau was led by a former Union general, Oliver Otis Howard. Howard handled his primary duties in Washington, DC, but selected likeminded military officials to execute his policies at the state level. Every state under the authority of the Bureau was headed by an assistant commissioner. Underneath the assistant commissioner were the sub-assistant commissioners. These commissioners controlled the individual districts in the state. Under sub-assistant commissioners were assistant sub-assistant commissioners who were responsible for the routine office work.

From 1865 to 1879, Bureau agents administered rations, shelter, and clothing to freedpeople. Rations consisted of pork, bacon or beef, hard bread, soft bread, flour, beans, peas, hominy, cornmeal, sugar, and vinegar; as well as candles, soap, salt, and pepper.[33] Although the Bureau distributed rations, they made many attempts to stop "pauperism." Since the Bureau only planned to provide support for a short time, they regularly debated who was most "deserving" of need. Agents quickly determined able-bodied men were omitted from this group. Men were required to "furnish employment" near their homes, and if they could not find jobs near their residence, they were told to look "elsewhere." The Bureau's push for African Americans to enter the labor market remained a constant issue. Agency leaders believed that without assistance, Black men and women would depend solely on the government for assistance. Many times, local officials disputed this point. On the ground, they saw Black women who wanted to work, but faced hostile work environments. Local officials frequently corresponded with the Bureau leadership on issues such as payment for labor performed. One agent bluntly stated, "without a military force in hand these persons cannot be compelled to pay freedmen."[34]

While the Freedmen's Bureau struggled to enforce labor contracts and acquire payment, officials found themselves befuddled about the fate of single Black women. The agency proposed relocating Black women to advantageous labor markets, but this proposal was unpopular. When the agency could not adequately meet the needs of the destitute population, they frequently called on the community members to take up responsibility for single women. Bureau agents counseled destitute residents to go to county-funded poorhouses and orphanages. In counties where these organizations served Whites only, agents called on residents to create alternate institutions for African Americans. This plan relied on the dubious participation of White Virginians, and it quickly became apparent that they were not enthused about aiding freedwomen. White residents fabricated various reasons to circumvent the task of caring for poor African American women. Many claimed the free population was transient and, therefore, unable to gain access to county institutions or benefits that came along with being a resident. Residents also reminded Bureau agents that local welfare services were already being depleted by poverty-stricken Whites.[35]

Just one year after the Bureau's creation, the welfare situation was further muddled. In 1867, Commissioner Howard passed down orders to discontinue aid to all but those who "were sick in regularly organized hospitals and asylums." Almost immediately, correspondence flooded in warning Howard of the dire consequences that would occur if his orders were followed. Some local Bureau administrators ignored Howard's pressures outright and continued to aid women who did not have "husbands living or present." Although Howard intended to decrease the number of African Americans who received help from the Bureau, in some cases agents thwarted that effort.[36]

Single Black women frequently reached out to officers for assistance. In 1867, Malima Robinson requested the Bureau support her. After caring for her family members for over a year, Robinson contracted consumption. Unable to support her family any longer, she asked the Bureau to take care of them. Other women approached the Bureau to help resolve temporary matters. Payne Ellen requested help in acquiring garments after her clothes were "taken in jail." Appeals from single Black women with children came across the desk of Bureau agents the most. This occurred for several reasons. Single Black mothers were largely excluded from the desired postwar workforce. Historian Mary Farmer Kaiser argues these women "faced a difficult labor market" because they were "no longer valued" for their reproduction.[37]

In enslavement, pregnancy represented an increase in labor despite the required downtime for birthing, but in freedom, pregnancy signified no benefit for employers. In fact, without the help of the plantation community, Black women were left with few options for childcare, and they were forced to dedicate work time to child rearing. Thus, women with small children were "labeled unproductives" and reached out to the Bureau for help. Their petitions were often successful. In 1866, when administrators decreased the rations for childless women, they noted single mothers should continue to receive the "same number" of rations but also supplemented their package with coffee and tea. Agents also bolstered the rations for the USCT widows, a population that was disproportionately represented on the destitution list. In an 1868 letter to his superior Bureau agent, Ian General took a census of the destitute population in Fortress Monroe. Among the ten freedpeople who were unable to support themselves, there were eight widows.[38]

Before the establishment of the Freedmen's Bureau, the federal government rarely interceded to help states or cities handle their poor residents. Instead, the work of welfare was designated to local charities. The Freedmen's Bureau was the nation's pioneering effort in aid to the poor. Subsequently, African Americans had the most to lose and gain in the experiment. This was especially true for single Black women since they were disproportionately represented in the indigent population. The Bureau's internal conflict with dependency impacted single Black women the most. Yet, Black women did not readily look to the Bureau for assistance. Bureau records illustrate how most women worked hard to avoid destitution and turned to the agency only out of necessity. This was particularly true in cases of women who wanted the Bureau's help in securing some sort of assistance in situations that left them unable to work. In 1867, Eliza Hackley asked the Bureau to help her gain economic redress after her husband "beat her." As a result, she was "disabled" and headed towards destitution.[39] Mary Staunton experienced a comparable situation with her husband. Staunton's husband abused her when she simply asked him about supper. He proceeded to beat her. The assault was so damaging it caused her to miss work, and her employer threatened to fire her. She asked the court to make her husband pay her for missed work days. These sorts of cases were not handled through local agents. Instead, they were often referred to Freedmen's Bureau courts.[40]

As early as 1865, Bureau commissioner Howard realized governing formerly enslaved African Americans who lived among the "disgruntled" population required close oversight. Although Union soldiers provided protection, African Americans still faced a prejudiced and discriminatory legal system. Black Virginians regularly suffered through unfair sentencing and prejudiced judges who refused to rule in their favor even when the evidence was favorable to their case. To solve the issue, Howard proposed the creation of a legal system that would help administer justice for African Americans – the Freedmen's Bureau courts. The courts were presided over by a three-person panel, which included a selected representative of the planter class, a representative of the freedpeople, and a bureau agent. This system ensured all interests would be represented and decisions regarding labor, landownership, and wages would be issued with compromise. The court was only given jurisdiction over "minor cases," so incidents that violated civil rights were referred to federal courts. As a result, freedpeople mostly used the court to resolve labor issues. In these cases, the Bureau often ruled on the side of the freedpeople. In many instances, the decisions of Bureau court agents remained unenforced. Still, the inefficiency of the court did not hinder Black Virginians from petitioning.[41]

In 1867, Marie Wallop petitioned Drummondtown, Virginia's court, complaining that Erastmus Donnis was her husband and he had "abandoned her." Wallop not only claimed "abandonment," she also stated all her clothes had been stolen. Wallop requested the court make her estranged husband return her clothes. Single Black women like Wallop continuously demanded Bureau courts aid them in securing financial support from their estranged spouses. Black women were conscious of the Bureau's efforts to curb dependency and therefore they understood the organization would take cases of abandonment seriously. In Wallop's case, the court looked for Donnis, but they were unable to find him.[42] In cases where abandoned women were aware of their husband's location, they asked the court to reach out to other courts and force their partners to return or send money. Ana Marie Brown was aware her husband, James Brown, was in Maryland and "doing well in the way of work." She complained he would not send his "wages" back to support her and asked the court to help her.[43]

Some women even used the agency to seek retribution against old partners who they believed had wronged them. Mary Jones felt she had been "seduced" by Joe Bullock, who "promised her marriage just to have intercourse." In the case of Mary Blizzard, the Bureau worked to mediate agreeable terms in her separation from James Blizzard "after he left her for another woman." The court heard testimonies from Mary's mother and other witnesses. Thereafter, her former partner agreed to "pay a set amount and furnish her with rations weekly."[44]

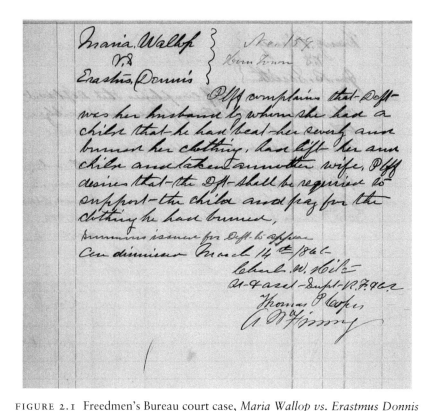

FIGURE 2.1 Freedmen's Bureau court case, *Maria Wallop vs. Erastmus Donnis*
for Drummondtown, Virginia, 14 March 1866.
Source: Virginia, Freedmen's Bureau Field Office Records, 1865–1872,
Drummondtown (Assistant Subassistant commissioner). Proceedings of
Freedmen's Court, May 1865–May 1867, M1913, National Archives and
Records Adminitration, Washington, DC

Single Black mothers also appealed to the court around issues concerning childcare. Martha Ann Dudley was married to James Dudley before the Civil War. They "lived together as man and wife" until 1867, when James deserted her, taking the oldest child with him. Martha filed a complaint at the local Bureau court, giving her former husband a choice to either return the child or support her. The love of mothers for their children extended into death as the case of Hannah Resell illustrates. Hannah took Jamie Bon to court after he "struck a blow" and subsequently killed her son. She demanded the court investigate the matter and send Bon to jail. This declaration demonstrates the ways formerly enslaved Black women asserted themselves in the first years of freedom.

Only a few years before, many African American women may have stood powerless in the decision-making processes concerning their children. After the war, Black mothers defiantly claimed their maternal rights in front of both White and Black men.[45]

In addition to their complaints regarding the treatment of their children, single Black women used Bureau courts to protect themselves from abusive partners. Abuse in African American relationships had been present in unions made during slavery. Katie Johnson from Washington County, Virginia, recalled "some good masters would punish slaves who mistreated their womenfolk, and some didn't."[46]

In freedom, Black women sought to ensure that abusers received punishment. In 1867, Margaret Davis took her husband to court for assault and battery. Davis's husband pled guilty, and he was sentenced to jail for five days. A few times, women failed or refused to bring charges on their violent partners. Instead, community members interceded on behalf of the victims. Although not married, Eliza Wheeler and William Thomas were brought before the court based on complaints of neighbors. Wheeler experienced abuse so frequently that her neighbors took her partner Thomas to court for "disturbing the peace." The judge confined him to jail for five days.[47]

Many Black women used the system to mediate the financial obligations of single motherhood. In numerous county courts, single women requested monetary support from men who fathered their children but refused to support them. Maria Sheppard experienced similar difficulties when she brought charges against Samuel Crittenden. He admitted to fathering her child and subsequently was ordered to pay one dollar per month. In 1867, Penelope Parker took Henry Duckett to Bureau court after he had "sexual intercourse" with her over eighteen months and left. Pregnant and alone, Penelope turned to the Bureau. Henry confessed the child was his but refused to support her. The court ordered Henry to pay four dollars a month. Agents who served as mediators were aware that if the women did not receive economic support for their children they would likely end up as dependents of the Bureau.

Bureau courts handled all aspects of minor cases pertaining to freedpeople. In many southern cities, African Americans had to contend with both the Union Army, many of whom were Bureau agents, as well as a provisional local force. The presence of multiple enforcement bodies may have been necessary for several reasons. The Bureau and the Union Army were wholly invested in enforcing the new labor relationship between Blacks and Whites. However, the presence of Union soldiers and the provisional local force ushered in years of excess surveillance. Black communities in urban terrains like Hampton and Richmond experienced Union soldiers who regularly perused the streets looking for offenders. In addition, Bureau agents traveled through the city, surveying their appointed districts. As a result, Black women and men were regularly brought in by Bureau agents and the Union Army for public offenses like street fighting and vulgar language. Single Black women were overwhelmingly charged with two infractions – vagrancy and prostitution.

Vagrancy was an umbrella term applied to criminalize perceived indolence. The large quantity of the charges illustrates how concerned the Bureau was with labor. Beyond protecting the rights of those who willingly entered contracts, the Bureau was also clear that African Americans "must be required" to obtain "a visible means of support." This rule was partially implemented to decrease the number of government dependents. Bureau officials' independent belief that progress in the reconstructed South was only conceivable if they strictly enforced the free labor structure was an added motivation. From June 1866 to June 1867, nearly forty Black women were arrested in Hampton, Virginia. Half of the women were charged with vagrancy. The crime was coupled with prostitution fifteen times. These statistics demonstrate that although Black women may have been charged with "idleness," they were engaged in an underground labor economy that was not deemed acceptable by the Bureau.[48]

By 1872, the Bureau was dismantled and no longer operating in Virginia and many southern states as the federal government transitioned away from reconstructing the South in favor of pursuing expanding commercial interests in the West. Black Virginians were forced to navigate the hostile and violent environment, during what Kidada Williams refers to as the war against Reconstruction, without assistance from the federal government. White southerners worked to undermine Black freedom and progress. But Black Virginians were equipped to create and sustain communities without federal aid. In the post-Reconstruction years, single Black women sought to build their lives on their own terms. In 1874, single African American women appealed to the county's overseer of the poor for assistance.[49] No longer having access to the Bureau courts, Black women used the local courts to file divorce petitions. Black women also worked together to create charitable organizations to take care of themselves and their community. The population was still economically vulnerable, but made a concerted effort to support themselves, their communities and their families.[50]

In 1898 Harvard-trained, Black historian and sociologist, W.E.B. Du Bois set out to study the African American population in Farmville, Virginia. The study was funded and supported by the Department of Labor. In his findings, he declared he was interested in exploring the "economic condition of the American Negro." Du Bois asserted Farmville was akin to most of Virginia, "easy going, gossipy and conservative." However, the city was selected for his study because of its prominence as a rural trading town. The town, with a population of nearly 2,500, was majority African American and in decline due to northern migration.[51]

For three months, Du Bois lived with Black families throughout the town and interviewed residents. The interrogation usually included questions about the resident's household composition, finances, and "conjugal status." Although Du Bois was primarily interested in the economic status of the residents, the study disproportionately concentrated on their social life. Moreover, he reserved his harshest criticism for one specific population. Under the heading of "conjugal status," he revealed the town had a low marriage rate and a large population of "single black women." Furthermore, he declared the single Black women in the town were the source of two evils, "illicit sexual intercourse and restrictive influence over family life."[52]

For years single Black women encountered hostility from White government officials and religious organizations. However, by the end of nineteenth century, their fiercest adversaries seemed to be members in their community. Du Bois and other reformers shared and publicized the belief that marriage was fundamental to Black advancement and morality. According to their beliefs, relationships not included in the normative family structure were harmful to the Black community.

Despite their presence in Union Army and Freedmen's Bureau records, single Black women remain understudied. Civil War and Reconstruction studies have been overwhelmingly focused on marriage and the reunion of family members following the war. This focus has ignored those not included in the normative family structure or those who chose to leave relationships. Telling the stories of single Black women in freedom illustrates how, collectively and individually, Black women fought to survive and define freedom on their own terms. Freedom was a complicated process that created new relationships to the state and federal government. The term implied equity, social, political, and economic equity, which remained illusive for African American women. Single Black women were not merely the helpless wards of governmental assistance. They were active in seeking employment opportunities that compensated them for their labor, resisted unfair labor contracts, and appealed to the courts to adjudicate poor treatment by partners.

3

"I Had Time for Myself"

Enslaved Women, Labor, and the Politics of Acquisition during the Civil War

Felicia Jamison

In December 1864, soldiers of the Union Army entered Francis Brown's home and requested her belongings. For several weeks the army had foraged through Georgia as a part of General William Sherman's "March to the Sea" military campaign. Soldiers routinely commandeered livestock, food, and other personal items from the abandoned homes of plantation owners and the enslaved folk who resided in the area. Enslaved women happily obliged them as the arrival of the forces signaled their freedom. In addition to yielding their belongings, enslaved women labored for the soldiers by cooking their personal food reserves, washing clothes, and doing manual labor at the Union camp at Midway Congregational Church, a site located near several plantations. However, the manner in which soldiers utilized the property disturbed these newly emancipated women. More than eight years after the event, thirty-eight-year-old Francis Brown remained aggrieved by how soldiers handled her property. After taking fifteen bushels of her rice, the Union soldiers then used her clothing as vessels in which to transport the seized goods. In her 1873 Southern Claims Commission testimony, Francis lamented, "I had three dresses taken. They were fine dresses. They had not sacks enough to take the rice so they tied up the dresses and put the rice in them."[1] As enslaved people were customarily allotted inferior clothing it is likely that these dresses were more than mere garments. When worn, they presented an opportunity for her to rise above the assigned status of field laborer and slave.[2] Equally as important, Francis had acquired the dresses and grown the rice by laboring in her personal time after completing strenuous tasks on the rice plantation.[3] Though happy that the soldiers' arrival ensured her freedom, Francis Brown and other enslaved people firmly believed that they should have some say in how their personal goods were used.

This chapter centers the lives and experiences of enslaved women in Liberty County, Georgia, to better understand how gender factored into accumulating property. Next, it turns to the period of the Civil War, paying particular attention to the month of December 1864, when soldiers from Judson Kilpatrick's cavalry raided the county for provisions. Enslaved women like Francis Brown willingly and enthusiastically yielded their property to Union forces, often to the detriment of their own physical and material wellbeing. The loss of personal goods such as clothing, livestock, and bushels of agricultural products severely hampered Black women's and their families' transition into freedom. Not only would newly freed women be forced to survive the winter without goods necessary for subsistence, they also lost access to items that would have been passed on to their children.

Using the politics of acquisition as a framework, this chapter argues that enslaved women in Liberty County, Georgia, used property to enhance their lives during slavery and to secure their freedom during slavery and during the war. It rests on several suppositions. First, enslaved women who acquired property were intelligent and skilled at managing their time and participating in the local informal economy. Second, it acknowledges the intergenerational effort inherent in property accumulation. Women, men, and children collectively worked to accumulate large amounts of goods in their personal time. As a result, children – male and female – benefitted by inheriting property from their parents. Finally, the framework recognizes that there was no one valid way to use the property once acquired.[4] Some purchased goods such as fine dresses and dishes because these items brought enslaved women immediate pleasure. Some also cultivated crops and livestock to supplement their diets, while others devoted years of their lives to accumulating goods to pass on to children. And a small number of property owners managed to acquire enough goods and money to purchase their freedom.

Historians Philip D. Morgan and Dylan Penningroth have highlighted the links between the task system and the enslaved people who owned property. Morgan's groundbreaking article "Work and Culture" explores the seventeenth-century origins of rice culture in Georgia and South Carolina and demonstrates the ways in which enslaved people used the task system to accumulate property throughout the eighteenth and nineteenth centuries. Ultimately, the skills acquired while working the task system aided freedpeople in the post-emancipation period as they participated in the southern economy.[5] In *The Claims of Kinfolk*, Penningroth examines the task labor system to analyze the manner in which bondpeople used a system of kinship and recognition to differentiate which person owned a particular good. In this extralegal sphere, community members verbally acknowledged and recognized each person's claims to property. Community members also used property to form or strengthen kinship ties.[6] Neither Morgan nor Penningroth, however, focuses on Black women's experiences as property owners. This chapter builds on these works and looks specifically at the manner in which women acquired and passed on goods to loved ones while legally classified as property. It also interrogates the varied meanings of property for Black women. As Deborah Gray White has affirmed, "Female slave bondage was not better or worse, or more or less severe, than male bondage, but it was different."[7] The same can be inferred regarding property ownership among enslaved women and men who accumulated property during slavery but in a different manner based on their gender.

Over the last three decades, scholars of slavery have examined how gender shaped Black women's experiences. Jennifer Morgan has demonstrated how plantation owners used enslaved Black women for their physical labor as well as for their reproductive labor.[8] Leslie Schwalm and Judith Carney have contended that agriculturally, enslaved women were integral to rice cultivation.[9] Stephanie Camp has shown that though their mobility was often limited to the spaces of the plantation, enslaved women used their bodies for pleasure to attend social gatherings outside the boundaries of plantations.[10]

Located along the southeastern coast of Georgia, Liberty County was populated with rice plantations that employed the task system. This labor system was organized around agricultural assignments that, if worked timely, could be completed before the end of the day, allowing bondpeople to work for themselves. During their "personal time," enslaved people raised crops and caught fish, and sold them in the informal economy to White and Black people alike. Many formerly enslaved people detailed this process of property accumulation in their testimonies to the Southern Claims Commission.[11] In the early 1870s more than ninety-one freedpeople in Liberty County filed claims to the Commission. Eighteen complaints were filed by women.[12] These interviews are representative of the thousands of enslaved women who lived, loved, and labored in the county during slavery and throughout the war. Their testimonies are filled with stories detailing the manner in which they acquired and passed on property, the culture of the informal economy, and the types of goods they purchased. Furthermore, their accounts reveal how enslaved women navigated the process of giving up their property in order to gain freedom. During the war, enslaved women affirmed their loyalty to the United States, showed their appreciation to Union soldiers who brought freedom to the county, and raised concerns for their loss of property.

FIGURE 3.1 Map of Georgia; Liberty County, located on the coastal region of southeastern Georgia. Many neighboring counties, such as McIntosh and Glynn counties, also included rice plantations which flourished due to enslaved laborers.
Source: A. Finley, Philadelphia, 1831. Courtesy, Georgia Archives, Historic Map File Collection, hmf0058

PROPERTY ACCUMULATION BEFORE THE WAR

By 1860, enslaved African Americans in Liberty County had produced more than 2.5 million pounds of rice.[13] Enslaved Africans and African Americans leveraged their rice cultivation knowledge and skills to gain some privileges for themselves. Patsey Campbell recalled that before the war she raised hogs and poultry and had managed "to plant a little corn for myself in front of my house and I planted some rice too." She had done so "ever since I was old enough." Working for herself afforded her the opportunity to eventually purchase a horse. When asked how she was able to acquire such goods, Patsey explained to the Southern Claims Commission officials, "I worked for my master by the task and afterwards I had time for myself."[14]

Through this informal economy, mothers taught their children important economic skills. For children, a skill could be used as "a valuable and portable kind of property" that could generate more income.[15] Skills could also be taught and passed on.[16] In addition to bequeathing them material goods, parents in Liberty County traditionally taught their children a number of skills relevant to property ownership. Mothers and fathers taught their children how to measure their work time on the plantation in order to have adequate time to work for themselves. They also showed them how to grow crops and raise livestock on the limited number of acres allotted them in the slave quarters. Parents informed their children on the particulars of participating in the informal economy. When the army came to Liberty County, Georgia, in the winter of 1864, Rachel Norman owned cattle, several bushels of corn and rice, chickens and hogs. She had inherited the livestock from her parents. Rachel learned the skills of property accumulation, and her expertise in accurately marketing these goods to community members, as a child while assisting her mother and father to acquire goods.[17] This was the case for other bondpeople who obtained property and participated in the informal economy.

The accumulation and passing on of goods were part of the politics of acquisition in which enslaved women sought to create and pass on intergenerational wealth to loved ones and to improve the material quality of life for themselves and their families. The accumulation of property was a collaborative effort involving numerous family members. It was customary for couples to jointly acquire goods, as was the case for Susan and Scipio Bennett. Susan was born about 1837.[18] She originally lived in McIntosh County on the plantation of William Y. King. When one of King's daughter, Mary E. King, married William G. Thompson, Susan moved to Liberty County with the newlyweds. There she married her husband, Scipio, who belonged to William G. Thompson.[19] The couple lived on the Thompson plantation for two years prior to the arrival of the Union Army. Susan recounted, "We got this property by working together on our own work after we got through our tasks. We bought a pig and raised from there. We both had pigs when we married."[20] Susan's case demonstrates that the work of accumulating property was a family effort. The Bennetts jointly grew fifty bushels of corn, sixty bushels of rice, and raised hogs. However, it is unlikely that the young couple received help from their children. Susan stated that in 1874 her oldest child was only ten years old, meaning that in 1864, at the time of the siege, her daughter was an infant.[21] Thus, it was largely the labor of Susan and Scipio Bennett, with the help of kin members, that produced the large bushels of crops and provided care for the hogs.

Married women acquired more property than single women, as they had assistance from their spouse. Whereas Nancy Bacon was a widow with young children during the war, Silvy Baker was married and had a number of children who could assist with labor on the plantation and help accumulate property for the family. In 1864 at the time of the raid, thirty-four-year-old Silvy was married to a driver on a local plantation. Her youngest child was an infant at the time, and it is probable that Silvy had considerable help from her husband and six other children.[22] Although the accumulation of property was a family endeavor, married women could devote more time to working for themselves as they had a partner who assisted them with growing crops and raising livestock. Enslaved women in the county greatly depended on the labor of extended kin members to assist in the accumulation of property.

Property accumulation was not an easy process. It often took strategizing and sacrifice to capitalize on one's personal time, even if one had the added labor of a partner and older children. This was the case with Joseph and Peggy James. When discussing the manner in which he and his wife accumulated property, Joseph explained: "My wife and I worked about three acres of land and we saved our rations and ate rice instead in the winter. I wanted the corn to feed my horse and hogs and eat myself."[23] The family of four regulated their eating habits in order to earn a better yield for their crops and to acquire more goods, further emphasizing the effort needed to effectively accumulate property under the task system. Although afforded personal time in which to work for themselves, acquiring property was no easy feat for enslaved women, men, and their children.

Ready access to large markets also determined the amount of property one could acquire. Black women in urban locations such as nearby Savannah regularly participated in a robust market economy.[24] In rural counties such as Liberty County, the majority of Black women did not travel beyond the city limits but participated in the local informal economy and sold goods to community members, both on the plantation on which they lived and to others on neighboring plantations. In several Southern Claims Commission interviews, Black women demonstrated that they participated in the local informal economy. For example, sixty-year-old Linda Jones recounted that she had raised and sold chickens in the community for "about all my life."[25] Although confined to the spaces of plantations, enslaved women used kin networks to sell their goods to larger markets in nearby cities. In her memoir, army nurse and educator Susie King Taylor recalled her grandmother, who lived in Savannah, traveling thirty miles to visit her mother in Liberty County every three months to barter with the local enslaved community. Taylor recalled that "She would hire a wagon to carry bacon, tobacco, flour, molasses, and sugar. These she would trade with people in the neighboring places, for eggs, chickens, or cash."[26]

The final aspect of the politics of acquisition is the purchase and accumulation of goods as an avenue in which to pass on generational wealth. These goods were used to materially demonstrate love for their children through the passing on of goods.[27] The acts of enslaved women who purchased and passed on goods to children were in direct opposition to their legal classification as property.[28] Daina Ramey Berry provides a detailed account of the manner in which enslavers valued bondpeople from the time that they were in their mothers' wombs until well after their death. In an attempt to show the latter's resistance, Berry "traces the internal self-worth African Americans held on to when external forces literally and figuratively sought to strip them of humanity."[29] Enslaved women effectively reclaimed their bodies and their personal time by strategically acquiring goods and methodically passing on those goods to their children. Jane Holmes recounted, "I labored for this property. I worked by tasks. My master gave us tasks and when we done we worked for ourselves."[30] Working for themselves was doubly significant for enslaved women: it enabled them to use their labor to acquire goods and to purchase items that gave them pleasure, and it also afforded them the opportunity to leave some goods to their children who were born into a life of servitude and bondage. Bondwomen like Francis Brown also resisted their classification as simply laboring and reproductive bodies by acquiring property that provided a source of pleasure for themselves and served as an inheritance for their children, even if the goods could only be enjoyed within the confines of slavery.[31]

Though enslaved women used property to enhance and supplement their material lives, property ownership was not a benevolent act bestowed upon the enslaved population by enslavers. Slavery was a system of power, control, and coercion. The owning of goods was yet another manner in which enslavers displayed control. In his study of African American political organizing in the rural South, Steven Hahn affirms that "while the task system allowed enslaved workers 'an economy of time' to plant and tend their own gardens and raise livestock, coercion and brute force remained the central elements of the labor system."[32] Such was the case in Liberty County. Enslavers' acceptance of this local, property-owning tradition should be positioned alongside benign scenes of slavery. Saidiya Hartman argues that "innocent amusements," such as holidays in which bondpeople did not have to labor, weekends off, and dances, created by enslavers in fact "constituted a form of symbolic violence."[33] These benevolent acts "must be considered in relation to the dominant imposition of transparency and the degrading hypervisibility of the enslaved, and therefore, by the same token, such concealment [of their feelings by the enslaved] should be considered a form of resistance."[34] Opportunities for enslaved women to acquire goods should be not be viewed as acts of benevolence but rather as one of the many coercive means to create a more malleable labor force.

By the period of the Civil War, enslaved women in Liberty County had established a flourishing tradition of property ownership. But although equipped with the skills and collateral to do so, enslavers in the county ensured that they were unable to purchase their freedom and the freedom of their loved ones.[35] Of the 6,083 African Americans listed in the 1860 census, there were no free people listed.[36] County records reflect that in 1861 at least one person registered as a free person and in 1862 that number had grown to two free women.[37] Free people accounted for less than 1 percent of the African American population during the war, further highlighting the insurmountable barriers to freedom faced by the enslaved population. Silvy Baker recollected that there had been several cases in which enslaved people in the county had paid for their freedom only to be taken advantage of by their enslavers. She detailed, "Many slaves made enough in that way to buy their freedom but they so often got cheated out their freedom. Few would risk it."[38] It seems that by the Civil War period enslaved women and men had come to realize that they would not be able to successfully purchase their freedom and thus sought to enjoy some benefits of their labor by acquiring property and passing it on to their offspring.

NAVIGATING FREEDOM DURING THE WAR

Black women in Liberty County had ready access to freedom due to the proximity of soldiers fighting and camping in the county. Women had begun fleeing plantations at the start of the war. By July 1862, according to local reverend and plantation owner Charles Colcock Jones, at least fifty-one people had escaped from the county.[39] This accounted for less than 1 percent of the enslaved population.[40] Many others would remain in the county and only choose to leave after the Union Army's arrival. Eliza James recalled that after the raid, "I then went with the Yankees and staid about a year."[41] Jane Holmes too would follow the army to Savannah but later returned as she had family and roots in the county.[42] Lucy McIver stated that "after I became free I went to Savannah and went to washing."[43]

Other women claimed their freedom and decided to stay in the county for the remainder of the war. Silvy Baker noted, "I did not change my residence or occupation" and continued living on a local plantation.[44] Clarinda Porter did the same and "worked fixing the ground to plant."[45] Susan Bennett and her husband, Scipio, participated in the emerging free labor system.[46] After the soldiers left the area, the couple remained on the same plantation and worked for their former enslaver for shares. Susan recounted that "He took two days and we four days work."[47] Whether they later followed the army to Savannah or stayed in the county and labored, each woman helped Union soldiers by giving them their property.

Black women gave their property to soldiers often to the detriment of themselves and their families. In Union-occupied cities and towns, "Union soldiers stripped slave cabins of their meager contents with the same spirit in which they rifled masters' mansions, often leaving slaves without food or clothing."[48] Black women in Liberty County supplied the army with bedding, cookware, food supplies, and livestock. Clarinda Porter testified that the soldiers took a horse, beehives, pots and spoons, and three quilts.[49] In addition to taking livestock and food reserves, Eliza James recounted they took "two wool blankets, two quilts, two sheets, and a mattress and all my plates, pots, kettle, and everything I had."[50] Seamstress Matilda McIntosh had eighteen blankets and four or five quilts taken from her during the raid.[51] Lydia Baker testified that during the raid, soldiers had taken five hogs, several bushels of corn, ten chickens, a jar of lard, and a blanket from her.[52] Goods such as bedding and quilts could have been used to warm the claimants on cold December nights.

Furthermore, women most likely depended on their personal reserves of food and clothing to survive the winter months each year. Though they were allotted a weekly portion of corn, sweet potatoes, and at times bacon, it is probable that the conflict of war disrupted this established distribution system.[53] Women supplemented their rations by growing their own foodstuffs and raising livestock to eat for protein. The three cows and three hogs that the Union soldiers took from Nancy Bacon could have certainly fed herself and her child. At the very least, Nancy could have sold one of the animals to purchase items that would have helped her family survive the winter.[54]

Many women also gave the soldiers personal items that held sentimental value. As Francis Brown noted, the dress the soldiers used to carry commandeered goods was one of her "fine dresses." In the county it was customary for enslaved people to receive two sets of clothing, one in the winter and one in the spring or summer. Often the clothing would be made of wool or cotton.[55] In her autobiography, abolitionist and former slave Harriet Jacobs recounted, "I had a vivid recollection of the linsey-woolsey dress given me every winter by Mr. Flint. How I hated it! It was one of the badges of slavery."[56] In this same vein, it seems Francis Brown's fine dresses afforded her a sense of freedom. Perhaps she had worn them on Sunday mornings to Midway Congregational Church or to one of the plantation services, an occasion that was both religious and social. Community members would have marveled at her fashion sense as the garments drastically differed from her usual wardrobe worn while laboring in the fields. Francis could have worn the dresses at any of the social events held in the county, including Saturday night parties, secret barbecues, or wedding celebrations.[57] Celebrating in or simply wearing one of her "fine" dresses would allow her some control over what historian Stephanie Camp terms the "third body" – a contested site "to be claimed and enjoyed, a site of pleasure and resistance."[58] Whatever the scenario, the use of her fine dresses in such a careless manner affected Francis so much that she felt moved to talk about it in her Southern Claims Commission testimony, almost more than a decade after the raid.

Patsey Campbell too lost a valuable object during the war. But unlike Francis, Patsey did not voice her concern about the loss of her property. In her claim, Patsey followed the rudimentary procedure of describing the pot and providing evidence supporting her claim that Union soldiers took it from her house. However, the testimonies of the two witnesses who corroborated Patsey's claim may offer some insight into how the claimant may have truly felt about the mistreatment of her pot. Her first witness, Rosa Jane Quarterman, was there when the property was taken and in great detail recounted that Patsey's pot "was in the kitchen when they took it. It had dinner cooked in it. They took the dinner and all and carried it off." The inclusion of this information about the soldier's taking the pot as food cooked in it was not pertinent to the claim. Rosa Jane's inclusion of this fact served to highlight the perceived disrespect inherent in the soldiers' taking the pot with the food cooking in it. William Bacon, Patsey's brother and second witness, further elaborated about the subsequent usage of the cookware. After the raid, William visited the Union camp site at Midway Church and suspected that the army did not use the pot but instead only ate food out of it. He stated, "I don't suppose they could have made any use of the pot but to cook in it. I didn't see them use it."[59] Both Rosa Jane Quarterman and William Bacon witnessed the taking of the pot and provided details that Patsey Campbell may not have felt comfortable including in her Southern Claims Commission claim as she sought to be compensated for her property.

The testimonies of Patsey Campbell and her witnesses also raise concerns as to how the commandeering of property may have impacted Patsey's livelihood after the war. It is likely that enslaved people were customarily given pots and pans in which to cook food, but according to Patsey the one taken by Union soldiers was very large and could be used for baking and for washing clothes.[60] It may have been difficult or very time-consuming to labor and purchase a pot of equal quality in the postwar period. This pot would have benefitted Patsey in freedom. In her claim, Patsey noted that she was currently cooking for a family. Perhaps she could have used that particular pot to earn additional money as a cook in the county. Additionally, she could have used the large pot to work as a laundress in the community. Patsey Campbell's oven "was as large as a family wanted. They could boil clothes in it."[61] If she chose to become a laundress or a cook, having such a high-quality pot would have certainly made either job much easier. Unlike many freedpeople whose property was taken, Patsey Campbell was compensated for her property in the amount of $100. The money most likely improved her material life. However, she was not awarded the funds until October 1876, more than a decade after the goods were taken from her.

The loss of goods likely hampered the employment opportunities of a number of freedwomen like Patsey. Matilda McIntosh was a seamstress who listed a buggy, a mare, a wagon, and two harnesses among her commandeered property. During slavery she "used the horse to go to church and down to the plantation." While enslaved, she had labored to acquire the goods. When not working on the plantation, she had "worked for myself at night. Sometimes I hired myself and I sewed by the task." Perhaps Matilda could have used the horse and buggy to travel to her clients' homes for fittings or to sell her goods in places outside of the county.[62] The practical use of these goods to continue generating money following emancipation cannot be overstated. These goods may also have been valued by women as they were acquired during their personal time, a time devoted to personal labor after completing tasks on the plantation. In discussing Black women's transition from slavery to freedom Thavolia Glymph highlights the importance of goods that were not bestowed on them by White people or that were considered secondhand. "The desire for a pretty dress or home with kitchen utensils and blankets was a small but central part of freedom making, of demonstrated control over one's life."[63]

Many elderly women whose property was taken in December 1864 had limited economic opportunities due to their advanced age. Seventy-year-old Lydia Baker stated that during slavery her enslaver had "dropped me down to a half hand before he died."[64] On rice plantations, a full hand would be a younger enslaved adult who completed one task, or a quarter of an acre of rice cultivation, per day. This labor classification illustrates that older women may not have been able to labor as vigorously as younger freedwomen and would not be able to earn as much money. Lydia had given soldiers five hogs, ten chickens, clothing, and ten bushels of corn. Having such large amounts of goods to barter or sell would have been useful to begin one's life as a freedwoman of an advanced age.[65]

Unlike Lydia, eighty-five-year-old Sylvia Walthour did not receive any funds for her commandeered goods. During the war, Union soldiers had taken a host of goods from her, including a horse, a wagon, chickens, ducks, cows, as well as her deceased husband's blacksmith tools. Her son Simon testified that his mother had inherited all of the property after his father passed away three years prior. Simon further elaborated, "Whatever she raised belonged to her. She was old and exempt from service for her long service to her master. No part of it belonged to her master. It was all my mother's."[66] It is likely that Sylvia's several adult children and grandchildren helped financially support and provide care for her in her old age.[67] The loss of the extensive property during the war, as well as her not being compensated by the Southern Claims

Commission several years later, negatively impacted her livelihood and limited her economic options in the postwar period.

The Black women who testified to the Southern Claims Commission did not vocally complain about their goods being taken during the war, for several reasons. Many people were simply happy to be free and gave generously of their property and labor. Francis Brown recounted that she "cooked and did everything I could for them all the time they staid [*sic*]." Silvy Baker "cooked and worked for them till they went away."[68] Joseph James testified that his wife Peggy and their daughter cooked and waited on the soldiers for three days.[69] Even if they wished to inquire about their goods, there was no specific person or system in which to state one's concerns. The James family's property was commandeered in 1864 and the Southern Claims Commission was organized in 1871, several years after the raid. Nonetheless, many of the women were anxious to be compensated for their goods at a future date. Though she raised no concerns at the time, Clarinda Porter recalled that "They told me when they came there that if they took them from me I could get them back."[70] That many of these women later filed claims to the Southern Claims Commission demonstrates the importance of this property to their financial and material wellbeing to better settle into their freedom.

The loss of property also negatively impacted the future wealth of the Black community. An important aspect of the politics of acquisition was strategizing and sacrificing one's time to create an inheritance for one's children. Sandy Austin remembered his mother raising pigs and hogs "and when she died she left it to us."[71] Pulaski Baker recounted, "My old parents used to raise poultry and pigs and they gave me some – that is how I got a start."[72] Rachel Norman affirmed that she inherited a sow and heifer from her parents when they died.[73] Although her father had rheumatism, Patsey Campbell's father helped her purchase a horse. She recalled that her "father helped me rake and scrape the rest and helped me out with it."[74] In addition to passing on goods to all of their children, parents also tried to be equitable in the informal passing on of goods. Joseph Bacon, a driver on a local plantation, inherited a mare from his father, but noted that after he died, his father "gave $50 to the other children for their share."[75] The small sampling of these interviews provides some insight into the importance of property acquisition and inheritance during slavery.

The arrival of war in the county and the Union Army's commandeering of property disrupted this generations-long informal inheritance practice. Susan Bennett stated that she and her deceased husband, Scipio, raised hogs and cultivated crops while enslaved. "No one but I and my children have any interest in this property." The four hogs, fifty bushels of corn and sixty bushels of rice or the proceeds of the sale would have benefitted the family in some capacity.[76] Silvey Baker asserted "I and my children are the only parties interested in this claim. I have seven children. Three girls and four boys."[77] Perhaps no case represents the intentionality of working to pass on property to children better than that of Linda Jones. Linda and her son Caesar jointly filed a claim with the Southern Claims Commission. Most likely they filed the claim together due to Linda's advanced age. She was sixty years old at the time of the filing. Linda made it clear in her testimony that she and her husband had accumulated the property for their son Caesar. She recounted, "When he died he left about six head of hogs and some poultry to my son and I brought them to my house. My husband's property and the increase of it I have got in my claim here for my son."[78] Linda Jones continued to accumulate property for her son years after her husband died.

CONCLUSION

In 1877, forty-five-year-old Silvy Baker testified to the officials of the Southern Claims Commission. She sought to recoup losses from her commandeered property which included a mare, buggy, livestock, twenty-five bushels of rice and ten bushels of corn, which she valued at $346. Like many enslaved women, Silvy had jointly acquired the goods with her now-deceased husband. If awarded, the money would be for herself and her children. She stated, "I have seven children. Three girls and four boys – all are living in Darien, McIntosh County Georgia." Though Silvy followed the proper channels of filing a claim and providing several witnesses to corroborate, the Southern Claims Commission only awarded her $136, an amount they felt proper and acceptable. Silvy had valued her property at $346, more than twice the sum the commission had allowed.[79] In losing her property, she forfeited the proceeds of years she had devoted to accumulating property, an inheritance for her children, and an economic boost to help her establish herself in a free labor society.

The politics of acquisition provides a framework in which to position Silvy Baker and other newly freed women as property owners. As such, it is imperative to understand how the loss of property impacted their transition into freedom. During Reconstruction, freedwomen in Liberty County built on their generational knowledge of owning property to acquire land. In1871 Black citizens owned 1,618 acres and by 1899 the number had grown substantially to 44,405 acres.[80] They purchased land from former enslavers through installment payments; in some cases, they sharecropped over several years in order to save enough money to purchase small plots of land, while others pooled their resources to purchase large acres of land. Black women acquired and maintained ownership of the land despite economic obstacles. They labored as sharecroppers to earn money to purchase the family land, toiled on the family farm to ensure that it was profitable enough to pay the annual taxes, and deeded the land to their children.[81] Freed women and men accomplished this feat in less than three decades following the 1864 raid. After the war, Susan Bennett had "bought a piece of land of Raymond Cay."[82] Jane Holmes purchased an acre of land in the county "to build my house on."[83] Francis Brown bought land that once had been a part of a large plantation.[84] And though all three women received some compensation for their loss of property during the war, the remuneration was less than the estimated value of their goods.[85] Despite not receiving full compensation for their property, they worked to build an economic foundation for their families through landownership.

PART II

WAR, GENDER VIOLENCE, AND THE COURTS

4

Black Women, War, and Freedom in Southern Louisiana and Low Country Georgia

Karen Cook Bell

In 1861, ten women from the Contrell plantation in St. James Parish, Louisiana, ran away along with twenty other men.[1] Living in the woods near Bayou Faupron, four miles from the plantation house, the escaped fugitives slept on logs and pilfered livestock from the plantation for three months until they successfully escaped through the swamps to Camp Parapet located above New Orleans and controlled by Union forces.[2] Similarly, on the Manigault family's Hermitage and Gowrie plantations in Chatham County, Georgia, the fields were not only neglected during the war, but Louis Manigault reported frequent escapes of men and women who "piloted boats through the creeks, swamps, rivulets, and marshes," and who assisted the "Yankees in their raids."[3] Dolly, Manigault's washer for eight years, whom Manigault listed as an "invalid" was among those who ran away in April 1863 while living with the Manigault family in Augusta.[4]

The women who escaped in southern Louisiana and Low Country Georgia found in their experiences and emancipatory struggles the sources of inspiration for their own individual and collective advancement. As political actors, their actions during the war were driven by the desire for freedom, which was oftentimes constrained by physical terror, wartime policies and practices. Freedom not only provided new and "socially liberated modes of being-with-others," but also created new opportunities to construct a liberated identity.[5] A comparative study of southern Louisiana and Low Country Georgia provides an important window into understanding the commonalities and diverse experiences of two coastal areas where African American citizenship and labor became contested arenas after the arrival of Union forces along the coast of both regions in 1862; followed by a sustained campaign to capture key cities, Shreveport, Louisiana and Savannah, Georgia, in 1864. By focusing on African American women's self-emancipatory actions and the socially created meanings, relationships, and identities organized around definitions of womanhood, this chapter expands upon the work of historians Leslie A. Schwalm in *'A Hard Fight for We': Women's Transition from Slavery to Freedom in South Carolina* (1997), Ella Forbes in *African American Women during the Civil War* (1998), Stephanie H. M. Camp in *Closer to Freedom: Enslaved Women and Everyday Resistance in the Plantation South* (2004), Hannah Rosen in *Terror in the Heart of Freedom: Citizenship, Sexual Violence, and the Meaning of Race in the Postemancipation South* (2008), and Thavolia Glymph in *The Women's Fight: Civil War Battles for Home, Freedom, and Nation* (2020), who provided regional and comparative analyses of the ways in which African American women contested slavery and gained their freedom.[6] As Schwalm argues in *'A Hard Fight for We,'* enslaved women were responsible for "the final collapse of slavery in South Carolina's rice regime."[7] Forbes argues that women "operated on whatever level they could to make a contribution to their community during the Civil War."[8] In a similar vein, Camp points out that African American women resisted enslavement in small and extravagant ways. Each act of resistance not only enhanced their cultural experience, but also brought them "closer to freedom." Rosen demonstrates in *Terror in the Heart of Freedom* how African American women were adamant about taking advantage of their newfound freedom by unabashedly taking former slave owners to court when necessary. In *The Women's Fight*, Glymph exposes the complex transformation the war wrought and underscores the fact that the experiences of southern Black women were distinct from those of Black men.

Historian John Hope Franklin was at the forefront of scholarship on self-emancipation, and critically examined the ways in which enslaved men and women freed themselves during the chaos of the Civil War by running away to the lines of the Union Army.[9] David Williams in *I Freed Myself: African American Self-Emancipation during the Civil War Era* (2014) argued that by the late 1850s, there were 50,000 escapees annually, temporary and permanent, and that the resulting freedom was neither an isolated event, nor an end in itself.[10] Williams demonstrates that African Americans contributed mightily to the war effort as well, noting, "They helped other refugees, black and white, escape to federal lines. They served as spies, guides, and informants to Union forces."[11] Resistance took many forms during the war, and enslaved African

Americans "staged work slowdowns, refused instruction, resisted punishment, demanded pay for their work, gathered freely, traveled at will,
and took freedom for themselves long before the Union Army arrived."[12]
Historians are still untangling the complicated skein of race, class, gender,
and legal status to illuminate the ways in which gender categories shaped
knowledge, identities, and power relations.[13] This chapter grapples with
the multiplicity of enslaved women's experiences by centering the analysis of war, self-emancipation, and free labor in southern Louisiana and
in Low Country Georgia. In both regions, African American women
engaged in oppositional politics aimed at breaking racially exclusionary
practices and creating new spaces of social and political action to claim
their freedom and contest their marginalization.[14]

THE GEOGRAPHY OF WARFARE

Opportunities for freedom in southern Louisiana and Low Country
Georgia were influenced by the natural landscape. The waterways, marshlands, and swamps provided transport and refuge from cruel enslavers,
mistresses, and overseers, even if only temporarily. For a few, the waterways brought the largest cities in the respective regions, New Orleans
and Savannah, within striking distance. In Louisiana, perennial flooding
determined the physical layout of cotton, sugar, and rice plantations,
with nearly every plantation fronted on water by either the Mississippi
River or one of the numerous bayous. The levees, which formed naturally, were maintained by slave laborers.[15] Similarly, rice and Sea Island
cotton plantations in Low Country Georgia were positioned near the
region's five large rivers: the Savannah, Ogeechee, Altamaha, Satilla,
and St. Mary's, which were vital to the growth of rice and served as
the focal point for settlement. The rice industry placed men and women
in agricultural and nonagricultural occupations such as ricemilling and
gristmilling. Additionally, men worked as carpenters, brickmasons, and
blacksmiths, and they manned ferry boats, tugboats, drays, and steam-
boats, which sailed down the coastal rivers to transport rice and cotton
to Savannah; and sugar, cotton, and rice down the Mississippi River to
New Orleans.[16]

   In this environment, the possibility of freedom in both southern
Louisiana and Low Country Georgia increased with the onset of military operations at the outbreak of war. President Abraham Lincoln's
"Anaconda Plan" imposed a naval blockade along the southeastern
coastline and led to Union control of coastal territory from Virginia to

Florida. In August 1861 the passage of the First Confiscation Act recognized self-emancipating men, women, and children who reached Union lines as "contraband of war" and their labor could be utilized to support the war effort.[17] As early as 1862, when federal ships threatened the Georgia Sea Islands in the counties of Chatham, Liberty, McIntosh, Camden, and Glynn, enslaved men and women escaped in the midst of what historian Clarence Mohr referred to as "refugeeing."[18] Georgia slave owners began relocating or "refugeeing" their enslaved workers, taking them further inland as the Union Navy blockaded the Sea Islands. In 1860, the enslaved population of this region numbered 28,011.[19] By the end of August 1862, the number of persons classified as "contraband of war" had increased to over 500 on St. Simons Island alone.[20]

In southern Louisiana, New Orleans and Baton Rouge were brought under Union control in April and May 1862 by naval commander David G. Farragut and General Benjamin Butler.[21] Farragut, a former resident of Louisiana, led an expedition of forty-four ships up the gulf along the Mississippi River with the intention of taking New Orleans, closing one of the Confederacy's main sources of supplies. After a five-day bombardment of Forts Jackson and St. Philip near the mouth of the river, Farragut successfully took seventeen ships past the forts on April 24, 1862, and two days later occupied the city of New Orleans without opposition.[22] On May 1, 1862, General Butler brought 15,000 Union troops to New Orleans and imposed military rule. Farragut continued up the Mississippi River and effectively captured Baton Rouge and Bayou Sara.[23] By the end of May, Union forces controlled the parishes of St. Bernard, Plaquemines, Jefferson, St. John, St. Charles, St. James, Ascension, Assumption, Terrebonne, Lafourche, St. Mary, St. Martin, and Orleans.

Geographic commonalities in both regions informed the process by which Union forces wrested these areas away from the Confederacy. The Atlantic Ocean and Gulf of Mexico facilitated the Union Navy's successful implementation of President Lincoln's blockade to cut off commerce in both areas. Moreover, the navigable rivers, bays, and inlets in both regions were complemented by marshlands, which promoted flight and rebellion by enslaved workers. In his study of antebellum Louisiana, C. Peter Ripley argued that the rivers, bayous, and swamps precluded the likelihood and success of running away. However, at Coco-Bend Plantation in West Feliciana Parish, disorder and chaos of war not only resulted in numerous plantation runaways of all ages making their way through bays and inlets, but also informed the Red River uprising in January 1864.[24] By that time federal gunboats had reached the mouth of the Red River, which served as a gateway to Alexandria and Shreveport. Union forces had previously launched a Red River expedition to take control of cotton resources in the area. When the retreating Confederate cavalry set fire to the cotton in the area, flames spread to the cabins of enslaved men and women who sought refuge behind the advancing Union lines, and many joined the federal troops as they marched through Rapides Parish en route to the Red River.[25] As the uprising spread, hundreds of self-emancipated men, women, and children reached Union lines, and nearly 600 African American men were recruited for army service.[26]

ENSLAVED WOMEN AND UNION OCCUPATION IN SOUTHERN LOUISIANA

Following the occupation of New Orleans and surrounding areas, Union Army officers searched for ways to organize labor forces and distribute relief to the poor. The August 1861 Confiscation Act allowed for the confiscation of Confederate property including enslaved workers, but on March 13, 1862, Congress passed legislation prohibiting the use of Union soldiers to return "fugitive slaves" to slave owners. However, the Second Confiscation Act, July 17, 1862, freed enslaved African Americans coming under Union control and authorized the president to use formerly enslaved people "in any military or naval service" to suppress the rebellion.[27] At the same time, Congress passed the "Militia Act," which freed the mothers, wives, and children of freedmen whose labor and service were used to suppress the rebellion.[28] The Act declared "forever free" the mothers, wives, and children of Black men who rendered service to the United States and had previously belonged to "disloyal masters," a qualification that excluded the families of African Americans who enlisted from the border states that remained "loyal" to the Union (Maryland, Delaware, Kentucky, and Missouri).[29] The federal government did not resolve this exclusion until March 3, 1865 when Congress, by joint resolution, provided for the freedom of the wives and children of all men serving in, or subsequently mustered into, the US Army or Navy.[30]

The Militia Act provided the official imprimatur for African American soldiers to claim freedom for their wives and children during the war. In Louisiana, African Americans in the First Louisiana Native Guards, who had pledged their support for the Union, seized horses, carts, and mules in St. Bernard Parish to transport enslaved men, women, and children from the surrounding plantations to the city of New Orleans. In August 1863, five Black soldiers successfully demanded the freedom of

their wives from planter E. Villerie who had claimed "loyalty" to the
Union.[31] Similar demands for freedom were made in other areas of the
South, particularly in the states that remained in the Union. In the border
state of Kentucky, Mary Wilson, the wife of Lewis Wilson of US Colored
Infantry (USCI), claimed her freedom under the Militia Act from slave
owner William Adams by leaving his plantation and setting up residence
in the city of Lexington. However, Adams reclaimed Mary Wilson, with
the assistance of the local constable, "tied her in a [s]laughter house ...
and inflicted upon her naked body a severe beating and bruising." This
incident was representative of the challenges that enslaved women faced
when they attempted to claim their freedom during the war.[32]

The Confiscation Acts also led to the formation of the Bureau of
Free Labor in wartime Louisiana in 1862 to address the conditions for
newly emancipated African Americans, who fled farms and plantations
and formed "contraband colonies" north of the city of New Orleans
where General Butler inaugurated a mass program of public works.
General Butler also promised Unionists the support of the US Army in
enforcing plantation labor in surrounding parishes provided that wages
were paid.[33] The Louisiana Bureau of Free Labor, a predecessor of the
Freedmen's Bureau, managed the affairs of freedpeople employed on
abandoned plantations. Under Louisiana's first "Superintendent of Negro
Labor," George H. Hanks, the first free labor policies were implemented
in Louisiana, and required work in return for support. In Terre-Bonne,
Louisiana, for example, freedmen received ten dollars per month, freedwomen received six dollars per month, and children between twelve and
sixteen received two dollars per month to continue working on sugar,
cotton, and rice plantations.[34] The devaluation of women's labor was
consistent with nineteenth-century cultural practices that marked masculine identity in hegemonic terms and reinforced patriarchal values.

In contrast, historian Julie Saville argued that African American
women in the South Carolina Low Country tried to control agricultural
production by "disputing what they would plant, where they would
plant it and in what amounts." The women also demanded higher wages
for task work.[35] Historian Amy Dru Stanley pointed out that emancipation meant "female self-ownership" which included the right to demand
fair prices for their labor.[36] On sugar and cotton plantations, each labor
agreement incorporated the language of "fair prices" for labor; however,
government-induced restrictions precluded fair market wages. In a fair
market, free labor removed government constraints and the paternalism
of the master–servant relationship.[37] During the war, the Bureau of Free

Labor created a market in labor, which contradicted free labor ideology. This contradiction undergirded federal policy during the Reconstruction period as labor contracts, which aimed to protect formerly enslaved workers from exploitative employers, restricted the freedpeople's ability to operate freely in the labor market.[38]

Between 1862 and 1865, the issue of wage labor emerged as the focus of military officials in the transition from slavery to freedom in wartime Louisiana. Previously, enslaved women in southern Louisiana labored on plantations, worked as domestics and market women, nurtured their children, loved their husbands, and endured episodes of physical and mental terror. The enslaved female population of southern Louisiana, which comprised twenty-three parishes in 1860, consisted of 43,898 women between the ages of fifteen and sixty.[39] During the Civil War, as Union forces occupied much of the region, newly freed women expected and demanded fair payment for their labor. Their expectations were often at odds with those of former enslavers, mistresses, and even military officials. In the case of "Dinah" and her three children, they were denied fair compensation for a day's work performed for "Mr. Elin" in New Orleans. "Mr. Elin told her he would pay her what was right"; however, he "gave her three [children] 10 cents each and refused to pay more."[40] Dinah received $1.00 for her labor.[41] This was not unusual. A sample of twenty-two registers and payrolls of freedpeople employed on plantations in Terre Bonne Parish from November 1863 to February 1864 indicates that the agency hired 139 women, 111 men, and 72 children to work on plantations. Women received $6.00 per month – four dollars less than the amount paid to men.[42] Government officials followed local custom and valued women's field labor above the domestic work they performed for their families.[43] In her examination of African American women's labor following the war, historian Jacqueline Jones found that newly emancipated women did not have the luxury of choosing between different kinds of work, and especially for women with children, "economic necessity bred its own kind of slavery."[44]

Historian Mary J. Farmer reports that in Virginia the Freedmen's Bureau agents believed that supporting "black women was more acceptable than supporting black men. Black men had to find employment or face persecution as vagrants."[45] However, court records from Louisiana's Bureau of Free Labor indicate that vagrancy charges were levied against a significant number of African American women, as well as men. But African American women filed complaints for nonpayment of wages and resisted charges of "vagrancy" leveled by military officials. By asserting their labor rights to the Bureau of Free Labor, they demanded full and fair compensation. In so doing, they relied upon a culture of resistance that had been forged in slave communities.[46]

As mothers, daughters, wives, and sisters, women had to contend with the problem of finding and keeping employment, while remaining dependent on the wages from White employers. Elizabeth White, Henrietta Henderson, Caroline Starks, Charlotte Ann Hall, and Amelie Candole were among the African American women who filed complaints in New Orleans for nonpayment of wages, and were representative of women who resisted "vagrancy" laws and charges and actively pursued fair compensation, equal treatment, and a liberated cultural identity.[47] While the records are incomplete on the final dispositions, in the case of Charlotte Ann Hall, she secured payment in 1865 from her employer, "Mrs. Pifer," for three weeks' wages; in other cases, the defendants were ordered to pay or appear in court.[48] Amelie Candole filed a complaint in 1865 against "Mr. Gastnell," the New Orleans Recorder of the Second District, for "not giv[ing] her justice" in *State vs. Annette Denis* 1865. Candole returned to the Recorder for a "satisfactory statement" to explain the dismissal of the case.[49]

Formerly enslaved women were persistent in their demands for payment for services rendered. Edith Williams, for example, worked for Mrs. Betsy Williams in New Orleans for one week in November 1864 and $3.00 in compensation was due. Edith Williams complained that "she had been after her money several times, but can't get no satisfaction."[50] In some instances, the economic consequences of war impacted employers' ability (or willingness) to pay formerly enslaved workers. Lucy Coleman worked for Martha King in New Orleans for six months at $3.00 per month. Coleman complained that King said she could not pay her because "she has no money." Coleman took her to court.[51] In other cases, children were held against their will to work for former slaveholders and the parents demanded their release and filed complaints with the Bureau of Free Labor. Esther, who was living in New Orleans in 1865, complained to Bureau officials that "Madame Mad Dog will not give her her child."[52] Bureau officials mandated the release of Esther's child. This practice was not confined to Louisiana. In St. Mary's, Georgia, in 1866, Dorca Samuels, the mother of Nannie Samuels who had been indentured for five years to "Mr. Miller Hallows," attempted to end the indenture and threatened to bring "a band of freed people to take Nannie by force."[53] The child was soon released to her mother.

Employers habitually defrauded African American women of the small amounts they had earned to sustain themselves and their families, forcing the women to leave without recompense. Unfortunately, agents of the Bureau of Free Labor did little to prevent these exploitative practices. Historian James Schmidt suggested that "Union Army officers did not act solely or even centrally out of racial reasons to create a free-labor system based upon Northern ideology."[54] However, racist ideas and attitudes influenced the behavior of White northerners and southerners, and their biases affected the way they formulated contracts, apprenticeships, and wage rates, and prevented the development of a "free-labor system."[55]

The contract system developed out of the assumption that freedpeople would work for former planters out of economic necessity. This system had its origins in the antebellum North where ideas about discipline and hard work determined the treatment of people considered "vagrants." The northern judicial system affirmed the right of employers with long-term contracts to impose labor discipline on apprentices and other workers. The contract system and passage of "vagrancy laws" in southern Louisiana limited the ability of newly emancipated women and men to exercise their civil rights and challenge the authority of employers and others in power. Yet, through their use of the Bureau of Free Labor courts, women engaged in oppositional politics to define freedom and labor rights.

FREEDOM AND WAR IN LOW COUNTRY GEORGIA

The chaos of the war created the conditions for many enslaved women in Low Country Georgia to experience freedom through flight. Despite what historian Stephanie H. M. Camp refers to as women's "spatial illiteracy," women in Low Country Georgia demonstrated a familiarity with the landscape and waterways and expressed a determined will to use flatboats and "dug-outs" to facilitate escape.[56] Strategies of escape brought women into spaces where they re-conceptualized the very meaning of political leadership to claim their freedom. In one poignant escape, a seventy-year-old Georgia woman used the marshlands to conceal her twenty-two children and grandchildren. Securing a flatboat, the fugitives drifted forty miles down the Savannah River, reaching a Union gunboat to claim their freedom.[57] Under the terms of the Second Confiscation Act, this grandmother and her children and grandchildren were free and could be used "in any military or naval service" to suppress the rebellion.[58] Such service often included serving as cooks, laundresses, and providing other forms of labor support. In Low Country Georgia, escapes were more numerous in 1862 than at any other period during the war.[59]

The Emancipation Proclamation, issued on January 1, 1863, broadened the scope of the Second Confiscation Act by sanctioning the enlistment of free African American men in the Union Army. However, the Proclamation had very little immediate impact on freeing slaves in Low Country Georgia since many had taken advantage of the chaos caused by the war to free themselves prior to 1863. In fact, General David Hunter's General Order No. 11 issued on May 9, 1862, had declared freedom to all slaves living in Florida, Georgia, and South Carolina.[60] Although President Lincoln rescinded the order two weeks later, Hunter's order furthered the cause of freedom among enslaved men and women who faced death from Confederate picket fire. Fanny, "a mulatto woman, a soldiers wife, and company laundress," escaped from the mainland near Liberty County in a boat with her two children. As she made her way through the marshes, swamps, and rivulets, her youngest child was shot dead in her arms prior to reaching Union lines.[61] The barrage of bullets which met fugitive slave women compelled them to locate hiding spaces in nearby woods where they remained for months seeking refuge before attempting an escape to Union lines.[62]

Beginning in 1863, federal policy mandated the conscription of Sea Island men by Union forces and this allowed them to join the all-Black regiments that had been raised in South Carolina and Georgia.[63] During June 1863, military officials inaugurated a special draft for the Third South Carolina Volunteers on Ossabaw Island, Fort Pulaski in Georgia; and Fernandina, Florida, on Georgia's southern border.[64] The Third South Carolina Volunteers combined with the newly formed Fourth and Fifth South Carolina Volunteers to form the 21st US Colored Troops (USCT). The 21st USCT numbered slightly over 300 men until December 1864, when its ranks were filled by additional men – of war and freedom – who had followed General William Sherman to Savannah.[65]

In June 1863, the 54th Massachusetts Regiment combined with General David Hunter's South Carolina Volunteers to form a special force sent on an expedition up the Altamaha River against Darien.[66] As Union troops, led by Colonel Robert Gould Shaw of the 54th Massachusetts Regiment, burned the city of Darien, Nancy, an aged African-born woman, asserted that she would not endure a second voyage on the "big water" and chose to remain in the ruins of Darien's destruction.[67] Union forces occupied abandoned cities such as Brunswick and Darien where women's marketing activities increasingly met the needs of US Navy ships near St. Simons

TABLE 4.1 *Prices charged to officers'*
messes and sailors for articles
purchased off former slaves on St.
Simons Island, Georgia, USS Florida,
July 1, 1862

Item	Quantity	Cents
Milk	Per quart	4
Corn	Per dozen	5
Terrapins	Each	10
Watermelons	Each	5–15
Eggs	Per dozen	12
Okra	Per ½ peck	10
Bean peas	Per ½ peck	5
Squash	2 for	3
Chickens	Each	12
Shrimps	Per 2 quarts	10
Rabbits	Each	10
Cantaloupes	Each	1–3
Whortleberries	Per quart	5

Source: Official Records of Union and Confederate Navies, series I, vol. 13, pp. 21, 159

Island. On St. Simons Island, the contraband population, which reached 500 by May 1862, had become self-sufficient. The commander of US Naval forces, J. R. Goldsborough, permitted self-emancipated women to sell goods and provide services such as laundering for Union men.[68] Women were also paid four to fifteen cents for milk, eggs, okra, squash, and other produce.

The Union military was a man's world and this was reflected in the language in recruiting posters.[69] One Union Army declaration stated, "[A]ll Negroes brought inside the lines at this place, will immediately on their arrival here, before any papers are drawn up, enlisting them as soldiers, be reported at the Provost Office in person." These orders ignored the self-emancipated women and children behind Union lines. Military orders and recruitment posters embodied cultural norms in existence at that time that marginalized women, especially formerly enslaved African American women.[70] Women's invisibility in military policies was countered by their overt presence as a result of their individual and collective actions to transform themselves into self-emancipated "soldiers" of war and freedom. In late December 1863, for example, thirteen fugitives from McIntosh County, Georgia, boarded the USS *Fernandina* in St.

Catherine's Sound. Led by a twenty-seven-year-old fugitive named Cain, the group had escaped from William King's plantation like most of the escapees. Accompanying Cain was twenty-two-year-old Bella, twenty-five-year-old Lizzie, and thirty-two-year-old Sallie who each escaped with their children.[71] Early in 1864, Cain left the *Fernandina* to rescue his relatives from the vicinity of Sunbury, Georgia. He returned on January 7, along with ex-slave Sam, bringing forty-five-year-old Grace and her five children, her son-in-law Charley, and her grandchildren.[72] Free Blacks from Darien, Georgia, likewise reached the Union lines together with those who were escaping slavery.[73] It was estimated that up to two-thirds of the self-emancipated people in the Low Country were women, and hundreds were mustered into Union service.[74]

Formerly enslaved women served as cooks, nurses, and seamstresses in Union military installations. The experiences of Susie King Taylor illustrate the ways women served as teachers for USCT soldiers. Susie King Taylor, formerly a slave, and her husband, Sergeant Edward King of Darien, Georgia, carried out their educational work in Union military camps providing literacy training to men, women, and children.[75] In Low Country Georgia and southern Louisiana, many literate Black women, along with northern White missionaries, taught in the "freedom schools" set up to teach the formerly enslaved men, women, and children. In Georgia by 1869, 8,415 students had been enrolled in the Freedmen's Bureau freedom schools.[76] In Louisiana, free Black teachers Caroline and Edmonia Highgate organized literacy training in churches, homes, sheds, stores, and White schoolhouses in New Orleans during the war. By 1864, 8,761 students in southern Louisiana had been taught in the freedom schools.[77]

African Americans' attempts at self-emancipation in many parts of the Low Country often led to violence. Confederates viewed attempted escapes as individual rebellion against slave owners, and collective acts of resistance were considered insurrection. Confederate soldiers often retaliated against African Americans who were captured after assisting the Union forces. On Hutchison Island near Savannah in 1862, Confederate soldiers from Fort Chapman in South Carolina burned Marsh plantation and murdered and terrorized over 100 enslaved men, women, and children.[78] These frequent skirmishes between Union and Confederate forces in the Low Country placed enslaved and self-emancipated women in dangerous situations. In 1862, after Union soldiers had left, Confederate soldiers, responding to drumbeating at night on the north end of Hutchinson Island, opened fire on a group of African American runaways, killing fifteen men, women, and children.[79]

Throughout the war, diseases contributed to the high mortality rates for African American women. The cycle of life and death continued as women gave birth and oftentimes unyielding diseases consumed the young and the old. At Hermitage and East Hermitage plantations, seven enslaved women gave birth in the early years of the war.[80] While precise figures on mortality rates for African American women in Low Country Georgia are not available, Louis Manigault, the medical assistant to Confederate surgeon Joseph Jones, reported deaths from the following conditions at Gowrie and East Hermitage plantations. Five enslaved women out of fifty-three died of dropsy, sunstroke, cancer in the stomach, and dysentery between 1861 and 1864. The most severe affliction occurred on the Gowrie Plantation, located near Savannah, in the years preceding the Civil War, when a virulent cholera epidemic swept through. The 1854 cholera epidemic was a national epidemic that claimed hundreds of men, women, and children across the nation.[81] On Gowrie and East Hermitage plantations, twelve enslaved men and women out of fifty-six died of cholera in December 1854.[82] On the battlefield and behind Union and Confederate lines, cholera, typhus fevers, dysentery, and other diseases were most prevalent. S. P. Moore, surgeon general for the Confederacy, authorized Joseph Jones in 1863 to identify the best treatments of fevers and study the relationship of climate and environment to disease. Fevers were associated with malaria, the foremost cause of morbidity among northern and southern troops, and African Americans – women, older people, and children – behind Union lines in Louisiana and Georgia died in large numbers.[83]

The arrival in Georgia of General William T. Sherman and his army provided additional opportunities for self-emancipation by enslaved African American women. The capture of Atlanta in September 1864, following Confederate general John Bell Hood's evacuation, led Sherman to propose to Union Commanding General Ulysses S. Grant a march across Georgia to force the Confederates to surrender.[84] Once given permission, Sherman's troops, numbering 60,000, made their way through central Georgia in November 1864. It was estimated that 19,000 formerly enslaved men, women, and children left the towns, plantations, and farms to follow Sherman's army.[85] Before the capture of Atlanta, General Sherman received some indication of what he might expect to find in carrying out his plan to slash and burn a path of up to sixty miles wide through central and southern Georgia. Wherever he encountered African Americans, a considerable following of women and men joined in what they considered a march toward freedom.[86] Sherman's

Special Field Order No. 120, issued on November 9, 1864, endorsed the inclusion of "able bodied Negroes" in the march who would comprise a "pioneer battalion" to repair and reinforce roads as they followed the advance forces.[87]

Sherman's army was divided into two wings: the right wing, the Army of Tennessee, commanded by Major-General Oliver Otis Howard; and the left wing, the Army of Georgia, commanded by Major-General Henry W. Slocum. The 14th and 20th Corps of the left wing of the Army of Georgia was under Slocum's command and was located in the section closest to the Savannah River and to South Carolina. General Slocum declared,

I think at least 14,000 of these people joined the two columns at different points on the march, but many of them were too old and infirm, and others too young, to endure the fatigues of the march, and therefore were left in the rear. More than one-half of the above number, however, reached the coast with us. Many of the able-bodied men were transferred to the officers of the Quartermaster and sub-sistence departments, and others were employed in the two corps as teamsters, cooks and servants.[88]

These refugees included many girls "too young" and women "too old and infirm" to travel.[89]

Escape to Sherman's army had its own dangers since the fleeing refu-gees were viewed as a hindrance to the troops' movement, and in the case of General Jefferson C. Davis, one Union officer reported that the general was "losing patience at the failure of all orders and exhortations to these poor people to stay home." At Ebenezer Creek, General Davis ordered "the pontoon bridge to be taken up before the refugees" following the Army's 14th Corps "had crossed, so as to leave them on the further bank of the unavoidable stream and thus dis-embarrass the marching troops…. [T]hose who could not swim as well as those who could swim, were drowned. The loss of life was still great enough to prove that … it was literally preferable to die free rather than to live slaves."[90] Sherman defended General Davis's actions as "militarily necessary," given his objective to reach the sea. Northern newspapers reported that hundreds of refugees had drowned or were eventually re-enslaved.[91]

General Slocum's left wing was under constant harassment from Confederate forces (General Joseph Wheeler's Calvary corp). The Confederate general believed this harassment led Union forces to abandon African Americans at Ebenezer Creek.[92] It was impossible to determine the number of African Americans who followed the army. Some joined for brief intervals, became discouraged, and returned to their homes.

Many found it difficult to associate freedom with the harsh measures applied by General Sherman's troops on their way to the sea. Frequently the inherent racism of many Union soldiers prevailed to give a grim view of what the future promised. When such treatment was encountered, African Americans soldiers of war and freedom turned away from the jubilant march and awaited an uncertain future.[93]

The ravages of war in Georgia left self-emancipated women destitute and in need of food, clothing, and medical care.[94] One month after Sherman's occupation of Savannah in December 1864, Sherman issued Gen. Field Order No. 15, which reserved the Sea Islands and abandoned inland rice fields for the formerly enslaved men and women. At the time, Sherman and other Union officers were under investigation by Edwin M. Stanton, Secretary of War, for "acts of cruelty" against the fleeing refugees. The issuing of Field Order No. 15, after meeting with African American religious leaders in Savannah in January 1865, represented Sherman's effort to recast himself as supportive of the cause of freedom, while simultaneously providing an alternative for the newly emancipated people residing behind Union lines. Under the terms of the field order, sixty-three formerly enslaved men received possessory title to 834 acres of land at Grove Hill and Grove Point plantations. Women who were heads of household received from five to forty acres of "abandoned land" under Sherman's order. For example, on Grove Hill and Grove Point plantations near Savannah, sixteen women held possessory title to 161 acres of land.[95] In 1860 in this area, there were 2,435 enslaved workers and 411 Whites (see Table 4.2).[96] Sherman's Field Order No. 15 remained in place until May 1865, when President Andrew Johnson rescinded it; however, many formerly enslaved people living in Georgia, Alabama, Mississippi, Louisiana, and Florida focused on the idea of receiving forty acres of land as compensation for their enslavement.[97]

CONCLUSION: POSTWAR TROUBLES

At the close of the war in accordance with President Lincoln's Reconstruction policy, the federal government imposed military rule on the state of Georgia, which lasted until November 1, 1865. Louisiana, Tennessee, Arkansas, and parts of Virginia met the requirements of Lincoln's "Ten Percent Plan" and were re-admitted to the Union prior to the end of hostilities. The framing of new state constitutions to include the abolition of slavery and the ratification by state lawmakers of the Thirteenth Amendment allowed the reinstatement of the remaining seven states by the end of 1865.

TABLE 4.2 *Possessory land titles issued to women at Grove Hill and Grove Point plantations, Georgia, March–April 1865*

Name	Acreage	Family Size
Hannah Butler	5	3
Jane Jones	6	3
Lucy Wilson	10	4
Mary Bush	30	3
May Anderson	10	7
Tina Jones	5	5
Jane Hargrave	10	3
Susannah Gordon	10	2
Polly Burroughs	10	2
Hannah Davis	10	4
Dinah Green	15	3
Lucy Barnard	15	5
Amy Wilkins	5	1
Rosanna Edwards	10	3
Susie Wright	5	3
Catsey Cheves	5	5

Source: List of Possessory Titles Issued to Freedpeople, Records of A. P. Ketchum, Savannah, Ga., Record Group 105, Bureau of Refugees, Freedmen, and Abandoned Lands, National Archives Building, Washington, DC

The wartime experiences of self-emancipated women in southern Louisiana and Low Country Georgia during the Civil War provide invaluable insights into freedom and resistance in the cultural value system of African Americans in the South. Their escapes, military service, and demands for equal treatment in the labor market underscore their desire to establish a liberated identity for themselves. In both regions, African American women seized their freedom before legal emancipation, many times without the assistance of the Union Army, and struggled against wartime practices that sought to marginalize them. The complex interrelationships of gender, class, and race produced a range of responses to self-emancipation, which gave meaning to freedom in a society that denied them self-determination. The myriad challenges they faced during the war represented distilled expressions of their freedom and desire for economic justice.

In southern Louisiana and Low Country Georgia, low wages and legal battles placed formerly enslaved women at a disadvantage; however, their labor aided their families and communities. Through the "contract labor system" in Louisiana and access to abandoned lands in Georgia, these women were able to improve their conditions in the short term. While some freedpeople derived marginal economic benefits from wage labor in the immediate aftermath of the war, in Louisiana these newly emancipated women were persistent in their demands for full and fair compensation from the Bureau of Free Labor, which adjudicated a significant number of cases in their favor. In Georgia, women made it through the "terror of emancipation" and secured remuneration from Union troops as market women providing goods and services during the war.[98] Women, like men, maintained deep-seated aspirations to invest in land. Land was a tangible manifestation of their independence as well as an asset that might strengthen kinship and family ties. However, single and widowed women, particularly in rural areas, found it difficult to purchase land because of low wages and familial responsibilities. In spite of these economic hardships, African American women in Savannah–Chatham County became landowners, and by 1876, 117 African American women in Chatham County, most of them formerly enslaved, owned land.[99] Gaining access to land after the end of the war gave new meaning to their efforts at self-emancipation.

5

Rape and Mutiny at Fort Jackson

Black Laundresses Testify in Civil War Louisiana

Crystal Feimster

The racial and sexual violence that defined slavery did not disappear with Lincoln's Emancipation Proclamation. In the context of war, however, formerly enslaved men and women did not hesitate to defend themselves. Just as runaways had forced the administration to begin to make policy about slavery in 1861, Black men and women who served and labored in the Union, whether defined as soldiers on the battlefield or laundresses in the contraband camps, put the question of free Black labor and equal protection under law squarely on the national agenda. Countless Black women, many of them laundresses who labored in the Union Army, were sexually harassed and assaulted by Union soldiers and officers. In the context of the Civil War and their military service, Black women, for the first time, were granted access to military tribunals that allowed them to bring charges of sexual assault against their assailants. The military's strict code of conduct that empowered commanding officers to court-martial soldiers accused of criminal activity, along with the 1863 Lieber Code that defined rape as a war crime, created a legal opening for Black women. Acknowledging rape as crimes against Black women, Union military courts ignored state laws and allowed Black women for the first time to testify against White men.

In Civil War Louisiana, Black laundresses took the lead in claiming rights and protections as free labor, by challenging White men's violent sexual power. As early as June 1862, Mary Ellen DeRiley, a twenty-three-year-old "washerwoman" for the 26th Massachusetts Regiment stationed at Fort St. Philip brought rape charges against Corporal William W. Chinock of Company F, 26th Massachusetts Regiment. Chinock was court-martialed and charged with "conduct to the prejudice of good order and discipline." According to the "specifications" of the charge, Chinock had "enticed" DeRiley into a boat, where he engaged in "unlawful sexual intercourse with her." Testifying in graphic detail, DeRiley recounted the assault: "He told me to lay down and let him ride me and I told him that I would not … he beat me with his fist, pulled my clothes over my head and rode me – for an hour." Even though the court found Chinock "not guilty" of the specifications "unlawful sexual inter-course," it found him "guilty" of the charge "conduct to the prejudice of good order and discipline," and sentenced him to be stripped of his ranks in the presence of his regiment and to "forfeit to the United States ten dollars per month of his monthly pay for four months."[1]

Undergirding Chinock's rape of DeRiley and the court's "not guilty" verdict was the common and long-held belief that Black women lacked virtue, sometimes invited, and always welcomed White men's illicit sexual advances. A dangerous fiction of antebellum "sexual economy of slavery," the trope of the lascivious Black woman, was the product of the systematic expropriation of enslaved women's productive labor, reproductive capacity, and sexuality.[2] Required to engage in physical and domestic labor, enslaved women, unlike Black men and White women, were also forced to perform sexual and reproductive labor. The legal doctrine of *partus sequitur ventrem* that established that children of enslaved women were born into slavery and the refusal of law to recognize rape as a crime against Black women engendered Black women's sexual vulnerability and enabled a sexual double standard that enforced chastity on White women and promoted aggressive sexual promiscuity for White men.

This chapter examines sexual violence against Black laundresses by White Union officers in Civil War Louisiana. The first part concerns the Union occupation of New Orleans in the spring of 1862 and General Benjamin Butler's orders and policies regarding the treatment of Black laundresses who labored in the Union Army. The second and third parts focus on the violent interracial interactions between White officers and Black soldiers and laundresses of the 4th Regiment of the Native Guard (also known as the Corps d'Afrique) stationed at Fort Jackson. Over the course of six weeks, in December 1863 and January 1864, these Black soldiers and laundresses engaged in open mutiny to protest the racial and sexual violence inflicted by White officers. Illuminating the connections between the mutiny of Black soldiers at Fort Jackson and sexual violence against Black laundresses by White Union officers, this chapter maps the shifting racial and sexual terrain on which Black women in Civil War Louisiana battled for their rights as free labor.

UNION TROOPS AND THE SEXUALITY
OF BLACK LAUNDRESSES

On May 15, 1862, two weeks after the fall of New Orleans, the 13th Connecticut Regiment dressed in their "best attire" and with "great pomp" marched down Canal Street to the US Custom House.[3] The designated Headquarters of the Department of the Gulf, the federal building took up a whole city block and stood four stories high without a roof. The newly constructed but unfinished Custom House had recently served as headquarters for rebel forces, who according to Captain Homer B. Sprague of the 13th Connecticut Regiment had left the building "filthy beyond expression."[4]

Within days of moving into the Custom House, the regiment was overwhelmed with the arrival of Black people desperate for work, shelter, food, and protection. Following the "contraband" policy initiated by Butler during his command of Fort Monroe (and made official with the passage of the Confiscation Acts of 1861 and 1862), the 13th Connecticut Regiment put the first arrivals to work "cleaning the floors, ceilings, stairways, walls, drains, casement."[5] The Quartermaster's Department hired Black people as blacksmiths, carpenters, shoemakers, wagoners, cooks, and laundresses. Sprague recalled that once the 13th Regiment "had established itself in the Customs House," most of the companies "employed, as laundresses, colored women, who had run away or been driven off to the Yankees."[6]

The US Army had a long tradition of employing Black women as laundresses in military camps and hospitals.[7] Adopted from the British, the practice was made official in 1802, when Congress passed an Act that prescribed four laundresses to a company and dictated a daily ration and quarters for each laundress.[8] Beginning with the War of 1812 until 1883, when the practice was officially ended, Black women were among the thousands of women who labored as military laundresses. The 1821 *General Regulations for the Army* dictated that "Laundresses employed to wash soldiers' clothes will be paid by the piece" at a rate set by the Council of Administration.[9] In other words, the regimental officers at a given post determined how much a laundress was paid. Regulations further provided laundresses with a common tent, straw for bedding, cords of wood for fuel, an iron kettle, two tin pans, and a hatchet.[10] In 1841, revised regulations stipulated that the Council of Administration could decide whether to pay laundresses "by the month, or by the piece." More importantly, regulations made clear that "debts due the laundress by soldiers, for washing" were to be settled at the "pay-table" and taken from soldiers' monthly wage.[11] Because the price of washing was set at each post by the Council of Administration, it is difficult to know exactly how much laundresses were paid. It seems, however, that by 1861 washerwomen were making on average between $6.00 and $12.00 per month and benefits had expanded to include rations for their children and access to military doctors.[12]

During the Civil War, Black women labored as laundresses in both the Confederate and Union Armies. Confederate muster rolls list Anne Green, a "colored (free)" woman, as a laundress at the Confederate General Hospital in Mount Jackson, Virginia; and Julia Bellman, a "free" woman, as a laundress at the Confederate Jackson Hospital in Richmond, Virginia.[13] In August 1864, the Confederate State paid Martha Bragg, "a free girl of color," $44.00 (eleven dollars per month) for "services as Laundress" at Breckinridge Confederate Hospital in Marion, Virginia.[14] The majority of laundresses who labored in Confederate hospitals and camps, however, were enslaved women pressed into service by the men and women who held them in bondage. Most likely, Andrew Green collected the wages earned by the four enslaved women, Fanny, Riney, Jennie, and Jennette, he sent to work as laundresses at Breckinridge Military Hospital in Marion, Alabama. For enslaved women who were able to secure jobs as laundresses in the Union Army, however, the position came with the dual benefits of freedom and wages.[15]

Under normal circumstances washing was grueling work, but in the context of war the relentless regime of soaking, washing, boiling, rinsing, drying, starching, ironing, mending, and altering war-stained and battered uniforms was dangerous work at best – and deadly work at its worst. Black women who traveled with the Union Army and labored as laundresses in "contraband camps," military posts, and hospitals were particularly vulnerable to sexual violence.[16] Those who did not have husbands or male relatives to protect them were easy targets. For many enslaved women, however, the combined benefits of freedom and reliable wages made the job a risk worth taking. In fact, many had already suffered racial and sexual violence at the hands of the men and women who held them in bondage.

Without question, the arrival of Union forces in Louisiana in the spring 1862 created opportunities for enslaved women to seize their freedom and to gain waged labor. Captain Sprague of the 13th Regiment did not hesitate to help Black women secure their freedom within Union lines. A native of Massachusetts and a Yale University graduate, Sprague was an abolitionist who had called for immediate emancipation with the outbreak of war. Thus, it is not surprising that he hired as a laundress Carolina, a twenty-two-year-old enslaved woman who had sought refuge in the Custom House to escape a whipping. In fact, the 13th quickly garnered a reputation as "an antislavery regiment."[17] Moreover, the commanding officer, Colonel Henry Warner, was notorious for allowing fugitives of slavery to seek refuge within the Custom House and refusing entry to slaveholders in search of runaways.[18]

On May 26, however, General Butler gave a Mrs. Benedict permission to enter the Custom House to search for and retrieve Caroline, the enslaved woman whom Sprague had employed as one of his company's laundresses. Catching sight of Caroline, Mrs. Benedict confronted the young woman, insisted on her return, and warned that she would never see her enslaved mother again if she refused. Unintimidated and confident in her status as a military laundress, Caroline declared: "You have treated me badly. You have beaten my mother over her head with a pan. I would rather stay and be free than see my mother again. You know you will be cruel to me. You can't take me from *here.*"[19]

While the commanding officers of the 13th Connecticut Regiment were committed to protecting the freedom of self-emancipated enslaved people, Butler was more interested in appeasing loyal slaveholders and preventing officers from harboring and protecting fugitives. On the same day that Butler gave the spurned Mrs. Benedict permission to search for Caroline in the Customs House, he issued Special Orders, No. 44: "All females, white and black, must be excluded from remaining in any portion of the United States custom-house after the hours of 4 o'clock p.m. or before the hour of 9 a.m."[20] The order's expulsion of "all females, black and white" from the Custom House included Black laundresses. Offended by the order's implications that the presence of Black women promoted sexual promiscuity and disorder, some of the officers, including Captain Sprague, protested Butler's removal of the laundresses. In Butler's office, Sprague advocated, "Many of our soldiers are debilitated by this climate, and it is a most welcome relief to have this work transferred to more skillful hands; besides contributing greatly to increased cleanliness, comfort and health."[21] More to the point, the officers argued that official regulations *allowed* every company four laundresses, whose rations, quarters, and fuel was to be provided by the army.[22] Butler flatly defended the removal of the laundresses "on the ground of the difficulty of preventing improper intercourse between soldiers and these women." The officers, however, managed to convince Butler to allow "rooms to be rented outside of the

Custom-house for the colored laundresses."²³ The issue, however, as far as Butler and the Benedicts were concerned, was not settled.

Despite Caroline's rejection of them, the Benedicts continued their campaign to return her to their ownership. On May 30, Mr. Benedict confronted Captain Sprague with a letter endorsed by Butler. Caroline, the letter explained, "was the property of a poor man whose wife is sick in bed and needs this negress for a nurse." It is unclear whether this sick wife was the Mrs. Benedict who marched into the Custom House four days earlier. In an appeal to "Capt. Sprague's humanity," the letter urged him to "drive [Caroline] out, so that she may return to her master."²⁴

In a written reply, Sprague explained his unwillingness to "drive" Caroline out. The Confiscation Act 1862, he argued, forbade "military officers to deliver fugitive slaves to their masters, on penalty of being cashiered."²⁵ The law, he insisted, "makes no exception in the case of 'poor' masters. No; not even if the 'poor man's wife is sick in bed, and needs the negress as a nurse.'" Nor did the law "make any exception on grounds of 'humanity,'" he reasoned. Moreover, he considered the choice clear if faced with a humanitarian appeal made by Caroline, "a young and helpless girl, innocent of any crime, pleading with me to save her from hopeless and perpetual slavery," and another claim made by Benedict, "'a *poor* man, with a sick wife,' and in need of this girl's unpaid toil, and the money which you might coin out of her body and soul, if you could only keep her degraded and enslaved, or sell her for labor or breeding or lust!"²⁶

Benedict took Sprague's letter to Butler, who in turn summoned Sprague to his office. Butler asked Sprague a series of questions in which he all but accused the captain of being involved in an illicit relationship with Caroline. Sprague challenged Butler's assumptions and insisted Caroline was not only "regularly employed as a laundress" and that her services were "very much needed," but also that she was "an intelligent, smart girl, anxious for her freedom." Moreover, he explained, she had "been cruelly treated by her mistress."²⁷ Uninterested in the "humanitarian" aspects of the case, Butler cut to the chase. The case raised "military questions" about how to best bring Louisiana back into the Union and how to promote discipline and morality. After a "long discussion" in which Butler reiterated the reasons he thought it best for Caroline to be returned to her "loyal masters," he directed Sprague to "procure a statement of the facts" from Chaplain Salter about Caroline's character. On June 3, Sprague sent Butler a statement from Chaplain Salter regarding Caroline and a letter in which he addressed head-on Butler's "objection" to employing Black women as laundresses. Sprague recounted how in two separate meetings, Butler had charged enslaved women with licentiousness and having a demoraliz-ing influence on the regiment. The problem, if there was one at all, wrote Sprague, had been "entirely obviated" by moving the laundresses out of the Custom House and into nearby private quarters. "These women are almost completely isolated from the world," he explained, "their seclusion is unbroken by any male person, except momentarily for the transmission of laundry articles or rations."[28] More to the point, Sprague challenged Butler's assumptions regarding Black women's sexuality: "Whatever may have been their habits at home – obliged to submit of course to their mas-ters' lusts, as you told us in that interview – they are necessarily virtuous in their conduct *here*, and are likely to continue so while in this service."[29]

Even though Butler allowed Caroline to continue to wash for the reg-iment, he was not convinced that the relationships between the "col-ored laundresses" and the men of the 13th Connecticut Regiment were purely professional. In fact, no sooner had he received Sprague's letter and approved Caroline's appointment, he issued General Orders No. 38: "The Laundresses of Companies are not permitted to come into the quar-ters of the men. They must be kept in their own quarters, and the clothing sent to them and sent for." More to the point, the order warned, "Any officer who permits a woman, black or white, not his wife, in his quar-ters, or the quarters of his company, will be dismissed the service."[30] Butler's order mobilized longstanding ideas that simultaneously defined Black women as lascivious and poor working women as promiscuous. According to Butler's logic, laundresses who dared to enter the "quarters of the men" were engaging in illicit sexual behavior.

Even as the order sexualized Black laundresses, it challenged the racial sexual double standard that permitted White men unfettered access to Black women's bodies. Indeed, Butler's order suggested that Black laun-dresses were no different from prostitutes and implied that Union officers were not above sexually exploiting them. It was one thing for Butler to issue a public order that perpetuated the myth of unrestrained Black sex-uality, but it was something else altogether to suggest that federal officers were sexually exploiting the Black women who labored under their com-mand. The order was printed in every issue of the New Orleans *Daily Delta* for the next two months and was reprinted in newspapers, north and south.[31] The Confederate press took the opportunity to mock Union soldiers. The *Louisville Daily Journal* reported, "General Butler has issued an order at New Orleans forbidding the admission of laundresses to the quarters of the men. It is probably thought a great hardship that the poor soldiers can't have a chance to court their washer-women."[32]

In defense of the 13th Connecticut Regiment, Chaplain Salter published an open letter in the *New York Times* protesting Butler's General Orders No. 38: "This order insulted the officers by intimating a state of things such as did not exist. It played into the hands of the rebels. It cast odium upon the retention of negro servants. If designed to counteract charges, it struck harder than it defended."[33] Less concerned with the "insult" against the laundresses, Salter defended the officers as men who "merited honor."

Ultimately, Butler remained unfazed by the insult that General Orders No. 38 offered to Black women. He, however, regretted the damage done to the reputation of the 13th Connecticut Regiment. On June 14, in an effort to diminish the aspersions his order had cast on the regiment, Butler issued Special Order No. 99, in which he praised the men at length and declared: "Soldiers, your behavior in New Orleans has been admirable. Withstanding the temptations of a great city so as to present such discipline and efficiency is the highest exhibition of soldierly qualities. You have done more than win a great battle; you have conquered Yourselves."[34] Without question, New Orleans was a city rife with "temptations," especially for many young men who were away from home and the moral influences of their families for the first time. Nonetheless the young soldiers, he insisted, had remained true to their "New England training" and "religious influences."

While Butler was willing to let the 13th off the hook, he doubled down on his critique of the Black women. Butler reiterated his belief that all Black women were eager for sex with White men, when testifying before the American Freedmen's Inquiry Commission in May 1863. Butler described the so-called "difficulty" that he had with Black laundresses: "I was obliged to make some stringent regulations in regard to them, because the women are all brought up to think that no honor can come to them equal to that of connection with a white man. And I am sorry to say that white men are not all above taking advantage of this feeling."[35] Butler, like slaveholders who justified the sexual exploitation of enslaved women with charges of licentiousness, ultimately blamed Black women for any and all illicit sexual relations with White men. The powerful ideology that portrayed Black women as sexually depraved made it difficult, for most White Union officers to see Black laundresses as victims of sexual violence. Butler's General Order No. 38, however, not only perpetuated the racist and sexist double standards that made Black laundress easy prey for White officers, but also exposed efforts to prevent Union officers from taking sexual advantage of the Black women who depended on them for employment and the protection of their freedom.

CRUELTY AND MUTINY AT FORT JACKSON

On the afternoon of December 15, 1863, Brigadier General William Dwight retreated to his new quarters at Fort Jackson, a Mississippi River garrison almost seventy miles south of New Orleans, and carefully penned a letter to his mother, Elizabeth Dwight, in Newton, Massachusetts. He recounted in painstaking detail the mutiny of the 4th Regiment Corps d'Afrique at Fort Jackson that had compelled Major-General Nathaniel P. Banks, Commander of the Department of the Gulf, to issue orders for him to take "temporary command" of the Fort.[36] According to initial reports on December 9, the 4th Regiment had risen up in arms against their White officers. It was rumored that twenty-seven White officers were murdered, the Fort in possession of Black soldiers, and the river blockaded.[37] "I was ordered down here to assume command, to enforce discipline, to arrest the ring leaders of the riot," he explained, "in short to deal with the difficult case – I was given white troops with which to force matters, if need be, with the edge of the sword."[38]

Organized by General Banks in February 1863 as the 4th Native Guard and renamed the 4th Corps d'Afrique in June 1863, the regiment was made up largely of men who had escaped plantations throughout Louisiana and Mississippi for Union lines. Unlike the 1st, 2nd and 3rd Native Guard Regiments that were organized in August 1862 by General Benjamin Butler and mustered in with Black officers, the 4th Regiment was commanded by White officers. When Banks replaced Butler as head of the Gulf Department in December 1862, he forced Butler's commissioned Black officers to resign and appointed less than capable White men to command the Corps d'Afrique. Indeed, it was difficult to find good White officers who wanted to command Black soldiers. The best men were able to secure promotions within their own regiment and as Banks later explained, "men disqualified by want of character and capacity for the discharge of the humblest duties in the regiments to which they belonged, and others, seeking promotion for personal objects, indifferent to the success of the corps, have in some cases been appointed."[39] Banks's promotion of Augustus W. Benedict to lieutenant-colonel of the 4th Regiment in the spring of 1863 was a case in point.

Benedict, who came from the Finger Lakes region of western New York, joined the war effort as a second lieutenant in the 75th New York Infantry in the fall of 1861. In February of 1863, Benedict wrote to Lieutenant-Colonel Richard B. Irwin to request the major's position in the Corps d' Afrique. Eager for promotion, Benedict saw the 4th as an easy opportunity to jump a grade or two. Benedict informed Irwin that Charles W. Drew, the 4th's newly appointed colonel with whom he had served in the 75th New York Regiment, had urged him to seek the position. With few if any qualifications, Benedict was appointed major of the newly organized 4th Regiment and four months later, when the unit's lieutenant-colonel resigned, he was promoted to second-in-command despite his inexperience.

Benedict quickly garnered a reputation as a brutal and cruel officer. He cursed and hit soldiers whose brass buckles or boots did not shine to his satisfaction. When a punch to the face or kick to the back was insufficient, he did not hesitate to use his sword.[40] At his worst, Benedict tortured men who failed to live up to his expectations. On one occasion he had a soldier tied up by his thumbs. Stationed in Baton Rouge in August 1863 the men had gone months without fresh meat or vegetables, and signs of scurvy had begun to appear. When Benedict caught two of his men "stealing corn to roast," he ordered the officer of the guard to "lay them on the ground, straighten their legs and arms out, and stake them – tie them down." Once the men were tied spread-eagle to the ground, Benedict had their faces, feet, and hands covered with molasses. For two days the men suffered in the blistering summer heat as ants, flies, and bees attracted by the sweet syrup swarmed their exposed flesh.[41]

The regiment's transfer from Fort St. Philip to Fort Jackson in December 1863 did little to change Benedict's behavior. The soldiers, however, were growing impatient with his brutality. On at least two occasions the men, to no avail, complained of Benedict's maltreatment.[42] For almost a year they had tolerated Benedict's cruelty and the failure of their commanding officers to act on their behalf. Thus, when it came time for the men of the 4th to depart for Fort Jackson, many of them requested "to remain at Fort Saint Philip, so that they would not have to be under Lieutenant Colonel Benedict."[43]

Less than twenty-four hours after their arrival at Fort Jackson, Benedict again resorted to violence to punish two of his men. With a rawhide teamster's whip, he flogged Harry Williams and Munroe Miller for attempting to leave the grounds of the fort without proper permission. The sound of the whip cracking on the men's backs and their pleas for mercy outraged the Black soldiers who watched in horror. Colonel Drew, as well as two other officers, looked on as Benedict beat the men like slaves. Their failure to stop the flogging or to reprimand Benedict for his abuse of power made matters worse. The soldiers knew that flogging was illegal; Congress had outlawed the practice two years earlier.[44] Moreover, the soldiers had "been constantly assured … that under no circumstances whatever were they to be subjected to the degrading punishment of flogging," and in a recent address by Adjutant General Lorenzo Thomas they had been promised that any officer who maltreated them would be dismissed.[45] For the Black soldiers the whipping was too reminiscent of their recent enslavement. More importantly, the racialized violence went up against their ideas of freedom.

The soldiers who had witnessed the brutal beatings grudgingly dispersed on Benedict's orders, but back in their quarters they decided it was time to put an end to the lieutenant-colonel's violent regime. Within an hour, they organized 250 men and, with muskets in hand, they rushed onto the parade ground in protest. Making clear their discontent, they demanded, "Give us Colonel Benedict; we did not come here to be whipped by him. Kill Colonel Benedict; shoot him."[46] Firing their guns into the air they declared, "We know what [Adjutant GeneralThomas] told us!" While many remained on the parade field shooting their guns into the air, others went in search of Benedict. As the mutineers continued to fire their riffles in the air, White officers tried to reason with them. Promising that justice would be meted out, Colonel Drew persuaded the men to put down their weapons and return peacefully to their quarters.

Dwight's mother would be relieved to know that initial reports had been "greatly exaggerated." Dwight assured her that the "trouble" at Fort Jackson was not with "the insubordination of the negro," but had everything to do with "the bad administration of affairs" and with "having inferior and incompetent officers over [the] troops." The primary cause of the mutiny, he concluded, "was a foolish and passionate Lt Col who so little understood his character as an officer as to raise his own hand against a soldier; and who had no more sense than to put the lash to the Negro whose idea of freedom is that he is raised by it beyond the pale of that worst degradation of servitude."[47] Indeed, here lay the crux of the issue – the violent gap between Black and White people's "idea of freedom" in the aftermath of slavery.

Twelve soldiers were court-martialed on charges of mutiny. After three days of testimony, the court announced its verdict. Two of the most aggressive offenders – including Private Frank Williams, who had tried to bayonet Captain Miller after declaring, "God damn you! I have been looking for you all night" – were sentenced "to be shot to death with musketry."[48] Private Julius Boudro was sentenced to prison for twenty years, while five other soldiers received terms ranging from one to ten years. Private James H. Moore was sentenced to a month confined in the guardhouse. Four of the accused were found innocent of all charges. At the same time, Benedict was charged with "inflicting cruel and unusual punishment, to the prejudice of good order and military discipline."[49] The court found him guilty. The sentence was dishonorable discharge. Banks heartily approved and immediately dismissed Benedict from the army. Banks, however, was more sympathetic towards the Black soldiers. While he endorsed the six prison sentences, he suspended the two death sentences and ordered both men to serve a sentence of hard labor instead.[50] By the end of the month, with Benedict and the mutineers removed, Dwight pronounced the regiment's discipline "excellent."[51] This, however, as Dwight would soon learn, was only part of the unsavory story of the mutiny at Fort Jackson.

SEXUAL COERCION AND THE RESISTANCE OF BLACK WOMEN AND MEN

On January 27, 1864, only a few weeks after the court-martial and two days after petitioning General Banks for reassignment, Dwight wrote again pleading to be reassigned. The delay, he complained, had required the "discharge of the most unpleasant duty."[52] Dwight reported in graphic detail the circumstances that compelled him to arrest four officers.

On the night of January 25, Dwight explained, "Officer of the Day" Captain Charles A. Goff and "Officer of the Guard" Lieutenant Henry E. Blakeslee left the fort "for the ostensible purpose" of inspecting the "contraband quarters." Captain William H. Knapp and Lieutenant William H. Odell were asked to join in the inspection of the quarters, which were "occupied by negro women," who served as regimental laundresses. The officers began their "inspection" by first forcing their way into "the hut" of Keziah Davis, a laundress for Company F, whom Dwight described as "an old negro crone ... whom more than fifty summers under the inspiration of the lash of the slaveholder, have not spared." The exchange between the officers and "Aunt Keziah" explained Dwight, "was characterized first by looseness, soon became indecent and obscene." The men insisted that Davis have sex with at least one of them. Dwight described Davis as a "hideous creature" and admitted that "it would appear strange" to Banks "that from this revolting embrace she was the one to shrink." Dwight found it difficult to believe a Black woman was capable of rejecting a White man's sexual advances. Davis, he admitted, eventually managed to drive the officers out of her quarters with the contents of her chamber pot.

The officers moved on to "the cabin" of "Mrs. Rose Plummer," a laundress in Company A, whom Dwight described as "a young octoroon widow not without pretention to good looks." Upon entering Plummer's quarters the men were allegedly "quiet and respectful, for the fair skin and bright eyes of the widow, scandal reports and she asserts, have obtained for her the protection of Captain Knapp." In this case, Dwight better understood the officers' desire and reported that Knapp was left "to the smiles and favors of this bewitching laundress." Plummer had confessed that, "he [Knapp] alone obtains from her the rights and acknowledgment of husband." Even as Dwight admitted that Plummer's consent was offered in exchange for Knapp's protection, he could not resist racist stereotypes of Black women as seductresses. Clearly, Plummer had consented to a sexual relationship with Knapp to "obtain" protection against the unwanted sexual advances of other officers. Rendering their relationship in the contractual terms of the rights and privileges of marriage, Plummer sought to position herself within the frame of respectable womanhood.

Leaving Knapp at Plummer's "cabin," Goff, Blakeslee, and Odell moved on to the "dwellings" of Emma Smith, Elizabeth Dallas, and Laura Davis. Davis told Dwight that she was so soundly asleep that she did not realize that one of the officers had entered her quarters until he was lying on top of her. Davis and Smith both reported that Goff and Blakeslee warned they "would lose their places" and be forced to leave the fort by the first boat "if they longer refused them the favors granted by Mrs. Rose Plummer to Captain Knapp."

By the time that the three officers arrived at Elizabeth Taylor's contraband quarters, the laundress was asleep. It was late now, and the officers who stood banging on Taylor's door had already forced entry into the quarters of at least four laundresses. Goff was particularly aggressive; he broke the door down when she refused to open it, declaring the men "were out on no very respectable business." Goff climbed into Taylor's bed and Odell tried to hold her down. Taylor screamed for help and fought the men as best she could. Eventually Goff gave up and called Taylor a "bitch" as he stormed out of her quarters. Hot on his heels, Taylor brazenly responded in like terms that he had "descended from a similar animal." Goff, not missing a beat, turned and struck her across the face with his sword.

Taylor's "appeal for help" drew the attention of Private Edward Idell of Company C, who lived in the boat house at the landing of the camp. Idell shouted from his doorway "that if he had a sister in those contraband quarters he would send her away from this 'Port' before she should be so abused by the officers." In response, Goff had Idell arrested and confined him to the guardhouse.

Dwight, explained that his account was a "very brief and inadequate description of the conduct of these officers during this pretend inspection," based on statements taken from five of the laundresses and four Black soldiers. The statements, he claimed, were "in some degree corroborated" by Goff, who conceded the inspection was not "properly conducted" and that he had in fact "pushed" Elizabeth Taylor with his sword. Blakeslee also admitted it was "not a proper inspection" and that Goff did strike Taylor with his sword, but added that because she had called Goff "a son of a bitch" he thought the Captain justified in striking her. Moreover, Blakeslee insisted "it would have been better to have shot Elizabeth at once." Dwight explained that "this would be woman-killer" declared "it is hard enough for a person to take *that* from a white man let alone a black woman." Odell, reported Dwight, denied holding Taylor down but admitted "to putting his hands upon her" and thought he might have struck her in "vindication of Captain Goff's birth." Knapp also admitted that the inspection was not properly made, but claimed he had no idea what occurred after the party left him with Mrs. Plummer. The four officers, concluded Dwight "are of course in close arrest."

The officers' assaults on the laundresses on the night of January 25 were just the tip of the iceberg. Dwight underscored that this kind of assault happened regularly. "These women, and the soldiers who live in their vicinity, as well as the soldiers who have from time to time for months past been placed 'on Post' near these 'contraband quarters,' all concur in stating, that scenes similar to the one of Monday evening have been of frequent, almost nightly, occurrences for a long time past," explained Dwight. The laundresses insisted that officers other than those arrested "have been at other times equally guilty." The names of many officers, reported Dwight, "have long been held up to the scandal and contempt of the soldiers of the Regiment."

Dwight hoped that Banks would agree with his assessment that "the disgusting details of the late affair render it unfit for the investigations of a military tribunal." The "publicity" of another court-martial, he reasoned, would bring more negative attention and further injure the reputation of "a most important corps of the service." Moreover, he maintained that the only witnesses to be produced against White officers would be "negro women, of more than questionable character, and the negro soldiers who stand in terror of all who have exercised authority over them – an inherited terror, increased by an average of twenty years of personal bondage, and only to be eradicated by the influences of time and the elevation of freedom." Dwight recommended "the immediate dishonorable dismissal of these officers from the service of the United States."

Banks, however, ordered Dwight to convene a military commission of officers from the 4th Regiment Corps d'Afrique "to inquire into the facts." Dwight appointed Major William Nye, Captain George E. Wentworth, and First Lieutenant Daniel C. Payne to the commission. Yet, within hours of the inquiry, Dwight found himself forced to "dissolve" the commission. In a letter to Banks' chief of staff, he recounted how one of the laundresses had testified that Captain Wentworth of the commission had also tried to force his way into quarters. Whether this was a case of mistaken identity, or merely a mistake as to time, Dwight explained that it was clear that "a similar occurrence with this actor [had] been so recent as not easily to be distinguished in the dull mind and dim memory of this heavy looking negress." Dwight believed it was of "no consequence" whether or not the woman's testimony was true. "The immediate effect," he explained, "can only be likened to the bursting of a shell loaded with Greek fire – it not only destroyed the efficiency of the commission but threw a glare of light upon the whole subject – a light which nothing could dim or put out." Moreover, he observed, "It completely dazzled Captain Wentworth who exclaimed with a pathos and simplicity seldom found combined with guilt 'that it would never do to prosecute such an inquiry as this, for that every officer in the Regiment might be implicated!'" Dwight insisted he had no choice but to dissolve the commission and requested permission to appoint Captain E. P. Loring of the 1st Heavy Artillery, Corps d'Afrique at Fort St. Philip to the commission.[53] He concluded, "I can find but one officer of sufficient rank in the 4th Regiment Corps d'Afrique fit to sit on the commission."[54] The problem, however, had less to do with finding an officer of sufficient rank within the regiment and more to do with finding a "fit" officer – in other words, an officer who was not implicated in the assaults.

Moreover, Dwight insisted the officers, under the direction of Colonel Drew, had "banded together for self-preservation." Prior to the convening of the commission, Dwight explained that the four officers "most implicated" in the attacks had spent the time "concocting" a unified story, which compelled him to put a sentinel over each man. Then three other officers, Captain James Miller (whom Private Frank Williams had attacked during the late mutiny), Captain Wentworth (of the commission) and Captain Charles H. Merritt "of notoriously bad character" had tried to intimidate some of the laundresses. According to Dwight, when Miller asked Keziah Davis not to mention him in her testimony, she berated him, "Go on! Go on! You know what you have done." As for Merritt, she reassured him, "Go long! You be not so bad as the worst of these – maybe I'll let you off this time." Davis's reprimand of Miller – "you know what you have done" – suggests that it may in fact have been his treatment of the laundresses in the contraband quarters that provoked Williams's attack on him during the mutiny.[55]

Taken together, the whippings of the soldiers and the sexual assaults against the laundresses left little doubt in Dwight's mind that Drew and the White officers under his command were "pro-slavery officers," who had entered the service "only for increased rank and pay." He believed they were just as bad as, if not worse than, southern slaveholders, who whipped and raped enslaved people. Dwight poured out his frustrations in a single sentence:

We are dealing with difficulties in a Regiment which has been driven to mutiny by one of the officers highest in command using in person upon its black soldiers the lash which even the slave-driver directed through other hands, – and in which the officers with great publicity have indulged with the colored women, or forced these women to indulge with them, in all the vices which have most stained slavery in the eyes of the civilized world as a curse and a shame.[56]

Whereas the slaveholder had delegated the whip to the "bad and brutal" overseer and sought discretion in the sexual exploitation of female slaves, Dwight argued that these White officers had "repeated in worse forms the methods through which the slave-holders ruled." He reasoned that the officers' "beastliness has not the virtue of the amalgamation practiced by the slaves-holder, for it tends to destroy, not to create." Moreover, he insisted, "It affords to those who desire to use them the best arguments upon what are called 'the curses of freedom.'"[57] Dwight promised to do his "part" to "purify" the regiment.[58] Responding on Banks's behalf, General Stone wrote, "Do the work thoroughly and fearlessly. Those men have no more right to the negro than the slave holder had."[59]

On February 1, the commission reconvened, with Loring taking Wentworth's place. Over the course of two days, the commission interviewed many witnesses, including six laundresses, three Black soldiers, and the four accused White officers. On February 3, the commission "after mature deliberation on the evidence" completed and submitted its official report. While laden with racist and sexual stereotypes, the report took seriously the laundresses' testimonies. "The testimony of Keziah Davis who is of a decent and respectable appearance was unmistakable, and was given in a straightforward and truthful manner."[60] More to the point, when the commission had asked Davis, "Are there officers here in the habit of doing the same thing?" she did not hesitate to name names, "Yes sir, Captain Miller." Miller had been the target of Frank Williams's bayonet during the mutiny.[61]

The commission praised Emma Smith, a laundress who was married to a soldier in the regiment, for giving "her testimony with apparent truthfulness but with some timidity."[62] Smith swore that the officers had threatened to get rid of her if she continued to reject their sexual advances. She also recounted that "Captain Merritt came and sat on my bed, and I told him that it was wrong to do so, because he knew my husband was under arrest. He said he knew it and asked my pardon."[63] Smith's testimony suggests that some of the laundresses tried to use their marital status to fend off assaults; and that some of the officers may have avoided sexually harassing laundresses who were married to soldiers in the regiment.

The commission, however, critiqued Laura Davis, as "somewhat heavy looking, and less intelligent in appearance than the other witnesses" and for exhibiting "more indignation and vindictiveness in regard to the Officers against whom she testified."[64] A close examination of Davis's testimony leaves little doubt as to why it was more forthright than that of the other laundresses. Davis took particular aim at Blakeslee, who was a lieutenant in the company that she served: "Lieutenant Blakeslee said ... he had as much right to stay with me as Captain Knapp had to stay with his laundress."[65] And it was Davis who had implicated Wentworth (of the commission), when she testified that he had come to her quarters "the night before ... and tried to do the same thing." Davis made it clear that the officers demanded sex as part of the labor they required of the laundress who served their regiment. In fact, the commission unwittingly exposed the implications of Davis's statement when it asked, "Whose laundress are you?" instead of asking her which company she served. Of greater significance, however, was Davis's answer: "I was Captain Cranes, Company K, but they have turned me off. I was turned off the day after this happened."[66] Without question, laundresses who resisted the sexual advances of the officers they served risked losing not only their jobs but their freedom in Louisiana, where Lincoln's Emancipation had not freed the enslaved people. Having lost her positions, it is not surprising that Davis's testimony was filled with "indignation" and bitterness.

While the report concluded that "nothing of importance took place" at Plummer's quarters and that the officers "unnecessarily annoyed"

Keziah Davis and behaved with "gross indecency" in her presence, it declared that in the quarters of Emma Smith, Laura Davis, and Elizabeth Taylor the officers "behaved with violence and gross indecency."[67] Furthermore, the report made clear that "scenes similar that of the night of January 25, in which other officers of the Regiment have been equally implicated, have been of not unfrequent occurrence."[68] The committee concluded "that the good of the service requires the summary punishment."[69] Dwight approved the report and attached his recommendation that six officers, including the four he had arrested as well as Miller and Wentworth, be "dishonorably dismissed the service of the United States."[70] Banks ultimately agreed. On February 10, he issued Special Order No. 36, in which he declared the officers guilty of "conduct highly prejudicial to good order and military discipline, and unbecoming officers and gentlemen, in disturbing the peace of the garrison by forcing an entrance in the quarter occupied by colored laundresses" and "dishonorably dismissed" them, "subject to the approval of the President."[71]

But Dwight was not finished yet. There was still the problem of Colonel Drew, who Dwight now believed was to blame for the "rotten" behavior of the officers under his command. In a separate letter written to General Stone, Dwight announced that he had arrested Drew and confined him to his quarters. He said that he had arrested Drew with "reluctance" but insisted his actions were necessary: "This Regiment will again rise in revolt if the abuse of the soldiers is suffered to continue, and the next revolt will not be bloodless."[72]

Dwight recounted, in detail, four acts of violence committed by Drew between January 24 and February 3. He described Drew kicking Private Idell (the soldier who had been arrested for speaking out in defense of the laundresses) twice in the back for "not moving quickly enough"; striking First Sergeant Williams (possibly related to the lead mutineer Frank Williams) in the face and kicking him several times for being out of his quarters without permission; striking Sergeant Eugene Charles twice with a pole, when he was sick and unable to drill; and threatening Private Sheldon with his pistol, for not facing properly in saluting and appealing to a higher authority for protection against punishment. The assault against Sheldon, on the very day that the Commission had concluded its investigation and submitted its final report, proved the tipping point for Dwight.

Drew's conduct was not discipline, declared Dwight; it was the kind of physical terror that, if endured too long, provoked mutiny. The problem, he suggested, was rooted in the fact that Drew and Benedict, two inexperienced young men with "violent passions and unchastened temper" and pro-slavery sentiments, had selected "many of the Regiment's worst Officers." There could be no mistake, Dwight explained at length:

In this Regiment thus commanded was practiced every species of disgusting vice; what should have been the performance of duty was made a means of low and vile licentiousness among the Officers, of outrage which could not fail to be known to these soldiers, towards the women of their race, and the demoralization thus caused was repressed by violent punishment miscalled discipline. These are the traditions possessed by this Regiment.[73]

Dwight again called for the regiment to be broken up and for the now seven officers under arrest to be discharged from the service.[74] Whether driven by his belief that truth will out, or inspired by the Black men and women who mutinied against the White officers at Fort Jackson, Dwight's vision of military justice was at odds with the racial and sexual hierarchies that justified White violence against Black bodies.

In the end, Banks refused to hold Drew responsible and President Lincoln revoked the commission's dismissals of the six officers. As for their laundresses, the *Weekly Times-Democrat* reported, it had "been found necessary, for the good order of the men and the good behavior of the officers, to send all colored women out of this camp, except a few who are lawfully married to privates in the regiment, and are retained as laundresses for the regiment."[75] Nonetheless, while the commission's report had failed to bring justice, the women hoped a proper court-martial might succeed. In September 1864, seven months after testifying before the commission, three laundresses, Keziah Davis, Emma Smith, and Elizabeth Dallas, testified at the court-martials of officers Wentworth, Goff, Blakeslee, and Knapp.[76] Despite the women's testimony, the court found the men "not guilty."

The case of rape and mutiny at Fort Jackson is an extraordinary example of how Black men and women sought to defend themselves against racial and sexual violence and raise questions about the links between slavery and Black women's wartime labor. Bringing into focus how sexual and racial violence informed emerging ideas about freedom, and not least of all, the capacity of Black women to refuse to be treated as enslaved labor, the Black laundresses at Fort Jackson spoke truths that had long been denied under slavery – truths rooted in ideas about the past, what was possible, what was likely, and what was just.

6

"I Told Him to Let Me Alone, That He Hurt Me"

Black Women and Girls and the Battle over Labor and Sexual Consent in Union-Occupied Territory

Kaisha Esty

It was the middle of spring in 1865, a month after Confederate general Robert E. Lee's surrender in Appomattox, Virginia. Susan was in the final days of her pregnancy. She was a woman of color residing on a plantation near Salisbury, North Carolina, owned by her former enslaver, George Lyerly.[1] Like many other freedpeople, Susan likely felt immeasurable joy knowing that her baby would be born free. The threat of routine family separation that plagued enslaved motherhood was, for the most part, behind her.[2] Susan could expect to negotiate her time and labor for a wage. She might commit herself to familial and collective duties as a wife, mother, and community member. As an emancipated woman, the many horrors inherent to the market in the sale and exploitation of human flesh and labor should no longer have been part of her lived reality.

But Susan's dreams of freedom were viciously interrupted when she was raped by a Union soldier.[3] The terror occurred on or about May 10, 1865. Private Adolph Bork of the 183rd Ohio Volunteers and four other soldiers had visited Lyerly's plantation. Along with several other Black women, Susan recalled standing on a porch and watching as the soldiers roamed around the plantation grounds asserting their power. Presuming the availability of the labor of the Black female onlookers, a soldier ordered them to prepare some dinner. Unable to help due to her condition, Susan left the company of the other women and headed over to her cabin. There she found three of the soldiers. She waited until they departed before entering her home, shutting the door behind her.

When Susan was done gathering her things, she confronted Bork at her door. Addressing her as "Aunty," Bork showed that he did not view Susan as a person. He asked if she had any Confederate money. She told him that she didn't but that her "old man" did and that he could have it.[4] He then asked her if she wanted to *make* some money. Seeking clarification, Susan asked Bork, "What sort?," to which he responded: "Confederate."[5] She refused Bork's offer, knowing that Confederate currency "was no account."[6] In doing so, Susan refused to participate in the games that men who rape deploy in their assaults.[7] Bork then threatened Susan at gunpoint, telling her that whether "you want to make money or not you will have to."[8] Susan, who had been holding the child of another woman on her lap, got up and laid the child down. Knowing Bork's intentions, she fearfully began removing her clothes. Susan pleaded as Bork – the supposed enforcer of her emancipation – raped her. In a testimony before a general court-martial, Susan asserted that she neither consented nor accepted any money from Bork. "I told him to let me alone," Susan testified, "that he hurt me."[9] In offering further "proof" that she did not consent, Susan emphasized her marital status as an indication of her sexual respectability. "I am a married woman," she stated. "I was married by a colored exhorter."[10] At the close of the trial, Bork was sentenced "to be shot to death with musketry," a sentence later mitigated to five years of hard labor.[11] Susan's experience transpired under the assumption that African American women were always prepared to negotiate sex in addition to, or as part of, their (nonsexual) labor.

THE CONSTRAINTS OF CONSENT

Scholars of nineteenth-century American liberalism have rightly exposed how the concept of consent as stipulated in relation to the "social contract" has been anything but universal in its historical application.[12] As the feminist scholar Pamela Haag argues, "The deployment of consent or violence in one type of relationship necessarily affects and is modified with reference to other social 'contracts' inherent to citizenship and labor."[13] Had Susan been sexually assaulted six months earlier, the outcome would have been different. Before the completion of Union general George Stoneman's raid on Salisbury, North Carolina, in early 1865, Susan's sexual assault would not have been prosecuted as an injury on her person, if appealed at all.[14] Sexual access to enslaved women was foundational to the accumulation of White capital and the culture of slavery as a whole.[15] The sexual availability of enslaved women was built into the definition and exploitation of their labor. Their enslaved status was rooted in the negation of their capacity to give consent.[16] Any power for legal redress would have rested in the proprietary rights of Susan's owner.[17]

The Emancipation Proclamation and the Lieber Code, each issued in 1863, marked a major turning point as much in the lives of African American women as in the American Civil War. The Lieber Code acknowledged Black women as victims of sexual violence for the first time in US history.[18] Still, this new legal recognition existed in tension with the everyday reality evident in Susan's case. For Black women, the right to refuse unwanted sex remained elusive even after the end of slavery. How does one account for a history of sexual violence against African American women of liminal status on shifting legal ground?

Refugee and freedwomen's testimonies of sexual violence must be read as part of a contestation over labor and sexual consent in the mid-nineteenth-century United States. In their petitions before the military courts, fugitive and refugee enslaved women and girls asserted themselves foremost as sexually sovereign, especially as respectable, morally sound, and virtuous women and girls. These women and girls understood the racist and sexist structure of southern rape laws. Victorian sexual morality, combined with narrow rape laws centered on the premise of (White) female chastity, determined the most "acceptable" representation of female sexual sovereignty.[19] The laws that previously prohibited Black testimony against a White assailant, and the cultural values that made no distinction among Black women's nonsexual and sexual labor, ensured that only White middle-class women could be considered "chaste." Black women were considered "unrapable" because any violence done to their person was either legally sanctioned or culturally beneath notice. The testimonies of Black women and girls in these courts-martial attempted to overturn all these legal and cultural attitudes. Through the language of sexual respectability, Black women in occupied territory who were not sex workers argued that sexual assaults interfered with their ability to be productive as women, wives, and mothers. Grasping the power offered them by the Lieber Code, these formerly disempowered women created a rupture in what feminine virtue meant and who could be said to possess it.

In the perilous and jagged transition from slavery to emancipation, fugitive and refugee enslaved women and girls embarked on a fight to renegotiate assumptions around their labor. This chapter illuminates some of their stories. Ushering in their own meanings of consent that drew sharp distinctions between their (nonsexual) labor and sexual availability, African American women and girls asserted their right to withhold consent on their own terms.[20] Using testimonies of wartime rape of Black women and girls by Union soldiers and other military personnel, this chapter explicates the ways Black women and girls fought for sexual

autonomy, and sometimes won acknowledgment of it, regardless of their
class, status, or statelessness.[21]

RACE, SEXUAL VIOLENCE, AND THE
CIVIL WAR MILITARY RECORD

Even by a conservative estimate, at least 250 Union soldiers faced military courts-martial on charges of sexual assault during the Civil War.
Scholars E. Susan Barber and Charles F. Ritter have counted around 450
cases.[22] Both historically and contemporarily, sexual violence is heavily underreported, with even fewer cases making it to legal proceedings.
The confirmed incidents of Union-perpetrated sexual violence during the
Civil War may be inferred to represent but a small fraction of a larger
phenomenon. With the number of cases in the Union Army court record,
the overrepresentation of Black women and girls as victims and White
Union servicemen as perpetrators underscores two essential points.[23]
First, it demonstrates that stereotypes of African American women's
sexual availability were not confined to the White South. White and
northern Union soldiers' sexual expectations of Black women and girls
were remarkably reflective of the attitudes of their White southern and
pro-Confederate counterparts. Second, the fact that such an historical
record of Black women's and girls' testimonies of sexual violence during
the Civil War exists shows the huge importance of legal developments
that empowered them to pursue justice.[24]

Sexual violence cases involving African American female victims reflect
the arbitrary and racialized nature of record-keeping during wartime in
the mid-nineteenth century. In some instances, Black female victims'
names are not identified. Unnamed women are sometimes referred to as
"a woman of color" or "a Negro woman." This was most prevalent in
courts-martial that did not feature the testimonies or firsthand accounts
of Black women. Union military courts often showed greater concern
with the conduct of soldiers than with the harm suffered by the victim,
meaning that statements invoking the voices of survivors themselves were
not always a priority. It is also possible that some of these women and
girls chose to remain anonymous due to fear of retaliation. Depending on
the outcome of these trials, many survivors could expect to live and work
within the vicinity of their assailants.

In addition to the erasure of Black women's personhood, the record
is problematic in its repeated reformulation of Black girls as women.
Born in enslavement, many victims could not accurately recall their age.

Few courts took this unique context into account in their treatment of younger victims. Where prepubescent girls may have received sympathy, adolescent girls were more systemically "adultified." The violence of "adultification" in the court environment dehumanized and further traumatized Black girls by diminishing their childhood innocence and undeveloped maturity.[25]

Despite these limits, though, Union courts-martial and commissions give a rare insight into the environment that refugee and freed female sexual violence victims navigated in their struggle for sexual autonomy. They offer a useful site for investigating the complexity of the interactions between contraband, fugitive, and refugee women and the Union Army. These women often conducted nonsexual labor in the company of soldiers, increasing their vulnerability to sexual attacks from soldiers. Black women and girls were compelled to seek justice from military courts, the same entity whose representatives were responsible for their ill-treatment.

TESTIMONIES OF SEXUAL VIOLENCE

African American women's and girls' testimonies of sexual violence during the Civil War and the emancipation era challenged cultural and legal assumptions around sexual consent in mid-nineteenth-century America. The battlefield of this rupture manifested primarily in relations of labor involving fugitive and refugee women and girls, and military personnel. During the first part of the Civil War, fugitives, "contraband," and refugees were mainly African American men. However, by 1863, with the passage of the Emancipation Proclamation, greater numbers of African American women, children, and elderly people assembled behind Union lines. "Attaching themselves to the rear of columns on the move," formerly enslaved people established makeshift communities.[26] Thousands of men, women, and children contributed to the war effort through noncombatant military labor. Refugee women and girls took on roles as officer's servants, laundresses, cooks, nurses, and plantation field hands, though it was not uncommon for Black women to engage in more physically grueling labor like hoisting wheelbarrows, digging ditches, building roads and bridges, clearing canals, and burying the dead.[27] As historian Thavolia Glymph notes, "For them, it was an opportunity to work for their own freedom and for Union victory."[28]

Scholars of sexual violence during the Civil War underscore the significance of groundbreaking wartime legislation in creating an avenue for

Black female rape survivors to seek justice. Clauses within legislation such as the Enrollment Act of March 1863 pried open a door. In section 30 of this act, the US military acquired "jurisdiction over common-law felonies," including rape, "when committed by US military personnel."[29] Thus, in language aimed at regulating the sexual conduct of Union soldiers, the government set in motion an unprecedented, albeit incidental, recognition of Black women and girls within the category of sexual assault victims. In a social and legal culture that narrowly defined rape as an assault on a chaste White woman, and rendered Black, especially enslaved, women unrapable, such legislation was innovative in its implications.

The introduction of President Abraham Lincoln's "General Order No. 100: Instructions for the Government of the Armies of the United States in the Field," also known as the Lieber Code, fortified both the Emancipation Proclamation and section 30 of the Enrollment Act. Issued on April 24, 1863, the Lieber Code further outlined the terms of conduct during warfare. In article 37, section 2 of the Lieber Code, the US government promised to protect "religion and morality; strictly private property; the persons of the inhabitants, especially those of women: and the sacredness of domestic relations" in Union-occupied territory.[30] In addition, articles 44 and 47 each invoked rape – among "all wanton violence" – as a punishable crime when committed by Union soldiers against "persons in the invaded country."[31] As historian Crystal N. Feimster emphasizes, these three articles collectively "conceived and defined rape in women-specific terms as a crime against property, as a crime of troop discipline, and a crime against family honor."[32] The absence of the language of crimes committed against specifically *White* women meant that African American women and girls gained access to the protections of the Lieber Code.

Amid these legal developments, as well as Black women's noncombatant military labor, refugee women and girls in Union territory navigated what historian Stephanie McCurry describes as a "different and more forbidding landscape than the men."[33] Many Union soldiers were volunteers from predominantly small White rural regions in the North. Most had little prior interaction with African American women. With ideas of Black women drawn from cultural stereotypes rooted in slavery, Union soldiers who committed acts of sexual violence on refugee and freedwomen abused their power and mistreated Black women in the belief that sex could be freely solicited as part of their labor. This contrasted sharply with Union soldiers' treatment of Confederate women, though it is not to suggest that White women were spared Union-perpetrated sexual violence. As historian Drew Gilpin Faust argues, "Most Yankee soldiers were reluctant to harm white southern women, particularly those who seemed to be ladies of the middle or upper class."[34] Class and race therefore contributed to laboring Black women's sexual vulnerability in Union-occupied territory. Though Union soldiers were supposed to represent the enforcers of emancipation, some directed their aggression toward Confederate property, including human "contraband." "In all likelihood," Faust continues, "black women served as the unfortunate sexual spoils when Union soldiers asserted their traditional right of military conquest."[35] Whether in the officers' quarters in a camp, a cabin on a plantation leased by the federal government, or in the homes of Black families living in occupied territory, "contraband," fugitive, and refugee women and girls were uniquely situated as targets of the kinds of gender violence that too often accompanies war.

It is crucial to stress that amid the uncertainty of war, refugee and freed women and girls in occupied territory did not wait for their legal status to be defined in order to protect their dignity and bodily integrity. As a class of poor, uneducated, and stateless workers, these women and girls launched arguments that hinged on their moral authority to compel the state to punish those soldiers who violated their person. Constructing their freedom from the ground up in the midst of war, African American women and girls were clear about what it meant for them to live, work, and provide for themselves and their families free from the constant threat of rape and sexual assault.

The well-known Port Royal Experiment offers a powerful case in point. Introduced in late 1861, this vast and profitable labor program put 10,000 former slaves to work the land on South Carolina's abandoned Sea Islands. "Contraband" and refugees picked and ginned cotton – valued at a premium rate from this region. They produced and distributed manure. Potatoes and corn that they harvested formed part of their main diet. Months without pay for Black soldiers meant that their wives had to help support their families. These women washed "for the officers of the gunboats and the soldiers" and made "cakes and pies which they sold to the boys in camp."[36] While the Port Royal Experiment was touted as assisting African Americans' self-determination, expectations around their labor – defined in slavery – were readily adopted by the federal government. For example, Charles Francis Adams Jr., a member of the prominent political family, was reluctant to dissociate emancipated African Americans from their previously enslaved status. As a Union soldier in 1862, Adams penned a letter in which he reflected:

The scheme, so far as I can see it, seems to be for the Government, recognizing and encouraging private philanthropy and leaving to it the task of educating the *slaves* to the standard of self-support, to hold itself a sort of guardian to the *slave* in his *indefinite state of transition*, exacting from him that amount of labor which he owes to the community and the cotton market.[37]

Calling refugees "slaves" and describing their transition to self-determined labor as disruptive to the market and deficit in nature, Adams's language revealed the logic that undergirded government policy towards former slaves. By 1862, the US Treasury projected upward of 2.5 million pounds of ginned cotton from the hands of refugees.[38]

Government agents viewed Black women at Port Royal with suspicion and contempt. "The women, it is said," wrote E. L. Pierce in a report, "are easily persuaded by white men ... a facility readily accounted for by the power of the master over them, whose solicitation was equivalent to a command."[39] In stating this, Pierce acknowledged the cultural presumption that sex constituted part of the labor expected of Black women. However, rather than criticizing White men who exploited the sexual vulnerability of Black women, Pierce consigned Black women's sexuality to pathology. "They have been apt to regard what ought to be a disgrace as a compliment, when they were approached by a paramour of superior condition and race," he concluded.[40]

Yet multiple sexual assault charges brought against Assistant Surgeon Charles F. Lauer in Beaufort, South Carolina, in 1863, proved that for many Black women, White men who abused their power were a nuisance and a danger in their working lives. Laundresses Sarah and Jane were among several women who testified against Lauer for offenses committed on the Milne plantation on Port Royal Island.[41] They asserted that Lauer sexually abused them under the pretense of a medical examination. In his defense, Lauer ascertained that he conducted an examination of their genitalia because he suspected they had contracted a venereal disease.[42] In doing so, Lauer brought the possibility that Sarah and Jane were sex workers into the military court's line of sight.

Captain S. S. Metzger, a witness for the prosecution who was present during Jane's examination, corroborated Lauer's challenge to Jane's virtue. In his testimony, Metzger confirmed that Jane initially resisted the examination. He went on to imply that Jane was a prostitute, noting the "general impression" being that "some of the members of the regiment had been diseased by her."[43] In a court environment that evaluated the sexual reputation of women to determine whether they were "true" victims of sexual assault, Lauer's view clearly aligned with this presumption. The belief that Jane was a prostitute – or at least sexually active – appeared to have forfeited her right to withhold consent to an invasive "medical" procedure. Lauer exploited this gray area in his assault.

Eda and Rebecca were among the women who testified to Lauer's violence and sexual harassment.[44] Eda told the court that Lauer visited her home on three nights trying to "knock" her. To avoid any further harassment, she told the court that she started sleeping in the cotton fields.[45] She described how the doctor punched her when she refused his advances. Similarly, Rebecca testified that the doctor approached her as she sat on a bench, asking if she "would do it." "I said no," she stated, "He asked why. I told him I didn't want to do it and then went into the house. He followed me. When I said again I wouldn't do it, he slapped me."[46] Rebecca's experience descended into further violence and a failed attempt to get immediate help. "He kicked me twice in the stomach and boxed me on the face," she continued.[47] Rebecca escaped and reported Lauer to Captain Nesbitt, who "said he didn't think the doctor would do such a thing."[48] In the moment of terror, the presumed respectability of the doctor as indicated by Nesbitt overshadowed Rebecca's claims. Substantiating Rebecca's account, Sarah spoke as a witness. "I am well-acquainted with him [Dr. Lauer]. I used to do his laundry," Sarah testified. "I heard him trying to get her to go to his tent. She didn't want to. He slapped her and I said to him. 'Doctor … when a woman did not give it up to him, he should leave her alone instead of striking her.'"[49] The testimony of these Black women in court was disruptive. Union officials were compelled to listen to refugee Black laundresses scold a White doctor about sexual consent. As stateless, noncombatant military laborers who may or may not have engaged in sex for pay, including survival sex, these women were clear about asserting control over the borders around their own bodies. They upended so many existing beliefs about race, class, respectability, and sexual consent.

Like Lauer, Union soldiers and military personnel who sexually assaulted formerly enslaved women not only upheld ideas about the availability of their sexual labor, but also deployed racist arguments that reinforced Black women's legal marginalization. Within months of the hard-fought Battle of Stones River campaign, which pushed the Confederate army from its post in Murfreesboro, Tennessee, Harriet Elizabeth McKinley and Matilda McKinley brought rape and attempted rape charges against Privates Perry Pierson and William Lindsey of the Indiana Volunteer Infantry.[50] Harriet was living on the plantation of her former owner, Joseph R. McKinley, when Pierson raped her. When Harriet was first called before the military tribunal, Pierson objected to her testimony on the ground that she "was not a qualified witness, being a colored woman."[51] Taking Pierson's charge of Harriet's social inferiority seriously, the commissioners cleared the court for deliberation. The mere existence of Harriet's body in a courtroom caused debate.[52]

The commission rejected Pierson's attempt at legal obstruction, but that was only Harriet's first challenge. Despite confidently recalling her experience with details attesting to her sound-mindedness and credibility as a witness to her own body, the court repeatedly asked whether or not she consented. Harriet was compelled to perform her trauma. She insisted that she screamed throughout the entire assault and told the court explicitly that she did not consent to the act. Harriet was also was forced to disclose that she was unmarried and a virgin. Pierson was found guilty. He was sentenced to a year of hard labor and deprived of pay for four months.[53]

Harriet and Matilda each offered testimonies that emphasized their militant protection of their sexual and bodily integrity. Matilda, who accused Lindsey of attempted rape, testified that she was prepared to have her throat cut when Lindsey threatened that as an alternative to sex.[54] Similarly, after Harriet professed her sexual innocence before the court, she added that when Pierson penetrated her, she "hollered so that you might hear me for two miles."[55] By stating that she was a virgin and emphasizing her pain, Harriet defied the stereotype of enslaved female promiscuity and availability for illicit sex as well as the common ideological belief that African Americans were less susceptible to pain.[56] She asserted her bodily violation before the Union Army despite her liminal status and demonstrated her sense of self-ownership. Formerly enslaved women made the best of a legal culture that invited them to testify within the narrow script of the (White) chaste female victim while equally subjecting them to suspicion and condescension because of their race.

Harriet and Matilda's defense of their chastity and sexual self-possession brings into view the fact that formerly enslaved women and girls adhered to their own codes of sexual ethics in defiance of White assumptions about their sexuality. Testifying in military courts enabled Black women and girls to define these sexual and moral values and, relatedly, their meaning of sexual consent. This was especially evident in cases involving violence against Black girls. It is important to stress that Black girls were not spared the violence of rape and sexual assault. Like Black women, prepubescent and adolescent girls faced sometimes hostile military courts that compelled them to recount in excruciating detail the horrors of their trauma, often with the assailant present. If their apparent young age promised to sever the suspicion that illicit sex occurred, their race and gender also subjected them to the violence of "adultification."[57] As a form of dehumanization, Black girls struggled with the violence of "adultification" in myriad ways. At the level of their assaults, perpetrators either approached them as mature women or later attempted to justify their attacks with arguments that Black girls were actually women who consented to illicit sex.[58] Additionally, Black girls were further traumatized by "adultification" within the court environment, from modes of questioning to the ways that their cases were recorded. In the mid-nineteenth-century United States, the legal age of sexual consent was set between ten and twelve across most states. But, as historian Wilma King notes, "enslaved girls, who had no legal protection against sexual violence, were assumed to be experienced without concern about whether or not they were sexually active."[59] While ascribing moral meaning to age helped to underline the innocence and victimhood of African American girls, their race, status, and the labor they were compelled to perform nevertheless depicted Black girls as fair game, like Black women.

Thus, Black girls experienced sexual violence as part of the normalized conditions of violence that Black women experienced. Their testimonies and statements offered repeated markers of their sexual innocence as well as the moral and cultural values that they developed from their enslaved upbringing. In Wilmington, Virginia, an unnamed sixteen-year-old described her terrifying experience of sexual assault by five men, one of whom was John Murray of the 117th New York Infantry. She did not testify in court but evidently shared with a nearby witness, who testified that "they tried to take my maidenhead" – an expression that underlined the scale of the soldiers' crime.[60] Jennie Green did not know her age when she was raped by Lieutenant Andrew J. Smith of the 11th Pennsylvania Cavalry in City Point, Virginia, in 1864. She was an enslaved girl who transitioned to fugitivity when she followed Union soldiers to federal lines sometime in late spring 1864. Yet Jennie carried with her a clear sense of right and wrong. Despite her young age, lack of formal education, and liminal legal status in a country in the throes of a civil war, she sought sexual justice.

Like most refugee and freed women and girls who were sexually assaulted by Union soldiers, Jennie's experience occurred as she was providing nonsexual labor. She was working as an officer's servant in a military camp. In her testimony, Jennie explained that she had entered Smith's

quarters to deliver his supper. When she turned to leave, he grabbed her
arm and locked the door behind her. She described how Smith forced
her on the ground and proceeded to rape her. Testifying to her sexual
innocence as well as her sense of sexual sovereignty, even as a young girl,
Jennie stated, "He did the same thing that married people do.... That was
what hurt me. I did not give my consent to have that done."[61]

One should not rush over the precise language Jennie used in her testimony. For an enslaved girl, barely weeks off the plantation, to use the
language of "consent" in this context speaks volumes about the kind of
consciousness that would assertively seek redress in a military court. What
Jennie said to the court reveals to what extent she possessed a moral code
and set of principles in enslavement that permitted her to make claims
about her power, privilege, and self-ownership in court. The term *consent* belies the assumed consciousness of an enslaved girl. The notion of
power, privilege, and self-ownership inherent in the language of consent
was incongruous to the logic of slavery. Jennie not only affirmed that she
did not consent to have sex but also defined her understanding of sexual
intercourse as a practice that should be reserved for "married people."
In a society where marriage between enslaved couples held no legitimacy
under the law, the fact that Jennie framed sex as part of a marital union
sheds light on the ways that sexual respectability operated as a subversive
script in the testimonies of fugitive and refugee women and girls.

By the summer of 1864, Jennie was at the center of a high-profile rape
case. The surviving record of her case reveals the kind of inconsistencies
that spoke to her struggle with systemic "adultification." In one statement, she is described as "a young negro girl"; in another, Jennie is presented before the court-martial as a "colored woman."[62] Nellie Wyatt,
an African American woman who testified as a witness for the prosecution, corroborated Jennie's youth and sexual innocence. She explicitly
asserted that Jennie was "nothing but a child."[63] Wyatt went further in
her defense of Jennie's challenged childhood by arguing that it was precisely because of Jennie's young age that Smith took advantage of her.
Understanding that Smith might just as easily have attempted an attack
on her, Wyatt testified, "I got off by being married."[64]

Smith was convicted with the endorsement of General Benjamin Butler.
The recommendation for his sentence consisted of years at hard labor combined with the loss of rank and position. A known enforcer of the Lieber
Code's policy regarding the conduct of Union soldiers, General Butler
expressed his disgust. "A female negro child quits slavery, and comes
into the protection of the Federal government, and upon first reaching

the limits of the Federal lines receives the brutal treatment from an officer, himself a husband and a father, of violation of her person," Butler wrote. "Of this the evidence is conclusive."[65] Butler's response revealed that some White Union officials were open to an inclusive understanding of sexual consent. Lincoln, however, was unconvinced that Jennie had accurately identified her assailant. After Smith had spent a short period in a penitentiary, the president issued repeated orders for his release. While Jennie likely never received full sexual justice, her self-presentation as a moral subject, assertion of sexual sovereignty, and insistence on sexual consent attests to the subversive potential of her testimony.

Jennie's case shows that Black female servants working for Union officials were especially vulnerable to sexual assault. Accessing the private space of officials' quarters made inappropriate contact much easier to execute. In addition, the threat of losing their provisions offered a potential reason to remain silent, while the authority of Union officials often masked their predatory behavior. Many Black women testified with arguments that demonstrated their demands not only around the question of consent, but also for a safer working environment. On April 22, 1865, at a contraband camp on the south side of the Cape Fear River, Julia Jennison told a tribunal that she had explicitly told William McManus of the 33rd New Jersey Infantry that she did not want to sleep with him. Working as a servant in the officers' quarters, Jennison recalled that she was in one of the officers' rooms, making the bed, when McManus accosted her. "He asked me if I would sleep with him. I told him no. He said I got to do it. I told him I wouldn't."[66] McManus then attacked Jennison, and she fought back. As she tried to protect herself, McManus punched her in the eye and stated, "Jeff Davis had but one eye and why couldn't [she] have?"[67] Jennison's case clearly highlighted the assumption that sex formed part of the service that Black women owed to Union soldiers.

The routine assertion of one's moral authority within the overlapping frameworks of Protestant Christianity and Victorian sexual morality was undeniably strategic. In asserting their identities as married women, for example, refugees made explicit claims to their sexual respectability as evidence of the absence of their consent. In the mid-nineteenth century, marriage constituted the cornerstone of a moral, civilized society.[68] For African Americans, this notion held consequences that affected their material lives. Slaveholders prohibited legal marriage among enslaved couples, while abolitionists pointed to the lack of legitimate marriage as the main cause of sexual immorality within the enslaved community.

For White Americans on both sides of the slavery debate, the idea that African Americans simply didn't value the covenant of marriage was commonplace.

Black women's self-presentation as wives did more than simply convey that they valued chastity, or even that they sought participation in conventions set by White American society. As wage earners as well as wives, refugee women brought attention to their uniquely situated racialized sexual oppression. The mention of husbands exposed the fact that even after emancipation, they could not expect the kind of patriarchal protection available to White women. For example, a woman addressed as Mrs. Cornelius Robinson was introduced as the "wife of a loyal colored citizen" when she appeared in court in February 1865. She was the mother of a five-day-old infant when George Hakes of the Sixth Michigan Cavalry raped her at her home, roughly two miles from Winchester, Virginia.[69] In her account, Mrs. Robinson stated that Hakes entered her family home and ordered her husband on an errand to buy some sheepskin. When Mr. Robinson left, Hakes pushed Mrs. Robinson into the bedroom and assaulted her: "He said if I did not give up to him he would shoot me. I said, 'Then you'll have to shoot me.'"[70] While the horror of the assault was central in Robinson's testimony, her husband's absence augmented both her defenselessness and the magnitude of the crime. Framing her assault as a violation of her individual self and the sanctity of her marriage, Robinson's testimony stood in accordance with the Lieber Code's definition of rape as "a crime against family honor."[71]

Refugee and freedwomen also emphasized their chastity and marital status as a form of sexual resistance and an assertion of their sexual autonomy, both individually and in relation to their husbands. On a Saturday night in March 1865 in Central Knob, near Chattanooga, Tennessee, a Black Union soldier entered the home of Mrs. Sarah Beuford and "did by force try to have dealings of a carnal nature."[72] Beuford was awakened by a knocking at her door. Her visitor, Private John Lewis of the 16th United States Colored Infantry (USCI), introduced himself as a patrol guard on a routine check. This puzzled Beuford, because two guards had already passed by earlier before she went to bed. Lewis used his authority to gain access to Beuford's home, and in doing so he established an expectation for Beuford's deference and service. He asked for some bread, and she explained that she hadn't had any for several days. He stole some meat from a pig that she had killed earlier that morning. Shortly thereafter, Lewis's pillaging evolved into the threat of rape. He informed Beuford that he'd thought she was "an old woman" – an ominous comment gesturing to his sexual interest.[73] Slapping her on the shoulder, he asked if she "had nothing else to give him."[74] "I asked what he meant and he said I know what," Beuford later recalled, "I asked him about a hundred times what he meant and he said I know."[75] By insisting that Lewis name his intentions, Beuford refused the terms of secrecy that empowered and protected sexual predators. Thus, when Lewis asked for "some skin," Beuford replied that it was "a pretty question to ask a married woman."[76]

Offering forty dollars, Lewis attempted to recast his sexual affront into an illicit, consensual exchange. He promised Beuford that her husband wouldn't find out about the encounter. In a court-martial testimony, Beuford was clear in her response to Lewis. She underscored that her chastity was a self-governing virtue and a reflection of her identity as a Christian and a wife. "I told him if my husband would not know it God would and that if I had done the like I could not be depended on by my husband," she declared. "[I] said I was a lady before my husband's face and behind his back."[77] In a legal culture where rape laws and statutes scrutinized the chastity, reputation, and character of sexual assault victims, Beuford was aware that her credibility as a respectable woman was also on trial.[78] She told the court that Lewis held her at gunpoint and threatened to have her gang-raped by "thirty of the boys."[79] "I told him if they come, I would have more Company to go to the Lieutenant with and asked if he had any objection," she stated.[80] Beuford succeeded in scaring Lewis off. Risking her life in the pursuit of sexual justice, she followed Lewis back toward the military camp where he was stationed, undeterred by his attempts to shoot at her.[81] The next day, she reported Lewis to Lieutenant John Scott, commander of Company C.[82] At the close of the trial, Lewis was found guilty of three charges, including assault and attempted rape.[83]

The resistive tension between Lewis's solicitation of "some skin" and Mrs. Beuford's riposte as a married woman is emblematic of the sexual precarity of African American women and girls in the transition from slavery to emancipation. Beuford's self-identification as a married woman was strategically encoded in the protections of a female liberal subject-position. That Lewis was an African American soldier, added to Black women and girls' dangerously confounding relationship to representatives who were at once their assailants and protectors. Living within the vicinity of a military base, Beuford may easily have been a Black soldier's wife – a point that augments Lewis's dishonor as a soldier and community member. As noted, notions of the safeguard of marriage were not readily available to Black women, including Beuford, a free(d) woman living in Union-occupied Tennessee in early 1865.[84] But the assertion of her identity as a married woman combined with her use of the language of sovereignty and inverted dependency – "I could not be depended on by my husband" – demonstrates how Black women like Beuford self-fashioned a position that claimed the prerogatives usually limited to the (White) female liberal subject.

African American women were intentional about spotlighting their respectability and moral character in military courts and commissions by differentiating themselves from sex workers in a society where prostitution was often publicly visible and not explicitly illegal. Presenting themselves as "not that kind of woman" emphasized their understanding of a distinction between women who engaged in illicit sex and those who chose the path of chastity, modesty, and Christian morality. Using gendered conventions of modesty and respectability, Black women sought to dismantle the assumption that their labor was indivisibly nonsexual and sexual.

Of course, in emphasizing their sexual respectability, refugee and freedwomen reinforced the problematic belief that women who had any past sexual experience outside of marriage did not deserve justice. In the early nineteenth century, prostitutes and other women of so-called "lost virtue" were often removed from consideration as victims of rape and sexual assault. "Virtuous" women were believed to be the true victims, as their lifestyles did not conform to the kind that invited male sexual attention.

Still, the precarious nature of life for African American women meant that their virtue was continuously challenged by men who sought illicit sex. Black women and girls contended with real as well as scam enticements of payment before, during, and after sexual affronts and violence. Detractors' efforts to recast an assault through offerings of money and gifts spoke to the common attitude that Black women were always prepared to negotiate sex as part of a labor transaction. In a court-martial on March 14, 1865, Laura Ennis similarly testified that Charles Clark attempted to bribe her with coffee and sugar in exchange for her silence after he attacked her.[85] Sarah Beuford told the military court that she refused John Lewis's offerings of money, gloves, and shoes after his attempted assault.[86] Women, Black or White, explicitly framed solicitations for sex in exchange for payment as an insult to their character. On September 12, 1863, Mrs. Ellie Farnan and her daughter beat up a drunken Private William Van Buren of Company B, 212th Illinois, after he tried to accost them. He had offered to exchange money for "some skin," and Mrs. Farnan and her daughter reportedly took this offer as an "insult and abuse." In a statement offered by a witness for the prosecution, Mrs. Farnan apparently said to Van Buren: "You god damned old son of a bitch, you had the impudence to offer a decent woman like myself a dollar and my girl, that I'm raising, three [dollars]."[87]

Indeed, not all Black women and girls were able to, or even desired to, define sexual consent within the frame of respectability. Some pushed for more sophisticated understandings of sexual consent in ways that deviated from the legal script of the virtuous female victim. In 1865, in Clarksville, Tennessee, a fourteen-year-old noted on record as "Rachel, a Negro Girl" told a court-martial that Private John Locker had attempted to rape her. Rachel was staying at a known "house of ill fame" when Locker met and attacked her. According to the court proceedings, Locker was intoxicated and initially groped Rachel on her bosom. Witnesses differ in their accounts of how much Rachel resisted this act, but Rachel testified that she told Locker "to quit."[88] She became more vocal in her resistance when Locker progressed with an attempt to penetrate her. Once again, Rachel, like other Black girls who sought sexual justice, was treated with the presumption of her fully developed maturity – regardless of whether she was sexually active or not. Interestingly, when the defense asked Rachel, "Why would you not permit the accused to have carnal knowledge of you?" she responded: "Because he was not of my color."[89] Rather than appealing to ideals of chastity, Rachel, who was likely a sex worker, invoked her own notion of sexual respectability. To be sure, the defense asked if "color was the only object," to which Rachel said yes.[90] Perhaps the taboo of interracial sex was where Rachel drew the line. What is compelling about this case is that Rachel claimed moral authority on her terms, and when the borders of her body were violated, she pursued full legal recognition and justice.

CONCLUSION

In their refusal to be reconstituted as sexually available laborers in the crucial period of Civil War and emancipation, fugitive, refugee and freed women and girls embarked on a contestation over labor and sexual consent. Intervening in, and weaponizing, nineteenth-century ideals of sexual respectability, refugee and freed women's and girls' testimonies resisted the persistence of cultural assumptions that sex could be negotiated as part of, or in addition to, their nonsexual labor. Survivors of sexual violence were especially positioned to intervene in existing definitions of Black women's labor, and many seized the opportunity to shape this reformulation. Married women also challenged the attitude that African American marriage was a mere inconvenience that a man wanting sex could easily evade or ignore. Their deployment of the language of chastity and assertion of their marital status subverted the legal premise of the chaste White female sexual assault victim. As a result, stateless working women and girls ushered in more sophisticated meanings of sexual violence and consent in mid-nineteenth-century America.

But appeals to chastity guaranteed these women and girls neither sufficient sexual justice nor protection. The window of recognition that wartime legislation offered them was not sustainable. Enforced to regulate the conduct of Union military personnel, legislation such as the Lieber Code acknowledged Black women and girls as rape victims within the specific context of war. The period of Reconstruction introduced a formal rights framework for freedwomen to define their sexual autonomy as citizens. To be sure, neither citizenship nor education, literacy, or middle-class status were ever prerequisites for Black women and girls to assert their moral agency, dignity, and desire for sexual ownership. Their struggle for sexual sovereignty joined a longstanding tradition of sexual resistance fashioned by enslaved women – the most marginalized and nontraditional political actors. As citizens, freedwomen gained access, at least in theory, to a model of female citizenship. But as Reconstruction came to a close, the resurgence of southern White male political power unleashed a nadir of extreme racial and sexual terror. Working-class, middle-class, and educated African American women within the Black Baptist community would deploy strategies of sexual resistance similar to those used by their fugitive and refugee forebears in what historian Evelyn Brooks Higginbotham has defined as a "politics of respectability."[91] The shifting legal ground and character of the state that Black women and girls confronted reveals their fraught historical relationship to notions of sexual consent within the framework of Western liberalism. Their strategies speak to the ultimately burdened ways that African American women were compelled to seek sexual freedom in the mid- to late nineteenth-century United States.

PART III

EMANCIPATION, THE BLACK FAMILY, AND EDUCATION

7

Making Their Place on the South's Ragged Edge

USCT Women and Place in Little Rock, Arkansas

Kelly Houston Jones

On July 4, 1866, twenty-five-year-old Lavinia Taylor, called Viney by those close to her, stood before her husband James Buckner (Jim, to his comrades in the US Army) and a Baptist preacher to re-solemnize the commitment she had already made to him several years earlier as an enslaved woman. The couple, now in Little Rock, had been held in bondage in Kentucky, possibly near Hopkinsville, and forced west to Arkansas at the beginning of the Civil War by Whites who surely viewed Confederate Arkansas as a safer bet for slaveholders. Laura, the couple's infant daughter, and Betty, Viney's young daughter from a previous marriage, probably looked on. The wedding represented a fresh start for the family. The war was over, their marriage legally recognized, and James soon to complete his service in the 54th US Colored Infantry. The couple became known as the Lucases, discarding the name of James's enslaver to proudly take on his father's surname. They would welcome two more children in the coming years.

As much as the moment meant to the Lucas family, only some Black Little Rock residents had looked forward to the Fourth of July as the couple's wedding day. Freedpeople in the city had spent weeks preparing a grand Independence Day celebration. Organizers raised as much as $1,000 to support the construction of an open-air shelter housing a dance floor large enough to accommodate hundreds of people. Celebrants stuffed themselves with barbecue and danced joyfully into the night. Organizers had chosen to locate their festivities in an area along the north side of the Arkansas River known then as Huntersville (and later, Argenta). Sparsely populated but considered part of Little Rock, this neighborhood sat just across the river in view of the main city.

It hosted a camp of US Colored soldiers soon to be mustered out, fringed by Black civilians, many of whom had connections to the soldiers posted there. South of the Arkansas River in Little Rock proper, White and Black federal troops guarded General Frederick Steele's headquarters, the federal arsenal, general army hospital, and other structures in view of ad hoc housing created by United States Colored Troops' (USCT's) friends and family, including hundreds of women. The river only *seemed* to divide Little Rock's Black soldiers and civilians, however – residents south of the river thronged across the pontoon bridge to the party hosted by their neighbors to the north that summer.[1] The July 4th celebration represented freedpeople's claim to Arkansas's capital city. Meanwhile, Little Rock's former Confederates declared themselves too "bruised and sore" to publicly celebrate Independence Day.[2]

White conservatives may have been in retreat for now, but the public advance of Black men and women in and around Little Rock required both hard-fought and ongoing battle. The story of that battleground, however, has often focused on men. This chapter explores the front navigated by USCT women – wives, daughters, sisters, and mothers of men who served in US Colored regiments – in and around this growing city at the western fringe of the South. While much of the information here represents research working outward from the starting place of documents associated with the 54th US Colored Infantry (which began as the Second Arkansas of African Descent), it includes stories related to other regiments, too.[3] The chapter reconstructs the geography of USCT women's family and community in the Civil War and Reconstruction to emphasize Black women's political placemaking during and after the war's refugee crisis. Black women provided support for their soldiers and the US Army presence overall, but they also constituted part of the occupation force of Arkansas's capital. They formed the backbone of Unionist Little Rock and forged alliances with White progressive allies. They fought for rootedness, gaining unprecedented control over their domestic lives, and claimed privileges via their association with Black soldiers. As the postwar decades passed, Black women suffered defeats and hardship. An essential strategy that helped them to survive and thrive as much as possible was to tend to the networks created during the war. Taken together, it is clear that USCT women's experience of the war and Reconstruction was uniquely spatial; they both created and reacted to political realities in relation to home and neighborhood.

Investigating the placemaking of Little Rock's USCT women provides an opportunity to link a handful of scholarly conversations regarding the importance of Black neighborhoods and networks, politics of space, assertions of citizenship, and Civil War occupation. This story pulls from and links histories like the Black neighborhood-building explored by Anthony Kaye, the political geography mapped by Stephanie Camp, and the material reality of community ties described by Dylan Penningroth with conversations about the war's redefinition of freedom, rights, and citizenship in relation to military realities as discussed by historians like Chandra Manning, Amy Murrell Taylor, and Thavolia Glymph.[4] The chapter also inserts Black women's activities into the histories of Union occupation highlighted by scholars like Gregory Downs and Andrew Lang.[5] All such discussions owe a debt to historians who turned scholars' attention to Black women in the Civil War era, like Leslie Schwalm and researchers like Tera Hunter who excavated Black women's economic and cultural agency as they created lives for themselves after the war.[6] Much of what follows here could be seen as a prologue to the realities that Brandi Clay Brimmer has explored regarding Black Union widows' influence over "the very boundaries of U.S. citizenship" as they navigated the US pension system and the tangle of gendered, class, and race assumptions that its concept of citizenship relied upon. Black widows' claims demonstrated that they saw themselves as true worthy citizens and the rights they defined emphasized autonomy. The seeds of that point of view, this chapter asserts, can be found in their wartime efforts to create independent roots in places like Little Rock.[7] This chapter also contributes to the spatial history of Black women and the Civil War by bleeding out from the boundaries of official US Army–controlled "contraband" camps. Finally, like so many other Civil War–era topics, we know much more about the realities of the refugee crisis in points east; this chapter pulls our gaze to the experience in the Trans-Mississippi.

For about forty years before the Civil War, enslaved women in and near Little Rock made their way on the frontier of the "second slavery" – the harsher, more capitalistic version of chattel slavery that hit its stride around 1820 and marched westward, fueled by cotton and facilitated by Indian Removal. Enslaved women on the rapidly transforming fringe of the Old Southwest understood the dynamics of environmental and spatial politics of slavery and worked them to their advantage when they could. A group of fugitives outside the city sustained a sort of Maroon colony for several years, raiding the town for provisions at night. Black women subverted the regime in the town when they could in this relatively urban space.[8] While some bondspeople there farmed – nearly 15 percent of enslaved people in Little Rock did such work on the fringes of town – women took advantage of the opportunities created by the slave hiring system. Angeline Jackson and her children who were enslaved, for example, assisted her husband, James, in tending a shop while he secured other work around town. Such opportunities were not guaranteed. The city's population only numbered 3,727 in 1860. Eight hundred and fifty were enslaved, 56 percent of whom were female.[9]

Free and enslaved Black women in Little Rock may very well have interpreted the bloodless yet extremist takeover of the US arsenal there in February 1861 as a harbinger of secession. They knew, however, that Unionists had a voice in the state. State leaders did not remove Arkansas from the Union until May 1861, after the firing on Fort Sumter. Although loyalists existed all over the state, Confederate power faced the fiercest contest both in battle and in the form of civilian pushback to the northwest and southeast of the capital.

Black women's lives in Little Rock went on as they continued working, caring for growing families, and striving for security. Minerva Anderson and her husband, William, nurtured their family amidst the turning points of the era in a one-room log house on Tenth Street near Center Street. Her oldest son and daughter had been born before the war. She then bore Robert in 1862 while Little Rock was under Confederate control; Susan after US occupation, and Johnathan during Reconstruction. At Third and Cumberland Street, the Jackson family leveraged their proximity to the arsenal and to Confederate (and later, Union) soldiers. Angeline made ginger cakes and her children sold them to Union soldiers.[10]

Families like the Jacksons and Andersons watched Confederate rule in Little Rock crumble on September 10, 1863, when Arkansas's rebel government fled in the face of an invasion by US General Frederick Steele. Federal forces had covered the nearly 100 miles from the Mississippi River post at Helena to Little Rock in about a month, suffering only 137 casualties. Their arrival in Arkansas's centrally located capital ushered in freedom for hundreds of additional fugitives from slavery who had thus far been unable to reach Union lines. Little Rock became Arkansas's center for Black refugees farthest from the Mississippi River. The city transformed with the influx of soldiers and civilians. Angeline and her husband, James, opened their family's rental property at Third and Cumberland to freedpeople in need of temporary housing. Their daughter Julia later recalled that her father converted "outbuildings into little houses and allowed the freed slaves to live in them till they could find another place." Only a block separated the makeshift camp from General Steele's headquarters.[11]

The federal advance to the capital had been made possible by the service of US Colored Troops at Mississippi River-side posts to the south and east, such as Helena's notoriously flooded, diseased, and guerilla-threatened Fort Curtis. Precisely three years before Black Little Rock's festive July 4, 1866 celebration, Black men who had been recruited (but not yet officially mustered as a unit) to the 2nd Arkansas of African Descent helped fend off a Confederate attack on the US position at Helena, not only laying the groundwork for recognition of Black soldiers' bravery but also contributing to the level of stability along the Mississippi River that made it possible for federal forces to set their sights on Little Rock. Just days before the capture of the capital in September, the 2nd Arkansas of African Descent (later the 54th US Colored Infantry) was officially organized and sent to Little Rock where they would spend the winter.[12]

Jane Williamson became one of many who made that journey from the Mississippi River to Arkansas's interior. If Black troops made possible the success of the US Army in Arkansas, Black women like Jane should receive some credit for the success of Black troops. Her actions made her one of the "black women [who] trespassed the space of men on the battlefront" described by Thavolia Glymph. Jane, by entering the lines of the troops, proclaimed that the war was going to mean more than simply the mobilization of and recognition of men who would fight the Confederacy.[13] As Amy Murrell Taylor put it, refugee women like Jane "chose to join the fight – to become a part of it and to shape it – rather than have it unfold around them." Years later, Jane spoke about this period and her partner, George Clay, stating that she had been "with him in service." Brandi Clay Brimmer has emphasized that the recruitment of Black men as soldiers and laborers competed with the immediate needs of the women and children in their lives. The service of men like George necessarily placed a burden on women like Jane to care for children and provide support for their families during their terms of enlistment. By the time George Clay had enlisted in August 1863, Jane at eighteen years old was already pregnant with or had recently given birth to the couple's first child, Henry Rector Clay. Jane had been born in Tennessee, and although the exact circumstances under which she escaped from slavery and arrived at US lines at Helena are not clear, she was determined to stay close to her husband.[14] Her bravery is especially striking when we consider that life at refugee camps was deadly, especially at Helena, and the fact that General Steele had become notorious for his mistreatment of Black refugees at Helena. Jane and little Henry came to Little Rock when George Clay's regiment relocated there; their union was legally recognized "in company quarters" in October 1865.[15]

Not only did the hopes of couples like the Clays arrive in Little Rock, but the horrors of the humanitarian crisis did as well.[16] Among the most destitute Black refugees may have been those who lived at the "home farm" several miles down the Arkansas River from town on the land that had been owned by William R. Vaughan (in what would be designated Ashley Township). Federal authorities settled freedpeople on such farms around the South, operating this one outside Little Rock from March 1864 until January 1865. Several hundred people lived and worked at the farm. Unlike federally leased plantations, "home farms" were directly administered by the US Army. Their goal was to shift some of the burden of providing provisions to able-bodied refugees. While it is not clear how many of the women at Little Rock's home farm had connections to USCT soldiers, it is plausible that many would have ties to the men. E. S. Peake, a chaplain for the 28th Wisconsin Infantry turned refugee agent, wrote that the farm "provided a temporary home for those able to work to the number of 200 to 300 men, women, and children." This group planted "gardens & have 150 acres in corn" and received some rations from the army. Residents tried to create as normal of a neighborhood for themselves as possible, holding preaching and Sunday school each Sunday. The school enjoyed some consistency, instructing 135 students by March 1865. However, like so many other Civil War camps, disease – which Peake attributed to contaminated water – ravaged the settlement. Some patients were transported into the city for treatment. In June 1864 alone, 295 freedpeople at the farm perished. Authorities eventually removed the supervisor for dereliction of duty. Although sickness devastated the camp, it is significant to note that residents there did not suffer the frequent danger of guerilla raids as did their compatriots to the southeast. Federal authorities came to allow freedpeople the opportunity to lease portions of the home farm – about 400 acres – in 1865. Authorities closed the farm sometime in 1865, after which time Vaughan took over the land.[17]

Newcomers to Little Rock faced bleak conditions in seeking refuge during the war. Peake described "destitute refugees who have reported here in great numbers" to Little Rock in a condition of "almost perfect helplessness." "Great numbers of them die from exposure or starvation," he wrote, adding that "Most of them are in some way involved in the war for the Union through relations in the Federal Army." Despite those connections, federal officials, as they had in areas along the Mississippi River, dispatched hundreds of refugees north to Cairo, Illinois.[18] Black women, however, continued to arrive in Little Rock and in doing so engaged the politics of war and freedom. Necessity highlighted the stakes for Black women's ability to shape power structures. "Hundreds of thousands of enslaved women," Glymph writes, "made the unauthorized declaration that the Union army and its geographical and political lines of authority were places both of refuge and retribution."[19] So they continued to place themselves, driven by both necessity and political motivations. Newcomers included Sarah Demsey who had been born and raised near Camden, almost 100 miles to the south. Like so many enslaved children, Demsey had been reared by her aunt, who took the risk to relocate Sarah to Little Rock, where the girl came of age.[20] Some Black refugees arriving to Little Rock congregated near the Wesley Chapel, while others situated on the western fringe of the city near the "government corral."[21] Caroline Andrews and her husband, William, founded the Wesley Chapel in 1853, a Methodist church for enslaved people. Their Sunday school may have been a front for teaching fellow bondspeople to read and write.[22] Amid the influx of refugees, several settlements with clear associations to USCTs dotted the Little Rock area. Available records suggest that the largest groupings most directly connected to USCT women would have been the following three: the congregation near St. John's College; the camp constructed adjacent to the state capital building; and the Black civilians gathered across the river near the USCT encampment in Huntersville/Argenta.

The largest camp of Black civilians, other than the "home farm," must have been the camp located behind St. John's College, a men's college one block east of the US arsenal. The US Army had taken the main building over as a hospital, constructing barracks and other buildings on the campus. At least 1,000 refugees inhabited the area, most of whom according to Peake, were families of US soldiers. A physician employed by the local relief committee attended to some of their needs while the US Army issued rations. Peake's description included the presence of a log cabin used as a schoolhouse, in which eager pupils received instruction from one of their own. The makeshift neighborhood included frequent preaching, too. Refugees found work cleaning, washing clothes, and nursing in the civilian hospital. Like so many others across the South, refugees at St. John's lived under the scrutiny of humanitarian associations and federal officials alike. Peake praised the camp as "well systematized, policed, and disciplined."[23]

The camp population at St. John's declined by at least half at the end of June 1865. While the end of the war allowed many of Arkansas's White Unionist refugees to return home, Black refugees had fewer options – the camps were their homes. By then, the new 113th and 54th USCTs

FIGURE 7.1 "Blissville, Little Rock, Arkansas," by Alfred Rudolph Waud, 1866. From the permanent collection of the Historic Arkansas Museum.

were stationed in Little Rock, supporting the Unionist government and detailed from time to time to stamp out guerilla activity in the river valley and protect rail lines. Wives and families of the Black occupation force understandably desired to remain near their men. Dozens of the refugees who stayed near the camps were widows and children of deceased soldiers. Freedmen's Bureau claim records reveal that several widows stayed close to the original camp site well into fall 1866. Women like Jane G. Kibby, for example, came to the Freedmen's Bureau office in Little Rock to declare their right to the back-pay owed to their deceased husbands, brothers, or sons. In doing so, they also registered for potential pensions that the Bureau of Refugees, Freedmen, and Abandoned Lands might be able to issue in the future. Freedmen's Bureau officials asked each claimant where she could be found for disbursement, providing a snapshot of the whereabouts of USCT women. Kibby, who lost a soldier of the 113th, lived "at Lawyer Rice's near [the federal] arsenal," while Ellen H. Waters, a widow of the 54th, resided "between [the] arsenal and US Gen'l Hospital."[24]

These notes indicate a lingering presence near St. John's even after many in the official camp had dispersed, and a desire by USCT women to remain near points of federal power. They also speak to some of the core domestic issues women faced. Jane Kibby had either taken work or simply refuge with a northern attorney named B. F. Rice, who was known to assist freedpeople in establishing autonomous homes. She was among the many women whom Glymph explains made alliances with useful loyal Whites in their struggle for survival and place. For her part, Ellen Waters occupied a space not designated in official US Army mapping. Agents described her home as between two places where a federal map made no acknowledgment of tents or cabins that sheltered people like Waters in the interstice. She inhabited a liminality that applied to many USCT women in Reconstruction Little Rock.[25]

Humble as they may have been, USCT women's habitations represented occupation. While it is not clear how long they had been there by the time *Harper's Weekly* reported on them in June 1866, USCT women claimed the space immediately to the west of Arkansas's capital building. There is no indication that this was a US Army–designated and/or –regimented settlement, although the women there would have expected some level of protection from federals. Some of them may have been women who previously resided at St. John's. *Harper's* specifically attributed the settlement to the wives and sweethearts of Black soldiers. They constructed cabins and outbuildings to create a neighborhood they called "Blissville." An 1864 federal map indicates that the site did not conform to the city's block layout, divided as it was by a gulley slicing down to the bank of the Arkansas River – visible in both the map and magazine illustration. On the riverbank just to the north, federal officials operated a sawmill, and another farther west. USCT women set up an independent neighborhood that transformed this otherwise undesirable location into a haven for their families. For them, it was a "picturesque retreat." *Harper's* described scenes of families cooking outside and enjoying each other's company despite the cramped conditions.[26]

Their choice of location not only made sense on a practical level – the women were unlikely to meet competition for this site – but also on a political level, situated as they were at the center of Little Rock's formal political scene. As Glymph explains, "Black women found myriad ways to make refugee camps more than they were intended to be and, in the process, laid claim to freedoms they were not intended to have." USCT women positioned themselves adjacent to the seat of political power in Unionist Arkansas, within blocks of General Steele's headquarters, the provost marshal general's office, and the home of the new Unionist governor. They declared their Unionism and relevance while ensuring as much security for their families as possible. Notes of Freedmen's Bureau officials might have named some of the residents of Blissville when they

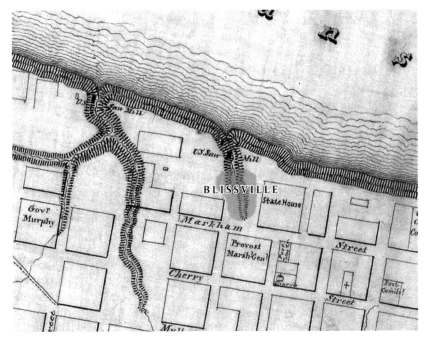

FIGURE 7.2 From US Army map, December 22, 1864. Map #0726, Butler
Center for Arkansas Studies, Central Arkansas Library System. Created by
Patrick Hagge.

recorded in late summer that Kitty Ann Waters, a 54th widow, could be
found at the "second door west of office" on the north side of Markham
Street; and described Venus Washington, mother of a deceased 54th
USCT soldier, as living near a steam sawmill, which may have been the
one on the river.[27]

Specifics regarding Black women's home camps in Huntersville (hereafter referred to as Argenta) are the most difficult to track in the 1860s
due to the general terms that contemporaries used to refer to the area.
By October 1864, the 112th US Colored Infantry (soon to be rolled into
the "new" 113th) had relocated from tents near St. John's College to
the north side of the Arkansas River, enjoying upgraded housing and a
hospital, and certainly accompanied by at least some civilians.[28] Upon
return from duty in western Arkansas, Indian Territory, and Kansas, the
54th encamped at Argenta rather than at their previous location to the
south. Mary Burns married Henry Kyles (who had been held by the same
enslaver before the war) of the 54th at the site on a Sunday evening
in March 1865. The time Mary spent at the Argenta camp also united

her with others she had known during slavery, like Lucinda Randolph and Henry's comrade, Albert Anderson. Mary and Henry's friend Isaac Gillam remembered that Mary "came to our camp at Huntersville, [Argenta] Ark as a young girl." Freedmen's Bureau agents' notes relating to claims also locate some USCT widows in the area during the fall of 1866. Sarah Horton and Ann Collins resided near a federal warehouse and Rachael Frazier inhabited a site "near the depot."[29]

USCT women's placement in Unionist Little Rock was inherently political.[30] It was Black *men* who gathered in the city for the Convention of Colored Citizens from late November to early December 1865 to make formal calls to the burgeoning Unionist government for equality under the law and access to the franchise. However, they did this in a city whose streets teemed with Black women asserting their humanity in public spaces and forcing civilians and military authorities to make room for their families. Legally registering their marriages alone constituted a declaration of humanity and citizenship, as other scholars have noted. When William Grey, one of the convention delegates, declared, "Here we have lived, suffered, fought, bled, and many have died. We will not leave the graves of our fathers, but here we will rear our children.... Here where we have been degraded, we will be exalted," he argued for a counternarrative to the displacement of slavery and war.[31] The rootedness he invoked was exactly the nature of the work USCT women had been undertaking on the ground. Scholars have explored the story of Black women's claims to rights based on who they married or had relationships with, as well as their claims to citizenship based on their labor, or as Manning put it, "usefulness to the nation." Less well mined, however, (but not wholly unrecognized) are Black women's claims predicated on their placement and movement. This is not to say that the places they made were warm, dry, healthy, comfortable, or completely free. But as Manning states in relation to the war's power to broaden citizenship, the "unleashed forces of war blew apart what had previously seemed intractable borders."[32]

USCT women drew new lines, not by prepared speeches or formal resolutions, but in their triangulation of spaces that asserted their loyalty, connected them to USCTs, and recognized the legitimacy of their families. The routes they took between their homes, Freedmen's Bureau offices, USCT encampments, hospitals, and worksites constituted their platform. They made their sense of place by walking their children from a crude cabin to the school supported by Freedmen's Bureau officials and the American Missionary Association, by carrying a meal to a loved one at the "colored soldiers" hospital, or by gathering for worship at

the Wesley Chapel on Sunday mornings.[33] Thus, as subjugation is a spatial act, Black women's "respatializing" in Unionist Little Rock declared
their autonomy.[34] Unlike White refugees, not only was the place new to
most of these women but so were the power structures surrounding their
daily routines.

Eliza McDaniel was born in Wilcox, Alabama, "but my white folks
brought me to Louisiana when I was a baby," she recalled, and kept her
there for a short time before settling in Union County, south Arkansas
near the Ouachita River. Eliza weathered the war, which began when she
was fifteen years old, in south Arkansas, but in August following peace
made her way north to Little Rock. Eliza had probably arrived in the city
with her mother Mary McDaniel and niece Sophia. But if she had been
lacking female company it wasn't for long, as she made a lifelong friend
named Charity Brown in the six months that she resided "in citizens'
camp up back of the St. John's college." Eliza later met Albert Hudson,
an eighteen-year-old private serving hospital guard duty. They courted
for six weeks before being married by a Presbyterian army chaplain
named W. G. Williams. Eliza described Williams as "a white soldier who
followed the dead to the grave yard, & who belonged to the regiment. He
married us in the house he was staying in."[35]

It may have been her new friend Charity who introduced Eliza to
Albert, linking the newcomer to other networks created by the war.
Charity had known Albert since 1863 as he was a bunkmate and prewar friend of her soon-to-be husband, Allen Love. Charity had experienced the upheaval of war and seen the misery of Black refugees along
the Mississippi River. Her enslaver, John Rosser, had moved a group of
bondspeople including Charity, who had been born in North Carolina,
from somewhere farther east to Coahoma County, Mississippi, early in
the war. After a few years, Charity, her first husband Tom Brown, her
future husband Allen Love, and his first wife Epsy, fled with a group of
fugitives to Helena. Epsy and her child died there. Charity and Allen
went separate ways. Allen enlisted, Charity's first husband Tom died,
and Charity and Allen crossed paths again in Little Rock, marrying in
April 1865.[36] USCT women like Eliza and Charity created a community
held together by linkages forged in the refugee experience and the military service of Black men.[37]

Black women in Little Rock readily employed the mobility that freedom from slavery offered, exploring the city and the people in it. They
reunited with friends and family and took up new acquaintances and
beaus. Women frequently availed themselves of access to the federals'

pontoon bridge crossing the Arkansas River in order to watch their husbands, brothers, sons, and friends in the army march in daily drills. When Fannie Garrett "used to go down & see soldiers parade here at Little Rock" she watched her stepfather Charles Banks and met the Lucases (mentioned earlier). Delia Burks was another frequent face, recalling, "I was in the camp every day nearly with my brother for several months."[38] Sarah Smith explained how she met her husband Henry in Little Rock: "I used to go over to see the soldiers drill and in that way became acquainted with him." Sarah lived south of the river while Henry's company of the 54th encamped just on the north side. "He used to come over to see me and I would go over to see him," Sarah explained, "We finally decided to be married" in spring 1866. The camp hosted the wedding and the celebration afterward, which took over a building "used by the soldiers as a dance hall." "There was quite a crowd present," Sarah remembered. After the wedding, she lived with a Mrs. Newsom who was married to a sergeant in her husband's company. Sarah resided with the couple until her husband's company mustered out. Even then, Frank Govan remembered, Henry "often brought his wife over to our camp and she often came over to visit him too."[39]

While USCT women and their children did not enjoy the support network that northern White Unionists could rely upon, they leveraged the connections forged by the service of their men to create a network of help. Bereaved and in precarious economic situations, many women came to the Freedmen's Bureau office to claim the pay owed to their deceased husbands, sons, and brothers. Eliza Brooks made a claim as a mother of a soldier of Company D, 54th USCT, and took shelter with her dead son's comrades. Freedmen's Bureau officials noted that she "could be found at Company D." Soldiers assisted bereaved USCT mothers in less direct ways, too. Harriet Greenleaf, who filed a claim for her deceased son, instructed officials that they could take any information they heard about her application to her son's comrade, Giles Harding. Carney Nevels registered claims for both the balance owed to her deceased husband (who died in November 1864) and her deceased son (who died June 1864). Agents noted that she could be reached by contacting Burgess Nevels of the same company. Whether Burgess was another son or a man held by the same enslaver, he agreed to take on the business of administering her claim.[40] These connections informed the networks revealed in pension claims decades later.

The context for all USCT women's efforts at placement and mobility was that of occupation. While plenty of USCT soldiers saw battle, the overall practice by the US Army was to apply them primarily as agents of occupation. The 54th, for example, had spent some time in Little Rock, had traveled across the state and seen action to the near west, but beginning spring 1865 their job became to act as the dedicated occupation force of Arkansas's capital. This was "when the companies all came together," Albert Anderson recalled. While it is unclear to what extent women followed their movements, as shown above, many USCT women clearly saw Little Rock as their home while their men served. According to Andrew Lang, USCTs "used occupation to their advantage, unbalancing traditional southern power dynamics" and "impressed their newfound martial authority on the very society guilty of enslaving them." USCTs and the women in their lives "envisioned the military to be *the* essential tool for social and political transformation." When USCT women made their homes, they extended that occupation and the transformational power it implied. Traditionally occupiers have somewhere to go home to, somewhere that they belong. Even the humblest White person had a place they called home somewhere. Black women, however, were busy redefining what home meant.[41] For many, like those described above, the concept became hitched to the spatial realities of their men's military service. After being married in camp by a chaplain in October 1865, for example, Jane Gray spent a lot of time in the camp and "occupied a cabin close to our quarters" in Argenta until her husband mustered out in 1866.[42] If Black women served as a wing of Union occupation in agricultural contexts by inhabiting and keeping plantations productive, in towns like Little Rock they filled public spaces with a loyalist culture, engaged in economic exchange with Unionists, educated their children, and otherwise filled the city's space with Unionism.[43] There was a limit to how far Black women could use social gatherings to display "loyalty, dominance, and conquest" like White Union wives, but it was not completely impossible. When Captain James M. Bowler wrote to family in 1864, he mentioned he had eaten in camp that morning, later having Christmas dinner "out in company" with officers of the 112th USCT, not at camp but "at Old Margaret's, the wife of one of our colored sergeants." Bowles claimed to have been served "roast chicken, several kinds of pie and cake, and everything in the best of style."[44] While White occupation wives' "true households lay elsewhere," such that they experienced lower stakes in their temporary domestic realm, Black occupation women in these exchanges engaged in fundamental meaning-making.[45]

While Little Rock's USCT women forged and strengthened relationships in place, they also busied themselves readying for the end of their

FIGURE 7.3 "Mustered Out," a drawing by Alfred R. Waud, depicting USCTs and loved ones in Little Rock. *Harper's Weekly*, May 19, 1866. www.loc.gov/resource/ppmsca.13485/

men's terms of service. In Blissville, "numbers of the mustered out colored soldiers betook themselves, their wives, families, or sweet-hearts having already secured habitations there."[46] Artist Alfred Waud's sketch reproduced as an engraving in the May 19, 1866 *Harper's Weekly* drawing is often used, especially by Arkansas's Civil War historians, to illustrate the joy of Black families coming together at war's end. Indeed, the scene features loving reunions between families and soldiers of the 113th who had recently mustered out months earlier than companies of the 54th. These companies had been on assignment about fifty miles to the east at DeValls Bluff. The energy swirling in the scene has made it an iconic representation of the hopes for the future held by Black families.[47]

The image's accompanying article several pages later, however, provides an even more revealing look, showing USCT women as more than wives in a dutifully static state waiting for their husbands' return. The troops' arrival, *Harper's* noted, "created a furor among the resident colored females" who "rushed into the arms of their husbands with an outburst of uncontrollable affection." Waud's sketch shows that these personal moments took place in public, out in the yard and street in front of Quartermaster Col. Page's office. If the quartermaster *Harper's* referred to is the district quartermaster, then the backdrop for this public emotional reunion was the Albert Pike house, a mansion owned by a Confederate general (and nationally known mason) that had been commandeered by federal officers upon 1863's takeover of the capital. The house sat merely a stone's throw from the Black civilian camp at St. John's. The iconic sketch, then, captures not only the emotions and hopes of Black families at war's end but also displays the extent to which USCT women asserted a public presence, in the orbit of federal power, of their designs on the future. This was their turf. Women gleefully embraced their loved ones, satisfied themselves that they were healthy and safe while also making new "introductions between comrades and wives." Meanwhile, they watched their children running about carrying their fathers' belongings and feeding off the excitement. *Harper's* described it as a generally smiling crowd, "with the exception of the faces of those who missed their husbands or brothers."[48]

Hard as they had worked to make these spaces their homes, however, USCT women did not convert their wartime camps into permanent abodes, nor did they leverage their occupation to real-estate ownership, a story common to the Civil War's Black refugees.[49] Universally, Black families expressed a desire to own land (or lots in town). Federal officials in Little Rock commented on the frustration of freedpeople trying to "get lands of their own to work." By the time most USCTs were released from service in 1866, at least half of the crop year had already passed, adding a complication to their ability to secure farm work outside of town.[50] Over the next few years, some USCT families remained in the city while others relocated out to the surrounding rural areas. Neighborhoods of USCT families in and around Little Rock, Arkansas, in the decades after their occupation duties ended included the following three: the main city's Third Ward, the northern section of the city called Argenta, and a belt of rural communities bending around east of the city.

By the 1870s, the majority of identifiable USCT households in Little Rock resided in the city's Third Ward – which in 1871 comprised the southwestern quadrant. There was a shift in residences from the Second Ward and farther into the Third Ward over time. While the causes for the shift are not clear, the Second Ward blossomed and became known as "Masonic Addition" by 1871. An 1871 city directory's ward map may have created a level of nineteenth-century "gentrification" that made it difficult for many Black families to remain in the Second Ward.[51] The Third Ward was home to women with varied journeys and stories. When Mary Williams came to the city's Freedmen's Bureau office to register her claim related to the service of her deceased husband, she identified herself as "Aunt Mary, cook on Col. Park's plantation near Pine Bluff." By 1870, she was employed in the Third Ward cooking for John R. Montgomery and family. Rather than return to her enslavers, Mary, only twenty-six, remained in Little Rock and leveraged her skills and perhaps new urban Republican connections. Her employer, John Montgomery, from Ohio, served as attorney general for Arkansas's loyalist Republican government. In 1866, Mary Crane, born in Virginia, and widow of Lindsey Crane of the 54th, registered her location with Freedmen's Bureau officials as Satterfield and Thompson's Plantation downriver from town. By the 1870 census, however, Crane, thirty, worked as a seamstress, living with a White family headed by boatman Isaac Benson in Little Rock's Third Ward. The 1871 city directory placed her residence at 609 West Eighth Street.[52]

Lucinda Campbell's circuitous route to the Third Ward may have been typical of many widows who had to rely on themselves for support. When she made a claim to the Freedmen's Bureau office in Little Rock, the notation did not specify whether it was based on the service of a husband or son. In either case, she indicated that she currently lived in the "rear of Parson Welch's yard." The note referred to Thomas Welch of Kentucky, a Presbyterian minister, who had been in Little Rock as early as 1860 and who had served as officiant for several Black couples whose marriages were recorded by the Freedmen's Bureau. Lucinda's work and residence there may have been an example, not unlike Mary Williams above, of Black women linking themselves with their labor to people with "loyalist credentials." Later, however, Freedmen's Bureau officials updated Lucinda's notes to indicate that she could be found at the farm of Peter Hanger, who had been a wealthy slaveholder on the fringe of town in the antebellum era. Hanger's farm sat to the northeast of the camps behind St. John's College. By 1871, Lucinda had made her way back into the city, working as a washerwoman on 305 West Thirteenth Street in the Third Ward.[53]

North of the Arkansas River, Argenta (which had been Huntersville) remained an important Black neighborhood with roots in USCT service. Some soldiers and their families remained close to the USCT site for several years before deciding to move on. Mary and George Champ of the 54th, for example, lived on the north side of the Arkansas River for the first five years after the war, then came south to reside in the heart of Little Rock where Mary died in 1875. Others stayed for the rest of their lives. The Kyles, Robinson, Lawson, and Lucas families' connections dated back to 1865. Many other families would leave Argenta to return in later years.[54]

In fact, several USCT families edged to the east and south from Argenta, still on the north side of the Arkansas River, as the years passed. In the process of clearing up the date of a potential pensioner's marriage, one veteran explained that his comrade Alfred Holmes had not married while in the service but after "we all lived down the river," referring to the fact that so many of his comrades' families had made the same journey outside of the city to farm. Many other USCT men and women described a similar journey within one to three years of mustering out.[55] After his service ended, Sarah finally got to live with her husband Henry Smith in "a little house" they rented "down in the bottom just outside of Little Rock" for three or four years before moving near Toltec, the next railroad stop after Scott's.[56] Overwhelmingly, these families farmed for their livelihood, and not usually as the owners of their own acreage. By the time these newcomers arrived, the new tenant farming and sharecropping system had taken hold.[57]

Households with USCT ties appear in clusters, suggesting that the experience of service together created lasting bonds. For example, the 1870 census returns for Eagle Township reveal a cluster of 113th families. Esther and Scott Fleming farmed there with their one-year-old boy Charly. Next door lived Harriet and William Hempstead, also of 113th. Both Scott and William's service records indicate that they had mustered out at DeValls Bluff in 1866, making it possible that their reunions with loved ones had been part of the scene that inspired Waud's 1866 sketch in *Harper's*. Nearby the Fleming and Hempstead household lived forty-five-year-old Hannah Kellogg, and Richard, who was probably her son, who had also served in the 113th. Other USCT clusters abounded in these townships. In Eastman alone at least sixty-seven households related to the 54th USCT appear in the 1870 census.[58] USCT families who headed to the countryside remained quite connected to the main city. Several came into town weekly, either to Argenta or into Little Rock proper, to trade.[59]

USCT families' political activism continued and men's formal political power was protected by Arkansas's 1868 Republican constitution. Henry Rector of the 112th US Colored Infantry (with neighbors from the 54th) served as a justice of the peace in Ashley Township in 1870.[60] Susan Water's husband George (also of the 54th) served as a justice of the peace for Ashley Township before transferring to Young Township; his term expired in October 1876.[61] At least eighty-four African American men would serve in the state's General Assembly between 1868 and 1893 (most between 1868 and 1874).[62] Little Rock's Black public servants included another 54th veteran as justice of the peace, a chief of police who had been a sergeant in the 113th, and a 54th veteran for a deputy constable.[63] Informal politics involving women and the use of public space continued as well. For example, at least as early as 1867, Black Little Rock residents organized public gatherings to celebrate January 1st as Emancipation Day, in which women figured prominently as speakers and performers. Philander Smith College, established at the site of the Wesley Chapel, was one of the most reliable hosts for that celebration. In the 1870s, women of that congregation founded the Benevolent Society of the United Sisters, which facilitated the pooling of funds to pay for what today might be termed "home health" as well as a death benefit. As they had in the 1860s, Black women in Little Rock crafted what Tera Hunter described as a "web of social services and institutions" to not only advance political goals but to serve economic needs that the lack of formal political power made more difficult to solve.[64]

USCT woman Cora Gillam's family ranked among the best known in Little Rock's public life. Fathered by a White overseer from the North and born to an enslaved mother in Greenville, a town just across the Mississippi River from Arkansas, Cora was held by a family named Warren. She had half-siblings who were enslaved, whom her father had acknowledged, and whom he secured freedom for and sent to college in Ohio before he died. Cora's enslavers relocated her to southern Arkansas during the war. She must have accompanied her mother, who was sent to Little Rock to cook for Confederates after Helena fell to federal forces. Her uncle, Tom Johnson, fled and joined the 54th, and it was likely through him that Cora met Isaac Gillam, a blacksmith by trade and first sergeant in Company I of the 54th, whom she married in 1866 or 1867, as a teenager. After the war, Cora's mother returned to Helena to work for her former mistress while the Gillams leaned into their public life in Little Rock, living by 1870 and at least through 1871 at 912 Arch Street (with their first son) among several USCT neighbors. Isaac served as quartermaster of the Grand Army of the Republic for several years, as city jailor by 1872, and afterward as a city policeman.[65] Cognizant of her half-siblings' education and the power of fortunate connections, Cora probably held high hopes for her children based on what her husband could accomplish as a voter and public servant with a record of military service. Entanglement in a state-level civil war may not have been one of them, however. Yet, when Little Rock erupted into a battleground between competing factions for the governor's office in 1874, Isaac Gillam again picked up a gun.

The growing tensions among Republicans (Black and White), as well as between Republicans and conservatives, are what embroiled the capital city in violence and darkened Black futures. Military Reconstruction and Governor Powell Clayton's tough stance against its insurgency inflamed conservatives in Arkansas and Little Rock while the Republican progressives splintered, leading to a fiercely contested gubernatorial election of 1872. In the violence that followed, each side asserted their candidate's claim to the governor's office, refusing to back down until President Grant intervened and a new constitutional convention was promised. Again the grounds of the state house and surrounding area became a site of public Black political activism closely tied to the martial activity of Black men. Would-be governor Joseph Brooks's supporters seized the capitol with the force of White and Black militia. Brooks was overwhelmingly preferred by African Americans like Isaac Gillam who served as a militia captain. He represented the less conservative wing of the Republican Party, and some of his appeal surely related to the fact that he had been a chaplain for a USCT regiment.[66] For his part, would-be governor Elisha Baxter commanded some Black support but held a reputation as more conservative than Brooks, winning over Democrats who had initially sided against him by proving more convincing and dedicated in his efforts to remove voting restrictions on former Confederates. Although the election was held in 1872, a court decision in April 1874 in Brooks's favor, after Baxter had been installed, kicked off a weeks-long firestorm that included street battles and harm to civilians.[67] Both sides pressed for Black militia support and both sides included former Union and Confederate leadership, eventually creating a collective troop buildup of as many as 3,000. Significantly, the US Army, whose presence had withered by then, did not serve as the protectors of Black civilians' persons or rights in the conflict. Neither were they in a position to dictate Black action in this contest. Having been criticized for intervention in Louisiana in 1872, President Grant hesitated before finally issuing a statement on May 15 pledging federal support for the more conservative Baxter government, bringing Arkansas's Reconstruction to a close and setting in motion the forces of disfranchisement and segregation in Arkansas.[68]

Many Black families in Arkansas remembered the events in their lives not only in terms of whether they took place before the Civil War or after peace was declared, but also in terms of whether they occurred before or after this "Brooks–Baxter War." When Jane Harris married 54th USCT veteran Austin Allen in 1874, the reverend who solemnized their union was too afraid of political violence in Little Rock to register the marriage certificate with the county. This complicated her pension application in 1889. He explained, "My recollection is that their marriage was a short time after the Brooks & Baxter war and the clerk office of Pulaski Co was at that time in the state-house building where Baxter['s] soldier[s] were camp[ed] and they were White men unfriendly to colored men who are known to be Brooks men and for that reason there was no good feeling." He further explained that "I did not care to be around them" and so did not file the marriage.[69]

The conclusion of the Brooks–Baxter war paved the way for the conservative constitution of 1874 that would roll back Reconstruction and remake the city. Democrats implemented a series of disfranchisement measures; never again would Arkansas see the height of Black representation in the General Assembly that had existed in the state's House of Representatives in 1874.[70] Cora Gillam watched her husband's public career continue, but saw that he would not be exempt from the long-term decline. In April 1877, voters elected Gillam to the Little Rock City Council and then appointed by the mayor to the Ways and Means Committee. She remembered, "I used to dress up and go out to hear him make speeches." That was, she said, until "colored folks got put out of public offices." The family continued building a life with what they could control. The couple had nine children and built a home at 1023 Arch Street, which was still wooded at the time. Cora's son Isaac Jr. went on to higher education at Howard University and Yale. Her daughter Cora Alice became a teacher and president of the National Federation of Women's Clubs, carrying on a tradition of women's political activity in creative ways.[71]

Viney and James Lucas (discussed at the beginning of this chapter) settled just on the edge of Argenta. They stayed in touch with friends and comrades, often catching up on Saturdays "when the farmers came in to trade" and Sundays at church. Or as their friend Albert Anderson put it, "nearly every Saturday from discharge until death." The couple had sons Austin (in March 1868) and Sammie (in May 1870) but were devastated when Sammie only lived a few days and Austin died the next year at only two years old. Adding to the trauma, Viney had endured losing a partner and children under slavery. Viney and James's daughter, Laura, who had witnessed their wedding as an infant, survived to adulthood and remained close with her older half-sister Betty. When Laura was only fourteen, however, both James and Lavinia died. Laura leaned on the network her parents had created. It was the Reverend Richard Lawson of Argenta, who had served in the 54th with James, and had known Laura since she was an infant, babysitting her from time to time, who "preached his [James's] funeral." The network that included Lawson helped Laura to apply for a pension based on her father's service. When asked to produce a record of her family's history, she pulled out a Bible, "her testament," published by the American Bible Society in 1864, within which her mother had recorded family birth and death dates. When it was Laura's turn to marry in spring 1883, her father's old comrade Lawson officiated.[72]

As pension applications in later years show, women who camped with, married, and befriended soldiers of the 54th USCT began families in their respective communities and consistently relied on networks forged by the men in their service, but also by the women during and after the war as they delivered each other's children, cared for each other in illness, farmed alongside one another, and ultimately buried their men. That history had been set in motion by Little Rock's wartime transformation at the hands of Black refugees and soldiers, who shaped a city ringing with proclamations of freedom symbolized not only by the blue uniforms donning the arms upon which so many Black women leaned, but by those women's determination to make homes, claim public space, assert the legitimacy of their relationships and families, provide for those families, and plan futures with their men. In doing so, USCT women acted out Union occupation in their habitations and routes in daily life, socialization, and work. While their experiences were hindered by death, disease, and precarity, USCT women enjoyed relatively more insulation from the guerilla activity that so many of their compatriots had suffered in the Mississippi Valley. Black women converted the connections related to federal power and men's military service into a meaningful sense of placement knit together by women as wives, friends, and neighbors, which anticipated the pension network to come and undergirded Unionism in this capital city on the western margins of the South.

8

Black Women's Lives and Labors in Post-Emancipation North Carolina

Brandi C. Brimmer

In August 1861, as the Federal Army inched closer to Hatteras Island, North Carolina, Judge John R. Donnell, the owner of nearly 200 enslaved people in Hyde County, resettled his family in Raleigh. Two years later, Donnell's Hyde property was under federal occupation and some two hundred enslaved men, women, and children boarded "steamships" and boats en route to what would become the Roanoke Colony. Many other enslaved people who resided on Donnell's property stayed behind.[1]

The destruction of slavery on Donnell's Hyde County property and subsequent movement shows in compelling fashion how enslaved families imagined their lives in freedom as a collective.[2] This chapter examines the lives of the women and children who remained in Hyde County, fled to refugee camps, and worked in military encampments as civilians during and after the Civil War. Using the records generated by southern Black women who applied for survivors' benefits after 1864, it traces the common threads linking their life histories while also providing a sample of the challenges and obstacles they endured while building free lives on their own terms.[3] The voices of the newly freed captured in the records of the Freedmen's Bureau and US Pension Bureau in conjunction with local records and archival sources reveal the linked histories of Black women and children enslaved by Donnell while also providing a window into the diversity of Black life for enslaved people transitioning from slavery to freedom during and immediately after the Civil War. Freedpeople built an intricate web of support that sustained some of the most vulnerable during the war.

Black feminist historical analysis in the field of gender and emancipation has enriched and complicated our understanding of Black women in the Civil War and Reconstruction era in numerous ways.[4] Yet, assimilating the experiences of Black soldiers' wives and widows and orphan children into the larger narrative of the Civil War and Reconstruction is only now beginning to take a larger place in the historical conversation. Fanny Whitney and her peers consciously charted their future in freedom by establishing their families, communities, and exploring the terms by which they would live their lives, demonstrating an Afro-futurism increasingly visible in the scholarship.[5]

Fanny Whitney's lived experience was revealed through an index card at the National Archives in Washington, DC. Fanny's case file stood out because it seemed to be relatively straightforward – perhaps even uninteresting. But for an administrative glitch in her case in 1873 and a county-wide investigation conducted in 1900, Fanny managed to avoid the exhaustive and intrusive examinations that unfolded in other cases. Fanny Whitney was far more active in the creation of her case file than the record reveals. Maintaining herself within the context of worthy widowhood in her community was part of her strategy. When questioned about her daughter's paternity in 1901, she refused to disclose the man's identity. It is safe to assume that Fanny took issue with the pension examiner rummaging around in her personal life. She likely also understood the consequences of such a revelation: suspension from the pension roster and a possible prison sentence. Fanny Whitney and her extended kin group in the coastal North Carolina town of New Bern argued for her dignity and worthiness.

BEFORE THE WAR

Born in Craven County, North Carolina, around 1828, Fanny Fonville came of age on Donnell's family properties in the years leading up to the Civil War. Judge Donnell and his family owned a collection of property near Lake Mattamuskeet, a few miles inland from Pamlico Sound. Donnell, a prominent judge and slaveholder in Hyde County, added to his fortunes in 1840, when he purchased a farm in Craven County, just outside of New Bern, where he resided.[6] Relying mostly on their overseers, William Simmons and Henry Jones, to manage their properties, Donnell had little to do with the enslaved men and women who inhabited the properties he acquired in tidewater North Carolina. The world of Judge Donnell and his kin was far removed from the Black people held in bondage in Craven and Hyde Counties.[7]

Few details about the rituals of slave life and the inner lives of bondspeople living on the Donnell properties exist, making the pension files an informative group of sources. Testimonies from these records indicate that Donnell and his overseers allowed, perhaps even encouraged, marriages.[8] Alexander Williams, an enslaved minister, performed marriage rites for enslaved couples with Donnell's consent. Williams later explained: "I was formerly a slave and belonged to Judge John Donels deceased, of Hyde County, N.C ... it was my practice to marry the [colored] people on my said masters plantation, which ceremony I performed with the knowledge and consent of Judge Donel."[9] When Fanny Fonville married Harry Whitney in 1851, Williams performed the ceremony and "all parties present were slaves."[10] Harry "lived in New Bern as a boy," perhaps on Donnell's Craven County farm like Fanny, but moved to Hyde County years before the war. Harry had at least two brothers, Charles and Thomas, and six sisters, although it is not clear if they lived in Hyde County or made the journey to Roanoke with Fanny, Harry, and their children.

While the marriage ceremonies performed by Williams had no legal standing, these ritualized celebrations held meaning to enslaved persons living on the Donnells' properties, and members of the community honored these unions. Jane Cooper and Moses Longest sought consent from the overseer before they married on Donnell's plantation in 1845 and Fanny Whitney attended the celebration. Disley and George Donnell married on the Donnell Plantation on August 1, 1856.[11] After their marriage, Fanny and Harry Whitney, at least, lived together in a cabin.[12] In the years leading up to the Civil War, Fanny bore ten children, seven boys and three girls. Moses and Jane shared five children together. Rumors swirled about the identity of Jane and Moses's young son Isaac because of his fair complexion. "Isaac is light ... he goes by the name of Isaac Holloway because it is said a man name Nat Holloway is his father."[13] Among the whispers and opinions, these same people acknowledged that Moses raised Isaac as his own. Family was much more than blood relation; it was community mutual aid that gave shelter and love to enslaved, and later freed, people. This liberatory family structure unbounded by defined paternity and capitalism invokes the revolutionary power of love.

BLACK WOMEN'S WARTIME TRANSITION TO FREEDOM

North Carolina's "rehearsal" for Reconstruction unfolded along the state's eastern seaboard in refugee camps such as the Roanoke Colony and the Trent River Settlement (later James City).[14] As Black people migrated to these and other settlement camps along North Carolina's eastern seaboard at

different moments during the war, they expanded and extended the boundaries of their institutions, culture, and kin networks. Typically set up on the
outskirts of Union Army encampments in eastern North Carolina, historian
Richard Reid aptly described these sites as "public domains" where military
officials and Freedmen's Bureau agents surveilled freedpeople.[15]

As Union forces moved further south, occupying large swaths of the
state's eastern seaboard in 1863, enslaved people living on Donnell's Hyde
County plantation set out to chart their future in freedom. The destruction
of slavery unfolded unevenly across North Carolina's eastern seaboard with
community relocations, individual movement, and former slaves staying in
place. A combination of these scenarios played out on Judge Donnell's
properties. Nearly eleven months after the Emancipation Proclamation
took effect, enslaved men, women, and children boarded a "steamboat"
en route to the Roanoke Colony, but some remained on Donnell's land.[16]
Fanny Whitney and her family, the Longest family, and many others were
among those who left. When they made their way to the freedmen's colony
on Roanoke Island, only three of the seven Whitney boys had survived.

Located off the coast of North Carolina – inside the Outer Banks,
between the Albermale and Pamlico Sounds – the Roanoke Colony had
been set up to house the families of Black soldiers recruited to the Union
Army in tidewater North Carolina and Virginia.[17] Roanoke offered a
modest means of self-sufficiency in the form of gardening for the inhabitants – almost all of them women, children, and disabled or elderly
men.[18] A combination of military employment, missionaries, rations, and
freedpeople's labor sustained settlement camps, of various sizes, across
the state. Military officials employed about 1,500 Black people in the
Quartermaster's Department at Roanoke, although Black women were
largely confined to improvised service positions.[19] Freedmen and women
expected to collect wages in exchange for their labor; unfortunately,
however, this was not the case, and even when it was, Union authorities
deducted the costs of food and clothing from their pay, enforcing a kind
of indentured servitude.[20]

For Black men, service in the Union Army symbolized citizenship.
Black men embraced this opportunity to fight for their freedom and
exhibit their worthiness for full and equal citizenship. At the same time,
they challenged the unequal conditions and unfavorable demands placed
upon them. They also wanted their economic due and actively sought
military pay equivalent to that of Black soldiers from northern regiments,
assurance that food and housing would be provided to their families,
education for their children, and a government commitment that their

families would be treated as noncombatants. Of the estimated 180,000 Black men who fought for the Union, North and South, scholars estimate that more than 140,000 enlisted from slave states.[21] In North Carolina, 5,035 recruits enlisted. We know much less about the Black women who labored as cooks, laundered clothes, and treated wounds for the diseased and injured within these regiments. Two women, Judy Blackwell, a laundress in the US Navy, and Elizabeth Dempsey, a nurse who treated soldiers in a Black North Carolina regiment, appear in the pension files and the National Cemetery records. Dempsey even petitioned for compensation under the 1892 Nurses Pension Act, an archival record that is striking on its own.[22]

Enlistment patterns reveal freedom seekers' priorities and concerns, including their family obligations.[23] A group of young men from Donnell's Hyde County property bypassed Roanoke, made their way to Plymouth, and enlisted in the 37th Regiment of the United States Colored Infantry. In contrast, Harry Whitney and others assisted their families in settling on Roanoke Island first, enlisted, and then joined with the cohort of men who enlisted at Plymouth. Assisting his family and extended kin in relocating was a priority for Harry and other men.[24] The record is silent as to whether the Whitney family carried personal items such as blankets, clothing and shoes, or cooking utensils when they boarded the boat to Roanoke, although wartime observers frequently described refugees entering union occupied camps clinging to their personal property. Once Black men with families enlisted and completed their medical examinations, they often located their loved ones. Adorned in his uniform, "gun [and] honer sack," Harry Whitney returned to the Roanoke camp to embrace his wife Fanny and their children and said his goodbyes.[25]

Black families coped with their loved one's enlistment through numerous strategies. Historian Heather A. Williams notes that formerly enslaved people regarded "separation" much like death. At some level, the families of enlisted men must have considered the real possibility that they might never see their family members again. Veteran and Minister Elijah P. Marrs's narration of the time of preparation before a group of men left a Kentucky neighborhood to enlist highlights the mixed emotions attached to their departure.

It was known by nearly every one present that night that there were a number of young men in the house who were preparing to leave for the army, and they the best in the neighborhood, consequently there was great weeping and mourning – the wife for husband, the maiden for her sweetheart. Such a demonstration of sorrow I have never seen, before or since.[26]

When Harry Whitney and other enlisted men left Roanoke Island, it was the last time their families would see them alive.

The news of Harry Whitney's death came one year later for Fanny Whitney and her children. Thomas Silvy [Silver], a formerly enslaved enlisted soldier who resided on Donnell's property, returned to the Roanoke Colony to report that Harry died from a fever at a hospital in Wilmington, North Carolina. The certainty of Harry's death was a heavy blow to his family and the men and women who knew him at Roanoke. As one woman later described it, "there was right smart sorrow about it."[27] As it turns out, several men enslaved by the Donnell family perished around the same time. The outpouring of grief surrounding Harry Whitney's death was probably communal in nature.[28] The community collectively mourned the loss of the men's physical presence as well as the emotional resources they contributed to their household and larger community.[29] In their time of grief, surviving family members may have gained comfort from the detailed stories shared by the men who served alongside their loved ones. When Harry Whitney lay ill in the post hospital just outside of Wilmington, North Carolina, his nephew Nathan Whitney made periodic visits. One day Nathan arrived and learned that Harry died and had already been buried.[30] Since Harry was buried at the National Cemetery in Wilmington, it would be difficult for his family members to pay their final respects.

Deaths occurred among the refugees at the Roanoke Colony too. Contagious disease wreaked havoc on the refugees living on the Roanoke Colony, leading to tragedy and grief for the surviving relatives and kin. Eliza, Moses, and Benjamin Longest suffered inconceivable loss when their father, Moses, and their mother, Jane, died nearly one year apart. Jane, died on Roanoke Island in November 1865 after a bout with small-pox. In her final hour, freedman Emanuel Merrick "sat up with her" and witnessed "her dead body."[31] Next of kin and members of the children's extended family assisted the children in coping with the loss. Benjamin Longest, the eldest sibling, and other relatives provided care and support during the war. As orphans, the Longest children could have fallen victim to North Carolina's apprenticeship system. Eliza's aunt "adopted" her after her mother died.[32] As the Longest family's situation reveals, orphaned children's survival and connection to their families during the Civil War years was closely tied to their family and community.

Grieving family members depended on the mutual aid of an extensive blend of personal friendships, familial connections, and communal networks throughout the war. Freedmen's camps provided an unprecedented opportunity for women to forge new relationships while sorting out their lives as free women.[33] These relationships would then constitute what historian Steven Hahn characterizes as the foundational networks crucial to Black political solidarities along North Carolina's eastern seaboard.[34] Fanny's network spanned from Hyde County to the Roanoke Colony as well as to New Bern. These networks sustained women who, as Jacqueline Jones observed, "became responsible for the full support of their children while their husbands fought or until the government issued rations."[35]

The population of Black refugees at Roanoke constantly changed. As new arrivals adjusted to the conditions on the island, others moved away. At age eleven, Matilda Proctor recalled settling at the Roanoke Colony with her mother and hundreds of other freedpeople from Elizabeth City. Sometime after she reached the colony, she relocated to Morehead City and assisted a Black soldier's wife "wash and cook" for soldiers at Fort Macon.[36] Then, in 1863, Matilda journeyed further south to New Bern with her mother, Hannah. At New Bern, she joined a community of women in the Trent River Settlement whose fathers, sons, and husbands enlisted in the Black regiments. She reconnected with freedpeople from Elizabeth City, including Charlotte Banks. "We all got here around the same time," Matilda recalled.[37]

As of January 1864, a year after the Emancipation Proclamation had been issued, a federal count showed 17,419 Blacks living under federal protection in eastern North Carolina; 8,591 freedpeople resided in the Trent River Settlement, across the Neuse River, and five out of six residents were new to eastern North Carolina. By January 1865, the superintendent in charge of Black refugees counted 17,307 fugitive slaves crowded into the Union-held areas of the state, with over 10,000 living in and around New Bern.[38]

Despite the fact that the community was large and self-sufficient, families of Black Union soldiers remained subject to attack. Military officials did not view Black soldiers' wives and widows as allies or noncombatants, nor did they remain shielded from the violence and brutality of war based on their gender identity in refugee camps (during or after the war).[39] Freedwoman Elizabeth Howard met Peggy Slade and Delia Howard "when we all had to leave New Bern and go over to James City when the rebels came in on us."[40] Howard's testimony underscores several points theorized by historian Thavolia Glymph in her landmark study, *The Women's Fight*. The "hard hand of war" crushed enslaved- and freedwomen who, as Glymph argues, constructed "communities that could stand as critical sites of resistance," in the face of Confederate attack and Union policies.[41]

Against the backdrop of military recruitment and enlistment, disease, death, and violence, federal agents indoctrinated freedmen and women about the meaning and definition of legal marriage. Recognizing that many couples in the camps and colonies had been forbidden as enslaved persons to marry legally, northern military officials quickly moved to ameliorate the problem. Legal scholar Kathleen Franke maintains that the institution of marriage was one of the primary modes by which respectability, legitimacy, and citizenship were "both developed and managed in African Americans."[42] Freedwoman Harriet Barlow remembered, "A man by the name of Chaplain Green married us, he was a Chaplain in the Army."[43] Peggy and Miles Slade secured a provost marshal's license and married before Miles enlisted in the Union Army. After his discharge, the couple went to the county courthouse in New Bern where they paid the necessary 25 cents for the official license and were married by the clerk.[44]

Black soldiers' families qualified for claim rations, a demand Black soldiers made before agreeing to enlist.[45] Additionally, in the event of death, Black soldiers' widows could in theory petition for cash payments in the form of a Civil War widow's pension, which amounted to $8.00 per month. Even so, eligibility to claim benefits based on their standing as a soldier's widow did not always translate into securing actual benefits. Black women in the North and the South had difficulty gaining access to government resources, especially bounty money, army pay, and pensions. The existing pension system did not initially acknowledge the fact that formerly enslaved soldiers' marriages had been extralegal because southern law had prohibited slaves from entering into all civil contracts. Thus, while the federal government recruited former slaves into their ranks, it did not recognize the complexity of their legal standing and the then-recent history of enslavement within the existing wartime pension system.

The failure to compensate Black military service members and affiliated workers in a timely fashion (if at all) led to food and housing insecurity for Black soldiers' families. Free and recently freed Black women in the North and the South, however, did not remain silent on this issue. Many Black women complained about the government's failure to support them, despite their husbands' service in the United States Union Army. For example, on July 11, 1864, Rosanna Henson, the wife of a New Jersey soldier, wrote directly to President Lincoln about her situation: "I have four children to support and I find this a great struggle. A hard life this! I being a col [*sic*] woman do not get any state pay. Yet my husband is fighting for this country."[46] An enslaved woman in Missouri wrote to her soldier husband: "Send me some money as soon as you can for me and my child are almost naked."[47] While formerly enslaved men made the ultimate sacrifice in defense of the Union, there were no legal mechanisms in place to relieve the economic burdens placed upon their families in a timely fashion.

Worrisome letters Black soldiers received from their family members underscore the stress and anxiety they coped with upon enlistment. Without government pensions and other resources, soldiers' families had to fend for themselves on Roanoke Island and the Trent River Settlement. Women had no guarantees about if, or when, they would receive compensation from the government or their loved ones. If the government dragged its feet with respect to bounty pay due to Black Union soldiers, the soldiers themselves did not hesitate to care for their kinfolk. The financial support Black soldiers managed to send directly to their loved ones during the war proved crucial to women's survival in the refugee camps. Judith Lavenhouse's son, George, provided for his mother by "hiring himself out and he took home pension to her."[48] A neighbor observed that George, "brought her food and his contributions were necessary as she did not have enough to support her adequately without his help."[49] York Biggs "contributed toward the support" of his mother, Maria, "by his labor" and sent "eight dollars per month" to her while he served in the heavy artillery unit.[50] Julia Ann Foy said that her son, William, helped support her "up unt[i]l he come to New Berne N.C. March 1862." He worked in New Bern "up unt[i]ll May or June 1863 at $10 per month" and gave "money, blankets, food, and soap to give to his mother shortly after he enlisted."[51]

Financial support, however meager or inconsistent, did not stop the economic system of indentured servitude or forced labor. Clashes between freedpeople and the superintendent of the poor erupted at the Roanoke Colony when island administrators introduced a policy requiring young boys to work in exchange for food and clothing. Richard Boyle, a Black school teacher at Roanoke Island, sent a series of letters to the president of the United States seeking clarity on the new policy. Only fragments of Boyle's letter of protest remain.[52] "[H]as any wright to take our boy Children from us and from the School and send them to … work to pay for they ration without they parent Consint [?]" Government officials reportedly "put them on board the boat and carried them to newbern." Boyle highlighted the emotional toll these actions had on Black refugees, including Black soldiers' families stating, "here is a woman on the Island which their husbands are in the army just had a little boy to help them cut and lug wood & to Goe arrand for them." Separating children from their mothers inspired fear and distress across the island: "the mothers ... Grieved and beg for the little boys." Residents of the Roanoke Colony attempted to propose a solution to regain control of their children.[53]

Military officials continued to implement punishing measures on Black families living in the Roanoke Colony as the war for freedom continued. Horace James, an evangelical Congregationalist minister and abolitionist from Massachusetts who served as the Superintendent of Negro Affairs in North Carolina, reported, "boys fourteen years old and upwards are denied rations and told to work for their living."[54] Did Fanny Whitney's three boys – Milton, Adam, and Harry – fall victim to these policies? Perhaps she was one of many who expressed their "dissatisfaction" to Superintendent James.[55]

In the summer of 1865, Richard Etheredge and William Benson, two Black soldiers serving out their terms of enlistment away from the Roanoke Colony, penned a letter to the recently appointed commissioner of the Freedmen's Bureau, Major General Otis Oliver Howard.[56] Writing on behalf of the men serving alongside them, Etheredge and Benson criticized military administrators for their failure to redress the work performed and emphasized the inhumanity of island officials who withheld support from wounded disabled soldiers. Etheredge and Benson also shined a light on the long-held practice of uncompensated labor and demanded the removal of one of the army administrators who had been accused of withholding food and supplies from Black families. The commander of the 36th added his own endorsement to the soldiers' letter and forwarded it up the chain of command.

Around the same time that Etheredge and Benson initiated their communication, military Chaplain William A. Green and a group of White missionaries in service at the Roanoke Colony sent a letter to the commissioner of the Freedmen's Bureau on behalf of the inhabitants of the island. They wrote, "There are many who are sick and disabled whose ration has been cut off, and these instances are not isolated, but oft recurring and children crying for bread, whose husbands, Sons, and fathers are in the army today."[57] Conditions at Roanoke Island continued to spiral downward as the war came to an end. Roughly two months after official combat in North Carolina ended, Colonel Eliphalet Whittlesey assumed the position of the assistant commissioner of the Freedmen's Bureau for North Carolina.

While Colonel Whittlesey announced to his agents and the White people of the state that freedpeople were "entitled to all the rights of man," Union officials and local White residents nevertheless treated Black soldiers' families with a combination of "hostile indifference" and "paternalistic altruism."[58] Meanwhile, the crises of deprivation and poverty for the Black refugees worsened across eastern North Carolina as the war dragged on and deaths mounted. In his testimony before the joint Senate committee on Reconstruction, Whittlesey described the situation in the state. "We have at certain places large communities of Blacks who have been gathering during the entire war on the coast-places of refuge from the interior – where they came within our lines." Whittlesey continued, "At those points the men have enlisted in the army, and left a large number of women and children dependent upon the government for support. These principal points are Roanoke island and Newbern and vicinity. In all the rest of the State we have not more than five or six hundred who are receiving rations and support from the government."[59]

Armed with a belief that aid in the form of food and shelter would create a cycle of dependency and reliance on government assistance rather than allow for conditions to promote self-sufficiency, Whittlesey worked to promote wage labor and avoid expectations that the government would provide provisions to able-bodied men, women, and children. He reported the plans he had set in motion across the state, stating, "I announced to the people on the Island [Roanoke] in a public Assembly, that the supplies would be cut off as early as May 1, [1866]." This reduction of rations created a crisis on Roanoke Island, where Fanny Whitney and her children remained after her husband died.[60]

At the war's end, Black migrants from across the state resettled in towns and cities along the eastern seaboard, creating distinct communities and neighborhoods throughout the South. Gradually Black refugees, including freedpeople once owned by Donnell, began leaving the Roanoke Colony. Nathan Whitney, Clarissa Silver, Dilsey Donnells and many others returned to Hyde County while another cohort resettled in New Bern, North Carolina. No matter where they elected to settle, prevailing free labor ideology meant that they had the right to allocate the labor in their homes on their own terms.[61] The newly freed also prioritized locating family members and lost loved ones during slavery. The families of Black soldiers offered a warm reception to these men (and the women that supported them) who returned from war. Upon discharge, these men sought to reintegrate themselves into their families and communities. They did so by incorporating their new sense of masculinity engendered by their army service.

Black people's experiences at the Roanoke Colony sharpened the profound sense of betrayal Black soldiers and their families experienced. From South Carolina's rice plantations, Mississippi's cotton plantations (leased during the Civil War), to New Bern's James City, freedmen and women resisted the Freedmen's Bureau's relocation schemes, preferring their own communities and the opportunities to support each other in community mutual aid.

FROM WARTIME CAMPS TO FREE BLACK COMMUNITIES

After the end of the Civil War, Black soldiers and their families continued to struggle, including in Black communities that were either under Union control or originated because of the war. In eastern North Carolina, for instance, enslaved people had joined free Blacks already living in the vicinity of Union-occupied areas such as New Bern and the Trent River Settlement, which grew into James City. There, nearly 2,000 Blacks (many of them families of Union veterans) had settled.[62] An office of the Freedmen's Bureau established in North Carolina in 1865, including branches of the Freedmen's Bank set up in New Bern and Wilmington, put the federal government within reach of the Black masses. Fanny Whitney and others who lost their husbands in battle had to piece together their daily existence, infusing their own experience of widowhood with meanings that made sense to them.

Sometime after Freedmen's Bureau agents at Roanoke began implementing Whittlesey's rations policy, Fanny Whitney and her three surviving sons resettled in New Bern and connected with a multigenerational community of men and women bound together by extended ties of kinship and personal connections. Described by one observer as a "mecca of a thousand noble aspirations" in the postwar years, New Bern attracted Black migrant women because of the social and economic opportunities, as well as the sustained community ties that provided a buffer for the intertwined dilemmas of singleness, motherhood, and widowhood during periods of economic stress.[63] These relationships originated on Judge Donnell's vast holdings that stretched between Craven and Hyde Counties. Fanny had made this journey before, but in reverse, as she was born in Craven County and she may have left family and extended kin when Donnell moved her to Hyde County.

Adjusting to the demands of widowhood required women to balance the organization of their household with the social and economic demands of post-emancipation society. Black women also contended with an unforgiving labor market that was predisposed toward male labor. When they worked in the domestic service sector, they could expect to make only a little more than four to five dollars a month.[64] Widows would find it difficult to find employment in farming districts, where employers often dealt with women and children as the dependents of male heads of household.[65] New Bern's proximity to waterways and rural areas also offered Black women some employment beyond agriculture and domestic service. In most cases, they still had to string together a wide range of low-paying jobs with the hopes of earning enough money to support their families.[66] Though it was not listed as a profession on the census, prospective widows gave as their occupation "keeping house," which involved cooking and washing for single men.[67] In these working arrangements, women lived with men as "housekeepers" without any intimate ties.[68]

Black veterans' widows and care-taking wives had to balance the organization of their households with their hopes and aspirations for the future.[69] Indeed, parents wanted a better life for their children, which included education. Fanny's teenage sons Adam, twelve, earned wages selling cakes and "picked cotton" on J. L. Rhem's farm while Harry, fourteen, attended classes led by "Miss Hicks."[70] Fanny's decision to enroll her son in school in the early years of freedom represented an enormous sacrifice to the family economy – especially because young boys had wage-earning potential. Moreover, a child's schooling added to women's uncompensated labor within their homes. As scholars such as Linda Gordon have pointed out, school attendance required mothers and guardians to keep their children clean, clothed, healthy, and punctual.[71]

Notwithstanding the demands that marriage and family support placed on Black women, marriage served as a vital mechanism for Black people to enact citizenship publicly as well as to reunite their families and build communities across the South after the war. This was especially true for returning soldiers who fought for legal recognition of their families by securing marriage licenses in accordance with the North Carolina Marriage Act of 1866. This law mandated all Black couples register their marriages or face a fine.[72] Marriage ceremonies and other community celebrations for returning soldiers as well as the newly freed Black people fostered social interactions. Men borrowed suits and women hired seamstresses to sew their wedding dresses. One woman planned an elaborate event with six bridesmaids, and another recalled proudly and joyously people spilling out the church when she took her vows at the altar in a church in the center of New Bern. Family and friends who attended also took the opportunity to catch up on community news.

Marriage and intimate relationships – as freedpeople understood them – came with familial duties and obligations. Whether married or courting, men expected the women in their lives to keep house – that is, prepare meals, wash and fold laundry, care for children, barter with local venders for foodstuffs, and stay abreast of community activities. At the same time, the women saw themselves as contributors to their families' earnings rather than dependents whose husbands represented their interests. Women who could manage efficient households and balance childcare responsibilities attracted men's attention. In turn, women expected their husbands to work and turn their wages over to them in a timely fashion. As historian Leslie Schwalm points out, Black women in these communities seized upon the Freedmen's Bureau's rhetoric about men's responsibilities to support their families.[73]

The possibility of financial relief for Black soldiers' widows came in 1864, but most did not have the means or resources to apply for survivors' benefits. When federal lawmakers cleared the pathway for the widows of dead Black soldiers, who had just a year earlier gained the right to claim their husbands' back-pay and bounty, women gained the new right to claim themselves as Union widows to the US Pension Bureau. This recognition by the federal government entitled widows of Black soldiers to the possibility of a cash pension (paid on a quarterly basis) in the form of $8.00 per month – but not without intense personal scrutiny and political fights.[74] Black widows had to prove the legitimacy of their marriages to Union soldiers. This requirement, thus, recontextualized the meaning of the marriage rituals Blacks participated in before, during, and after the war.

In 1867, Fanny Whitney availed herself of the federal program designed to support the survivors of dead Black soldiers such as herself and several of her peers. Claiming these benefits and maintaining their standing on the federal pension roster, however, would not be a simple task for Fanny or the thousands of other freedwomen entitled to them. Women like Fanny Whitney, Gatsey Donnell, Dilsey Donnells, and thousands of other Black soldiers' widows, North and South, struggled to define Union widowhood for themselves and in ways that made sense to them. To endure and maintain their personhood, they crafted wholly different concepts of the meaning, definition, and function of widowhood within their communities and the Pension Bureau. More importantly, they unabashedly presented their conception of worthy widowhood to the Bureau in the face of criticism and personal scrutiny.

The federal government's application procedures and evidentiary demands all but eliminated applicants who could not read or write.

Widows depended on middle-class men, both White and Black, such as former veterans, ministers, notaries, attorneys, and claims agents who courted their business and facilitated their petitions over long stretches of time. In eastern North Carolina, Black women initially called on White northerners and federal officials to assist with their cases by securing documentation from the military, obtaining certified affidavits from witnesses, and filing paperwork. Fanny Whitney availed herself of the new pension law in 1867. She hired Augustus Sherill Seymour – a White New York–born attorney who migrated to New Bern during the war – to file paperwork on her behalf. According to Fanny, "He had the book of my husband and I went to him."[75] This book was a "complete roster and history" of the 37th Regiment organized at New Bern, the same regiment her husband enlisted in.[76] A year later, Seymour turned over the case to Edward W. Carpenter, a New York–born journalist, who came to North Carolina as a news correspondent for the Associated Press and the *New York Tribune*.

A group of freedpeople with longstanding ties to Hyde County filed petitions around the same time as Fanny Whitney and with the assistance of Edward Carpenter.[77] Freedwoman Francis Holloway, who was once enslaved in Hyde County (though not a part of Donnell's holding), filed a claim in 1868 seeking support for her children Nat, Matilda, and Mary J on the same petition. Gatsey Donald filed an application for herself and her six children in 1869. Benjamin Longest initiated a petition for minor's benefits on behalf of his younger siblings in 1868. Perhaps taking advice from Fanny Whitney, Francis, Gatsey, Dilsey, and Benjamin contracted with E. W. Carpenter. With the assistance of attorneys and claims agents, Black soldiers' widows and their descendants asserted their status as citizens and simultaneously sought to alter their relationship to the federal government as poor Black women, mothers, and citizens.

Claims agents played a vital role in New Bern's pension network. Despite its generic reference, claims agents helped prepare the application materials for disabled veterans, widows, orphan children and other eligible family members. After 1890, Emanuel Merrick and veteran Nathan Whitney, two men once enslaved by Donnell with deep personal ties to the Black descendants from Hyde County, regularly assisted men, women, and children present their claims to the Pension Bureau, although neither secured formal licensure from the Pension Bureau.[78]

Soldiers' widows' eligibility to collect their deceased soldiers' backpay and bounty money from the military provided significant sources of income and peace of mind for their survivors, especially since recognition from the Pension Bureau could take several years. Fanny Whitney collected a $300 bounty and her husband's back-pay on May 2, 1868. Pension officials recognized Fanny Whitney's petition in 1869.

Although not explicit in the records, the resources that war widows derived from the government may have enabled them to establish independent households and protect their children from the threat of apprenticeship. In North Carolina, discriminatory antebellum laws that provided for the apprenticeship of free Black children were simply extended to the children of former slaves in the postwar era.[79] Parents had to demonstrate their ability to provide for their children. Singleness – even in the case of widows – placed mothers at a disadvantage in apprenticeship cases, while married women held a slight advantage in the court cases involving questions of child custody in the southern legal system. Historians Rebecca J. Scott, Mary Farmer Kaiser and Karin Zipf have shown the particular vulnerabilities of unmarried mothers, Black and White, in legal forums and southern courts.[80] Black parents had to demonstrate that they "possessed the capacity to care" for their children and maintain "a reputable standing."[81] Fanny Whitney's ability to secure her husband's back-pay and bounty a full year before she gained recognition from the Pension Bureau as a Union widow gave her resources necessary to protect her family from White interference in her family's life.

A branch of the Freedmen's Savings Bank, set up in New Bern in 1866, provided residents a place to deposit their money. Before its collapse in 1874, the wives and mothers of Union soldiers set up accounts at the New Bern branch, as did several White families and government agents.[82] Zipf finds that approximately one-third of the freedpeople who opened accounts in New Bern's branch of the Freedmen's Bank were female. Their deposits, she writes, consisted mostly of the wages and military pensions of their deceased husbands and sons. According to Zipf, a little over 400 Black women opened accounts between 1866 and 1873 in New Bern. Nineteen percent of the women labored as cooks, 17 percent worked as laundresses, 15 percent said that they performed farm labor (independent).[83]

Some freedwomen formalized their independent households through the acquisition of property. Fanny Whitney purchased a home at the corner of Jones and New South Front Street in New Bern's Fifth ward. As of 1875, Dilsey Donnel[l]s reported "she [Fanny] has a house of her own and she and her children occupy it themselves."[84] Dilsey followed Fanny's example and bought a house and lot on the same street a short time later.[85] Dresses and trinkets formed a small but significant part of the economic landscape of these women. Before her death in 1883, Dilsey Donnell acquired an impressive set of household items including: a large iron pot, a rocking chair, a pine table, and a feather bed. Indeed, Dilsey's probate records reveal her special fondness for dresses and household appliances. As Tera Hunter observed, "these pursuits of pleasure also signaled [southern Black women's] embrace of a modern ethos."[86]

As the application process for survivor's benefits unfolded, prospective applicants directed Pension Bureau examiners to seek information about their complex marital histories and family lives from their owners, overseers, and employers. Freedwomen from Donnell's plantation knew that overseer Henry Jones scrupulously recorded the names and birthdates of all children born to enslaved women on the Donnells' plantation and they would need this evidence to secure support for their minor children. Freedpeople with ties to the Donnell plantation circulated information about their former owners and overseers and maintained distant communication, when possible. Fanny Whitney and Moses Longest's children tried to document birthdates with the assistance of Jones. Julia Benson worked in overseer Jones's family home and "frequently saw the book that [the] ages of slaves were entered in." At some point after the war, Julia asked Jones about "the book." "[H]e told me that the Yankees destroyed the records," Julia recalled.[87] Jones confirmed Julia's recollection in an 1877 letter addressed to Fanny Whitney: "the Yankeys Distroyed it During the war I am not able to tell the ages of your children.[88]

Fanny needed Jones to present the book of dates to the pension office so that she could collect support for her minor children. Fanny was hoping to clear up a discrepancy in her case file that occurred because the ages of her children appeared inconsistent. After the suspension of her benefits, Fanny tapped into the network of freedpeople who at one time lived with her in Hyde County. Attempting to pinpoint the chronological age of each child with fragments of information, Fanny contacted a "fellow servant" who also belonged to Donnell and "kept the record of the births on the plantation."[89] To Fanny's dismay, he had "little or no recollection" of her children. Worse, the magistrate misunderstood what was "required" and her "claim was left in greater disarray than it was before."[90]

Eventually Fanny became frustrated with the entire process. She directed her claims agent to express her desire "to have all of her children dropped from the Pension rolls" as she would be "content" to collect the pension "due her as the widow of Harry Whitney."[91] Fanny's pension was reissued four years later, by which time all her children had reached "the age of maturity." Examiners and local advocates freely expressed their assessment of Fanny Whitney as a "worthy woman," which certainly helped her cause. A local postmaster endorsed Whitney's application, describing her as a "very exemplary and worthy woman" and a bureau examiner later remarked: "I may add Fanny Whitney is a very respectable colored woman owns a nice house and makes her sons work instead of loafing around."[92] Recognition was due to Fanny for brilliantly mobilizing what historian Kimberly Welch calls the politics of reputation in her case.[93] According to Welch, reputation is "a malleable package of linguistic possibilities one claims or manipulates." Although she was not able to read and write, Fanny understood how the gendered logics of race operated within the pension system and used these tensions to maneuver.

Pension officials suspended paying out survivor's benefits to all women who remarried. No set of investigation procedures existed for examiners until 1882, almost twenty years after the end of the war.[94] Fanny Whitney opted to remain single rather than marry again. She did, however, nurture a short-lived intimate relationship, which resulted in the birth of her daughter, Malissa, in 1868. Fanny made sure that her daughter, like her son Harry, secured an education at one of New Bern's public schools.[95] No matter the investments Fanny made in the lives of her children, the revelation of Malissa's birth after Harry's death could have left her vulnerable under the Pension Bureau's cohabitation rule. Federal officials questioned Fanny Whitney about the circumstances surrounding her relationship with Malissa's father in a 1900 investigation. The proceedings must have been of great concern for Fanny as she was now aging and unable to generate the same level of income from housekeeping and domestic service. Bureau officials surmised, however, that Fanny's case did not violate the law of August 7, 1882, which terminated a woman's pension if she was sexually involved with or cohabited with a man while collecting survivors' benefits.[96] Fanny's relationship with Malissa's father – a freedman also enslaved by Judge Donnell – may not have been destined to move in the direction of marriage. In later testimony, Fanny Whitney revealed that Malissa's father never provided any support for her or her daughter; instead, he had married and returned to Hyde County.[97]

Ill and aging war-widows took intentional steps to protect their financial assets and ensure their surviving kin had access to their hard-earned assets. In her final will and testament, Francis Holloway set aside money to pay for her "undertaker bill, medical and provision bills, and the money loaned to me to purchase medicine and nourishment in my sickness." After paying for her "just debts," Holloway gifted the remaining monies to her two nieces, who provided care and comfort in her final illness.[98]

This composite portrait of the lives and labors of the wives and widows of Black Union soldiers during the Civil War and postwar era reflects some of the experiences of Black women across the South. Thirty to forty thousand pension files remain at the National Archives, and scholars of Black life in the US South have only scratched the surface of what these files can illuminate about freedwomen's lives and the communities they built. What set these recipients of pensions apart from their counterparts was their status as Union widows. Marriage to Black Union veterans qualified them to make claims within federal arenas during and after the collapse of Reconstruction. As a cohort, Black Union widows were self-supporting in the sense that they navigated the public world on their own and dependent in the sense that they earned their dollars from the federal government. Women who were able to secure survivors' benefits surely had more economic stability than those who did not, but their standing on the roster was never guaranteed. These women subsisted at a level slightly above the poorest women in their neighborhoods. Most of them worked until they became too old or disabled and then moved into the homes of family members or rented out rooms in their own homes. Some even organized intergenerational households of women, and no matter the arrangement, community care was at the core of their lives. Through federal recognition as Union widows, these women could buffer themselves from the social categories of "unmarried" or "single," and still maintain independent households. Formerly enslaved Black women's testimonies, preserved in the pension files, deepen our understanding of poor Black women's lives and survival strategies during the Civil War years and into the early twentieth century.

9

Remaking Old Blue College

Emerson Normal and Addressing the Need for Public Schoolteachers in Mobile, Alabama

Hilary Green

In reflecting on the history of the educational work of the American Missionary Association (AMA) in Alabama, L. B. Moore found much to celebrate. In establishing "industrial schools and normal schools and academies, and even universities in the darkness of this land," the American Missionary Association facilitated the growth of a class of leaders. "Oh, how my people need leaders!" exclaimed the African American missionary from Florence, Alabama. "I can take you to a place where the blind are leading the blind and they are both falling into the ditch together." From the organization's work at Burrell Normal School in Florence to Emerson Institute and Normal in Mobile, Moore cheerfully reported that the schools "have sent forth a thousand college-bred men who are going to teach that people; and I tell you the time is coming when that thousand will be increased by another thousand, and the ignorant and oft-times immoral leaders will have to give way before the light which is now rising." For these reasons, Moore concluded that the AMA needed to continue its educational work. Through obtaining advanced education, the AMA would help to provide justice "to the slave who toiled for two hundred and fifty years and accumulated the wealth of this nation" by adding a growing class of leadership comprising teachers and other educated professionals.[1]

Most Black Mobilians shared Moore's assessment of the AMA's work in Alabama. Their partnership with the organization aided in legitimating African American primary education but also allowed a select minority to obtain advanced degrees at Emerson Normal. The school was instrumental in permitting former slaves as well as the children born after the end of slavery to become teachers, administrators, and, most important, leaders within their communities. In becoming educated leaders, they prevented the blind from "leading the blind" and created the necessary leadership to carry African Americans out of the darkness.[2]

Emerson Normal represented the expansion and refinement of the educational partnership between Black Mobilians and the AMA after the creation of state-funded public schools. This partnership played a critical role in creating the corps of teachers required for the new public school system. Outside the classroom, graduates employed their preparation for middle-class leadership by actively participating in racial uplift organizations and campaigns. Never viewing their service as limited to the classroom, Emerson Normal graduates became an essential asset for Black Mobilians and their slow, arduous struggle for African American public education and racial equality in Mobile. Without the training of African American teachers and a renewed partnership with the AMA, the public schools and turn-of-the-century racial uplift activism would have been greatly impaired in Mobile.

As in Richmond, racial assumptions on the part of White educational partners thwarted teacher training during the initial years of the Freedmen's Schools. Influential White educational partners often viewed the African American educators in the independent Freedmen's Schools as incompetent and inexperienced. Charles W. Buckley, superintendent of education for the Freedmen's Bureau in Alabama, voiced this opinion in a report to Major General Wager Swayne. He wrote, "There are in Mobile several colored schools taught mostly by colored teachers. Some of these teachers are not competent for the position they fill. They need suggestions from experienced teachers … and thus bring those of the same degree of advancement into the same school." In the same report, Buckley noted that the school operated by E. C. Branch, a White educator, was "flourishing" and doing "great work for the colored people of the city." For Buckley and other White racial moderates, the existing educated class of African Americans was inadequate for the work at hand. Like his Richmond counterparts, Buckley could not overcome the racial assumptions regarding slavery or the "stages model." He accepted that slavery had prevented this class from attaining the formal education necessary for teaching. Hence Buckley viewed guidance and supervision by experienced White educators, like Branch, as necessary until a sizeable number of African Americans reached the educational achievement for progression to normal training. He also discouraged independent schools with African American faculties and encouraged schools operated and administered by White northern missionary associations.[3]

The Reconstruction Acts of 1867, the purchase of Emerson Institute by the AMA from the Freedmen's Bureau, and the establishment of public schools in Mobile facilitated a shift in racial attitudes by some White educational partners toward African American teacher training. White educational partners who once opposed teacher training now deemed competent African American educators as essential for the future of African American education. State Superintendent R. D. Harper remarked in a May 1868 report to O. O. Howard that "obtaining competent teachers" was one of the "chief obstacles to our work." Harper, though, viewed Emerson Institute as a solution to this problem for Mobile and its county. He found encouraging the AMA's implementation of a normal program among its most advanced students by its current teachers. According to Harper, the principal selected ten of the "more advanced students, male and female," and met with them privately regarding "the importance of qualifying themselves for teaching." These selected students accepted and entered the program. Harper reported that school officials hoped to train additional teachers "who will be well qualified for the work of teaching the people of their own color or indeed of any color. This it seems to me is the way and the only way in which the freedpeople of the South can be educated." The struggle for control of the school board, though, stopped the nascent program.[4]

Resolution to partisan school board politics in the early 1870s never addressed the teacher crisis generated by the creation of public schools. The Mobile County Board of School Commissioners still faced tremendous pressure to adequately staff the White, African American, and Creole of color schools with teachers. Political rivalries prevented the state from assisting the board. Thus the board had several options. First, it could have employed any from the growing class of southern African American teachers who were educated in northern colleges or in normal programs created under the Freedmen's Bureau. Alabama, according to John Alvord's 1870 report, had five schools and 314 enrolled students. The Mobile County Board of School Commissioners found this option unacceptable.[5]

Second, the board could have continued the practice of hiring White northern missionaries and teachers for the African American schools. The AMA maintained its control over Emerson Institute instead of turning over operations to school commissioners after the Freedmen's Bureau departed the city. Rather than working with the organization, the board decided against an alliance with the AMA. It based its decision on complaints often mentioned in the White press pertaining to the invasion of northern outsiders who forced African American education, morals, and notions of freedom and citizenship onto the community. These invaders created a hostile environment in Mobile over the clash of ideas and visions for the postwar city. Therefore, school commissioners struck down this option.[6]

Instead, school commissioners in Mobile adopted a policy of hiring White teachers as the principal educators in the African American and Creole schools. The departure of the Freedmen's Bureau and designation of Emerson Institute as a private school gave the Board of School Commissioners full power and control over the public schools. Hence school commissioners decided who taught in the African American and Creole schools through this strict hiring policy. To be sure, Howard Hall and a few White Freedmen's School educators not directly associated with the AMA received positions. The hiring policy meant that the board rarely hired African American and Creole teachers. If hired, they often served as assistant teachers, aides, or supernumeraries in the schools and not in the capacity of principal instructors.[7]

Sara Stanley Woodward, former Emerson Institute teacher, was an exception. She found employment as the principal of the St. Louis School from 1871 to 1874. School commissioners were unaware of her racial background and interracial marriage to Freedmen's Saving Bank administrator Charles Woodward. City directories often mistakenly noted her race as White although Woodward publicly proclaimed her race as African American. This lack of awareness on the part of school commissioners spared her from sharing the fate of other African Americans in the public schools.[8]

Black and Creole Mobilians attacked these hiring practices by pursuing several strategies independently. The private and parochial school system was one option. M. H. Leatherman cited the poor quality of the public schools and the teachers as the reason for her and others' decision to send their children to private schools. According to her letter to the AMA, "There are a great many free schools about the city but as they do not amount to much, the people do not care to send their children, so long as there is any alternative."[9] Withdrawal from the public schools often gave African American and Creole parents more control over who instructed their children. Only a small percentage pursued this option. Demographically, these families belonged to the elite and middle classes in the community or had steady employment to cover the tuition costs. Creoles of color utilized the parochial schools created and maintained for the Creole parishioners by the Mobile archdiocese and Catholic charities.

Creoles as well as Black Mobilians utilized the private schools that individual educated members of their community operated, often out of their homes. Tuition and other expenses made this option unattainable for the majority of families and children in the public schools. This option, furthermore, never adequately addressed the lack of African American educators in the city public schools.[10]

Black Mobilians also directly appealed to the Board of School Commissioners by holding special mass meetings. From these meetings, they developed a course of action entailing petitioning and later providing the school board with qualified applicants. Petitioning had been a longstanding tactic employed by the community in dealing with the school board. For instance, the Colored Mass Convention of the State of Alabama held at the Stone Street Church in Mobile adopted a series of resolutions on May 2, 1867. One resolution called for the expansion of the Mobile schools and the state system to include African Americans. While the White conservative press viewed these resolutions as "poisonous doctrines," the board's response to this demand led to C. S. Bradford's proposal of partnership with the Freedmen's Bureau in August 1867. As a result, Black Mobilians felt that petitioning was an appropriate tactic in their campaign for teachers.[11]

Black Mobilians even encouraged educated members of their community to submit applications to the Board of School Commissioners. These candidates had attained an advance education and the majority had completed a normal school curriculum at a reputable institution. On paper, these individuals met the stringent state teaching requirements and were suitable candidates for a teaching position in the school system. However, school commissioners either rejected these qualified candidates or hired them in lesser positions. They defended the policy by arguing that all applicants were equally considered and ultimately based their decision on the applicants' meeting the stringent Alabama qualifications, which included prior teaching, and letters of recommendation. The board deemed White candidates as more qualified than nonwhite applicants. Hence the few nonwhite applicants hired met their standards. Despite its limited success, Rev. E. D. Taylor and other community leaders continued this course of action.[12]

After several consecutive teaching cycles, Black Mobilians sought another course of action. They turned to the AMA for assistance. This decision, though, was not made hastily. The society continued its operations at the Emerson Institute, which offered primary, intermediate, and advanced classes. Students who withdrew from the public schools often turned to this affordable private school. Yet the organization's handling of several school board crises left many in the community weary. After the dual school board affair, AMA administrators seriously considered their future in the city. Their contemplation resulted in the inadequate administration of the school and a revolving door of AMA missionaries and agents. As a result, many Black Mobilians lost confidence in the organization. Aware of their frustration, Rev. Edward P. Lord wrote his supervisors, "If anything is ever going to be done in Mobile, Emerson Inst. ought never to deceive the Cold'd people again. We have had uphill work all this year in gaining back the confidence which the Inst. had forfeited." Negative encounters with the Board of School Commissioners caused Black Mobilians to overlook any previous frustration and disappointment in their relationship with the AMA.[13]

Parents and community leaders approached the AMA regarding expanding the existing curriculum to include normal school instruction. They hoped that the proposed program would meet the stringent state teacher certification standards. Program graduates would then provide a pool of qualified applicants for the city to draw on and thereby circumvent any arguments concerning qualifications. Moreover, the location of the school in Mobile would lessen the expenses incurred if a student undertook a program at another institution in the state or region. By their estimation, a local normal school would greatly improve the chances of securing Black and Creole public schoolteachers. Black Mobilians had every reason to believe that a normal program would result from their appeals. Enrolled students and their parents previously made requests for additions to the curriculum with much success. As a result of student requests, the curriculum expanded to include Latin, French, vocal music, instrumental music, and courses in higher mathematics. The AMA yielded to these requests in order to ensure enrollment and tuition revenues. Although the historical record is silent on the specific requests made for the normal program, it is evident by the principal's correspondence with AMA headquarters that community pressure led to development of Emerson Normal.[14]

A White northern benefactor and a change in leadership made Emerson Normal possible. In 1872 Ralph Emerson, Jr., again provided the necessary financial support for the creation of a normal program at Emerson Institute. Without his generosity and pressure from Black Mobilians, the AMA would not have embarked on fundraising efforts for an institution considered a preparatory school for Talladega College. Moreover, the presence of Rev. Edward P. Lord, the new energetic principal of Emerson Institute, also aided their struggle. Lord was determined to make a viable normal program at Emerson Institute. In Lord, Black Mobilians found a strong advocate. The convergence of community pressure, funding, and a new principal allowed for Emerson Normal to become fully operational by the start of the 1873–74 academic year. Emerson Normal reinvigorated Black Mobilians' relationship with the AMA. City residents now had access to a local program that could aid their quest for African American teachers in the public schools.[15]

Emerson Normal transformed the nature of Emerson Institute from a feeder school for Talladega College into a normal and preparatory school. Advertisements announcing the opening of the 1873–74 academic year proudly publicized this new focus: "Special attention given to those who wish to Teach, and those preparing for the Ministry." In order to provide the "best Normal and Academic Institutions in the South," its curriculum included courses typically taught in the public school system and other normal programs, such as Latin, geometry, natural philosophy, and physiology. The curriculum also included hands-on training in the primary and intermediate classes conducted at Emerson Institute. Lord and his teaching staff strove to "draw the young people into the earnest Christian influence which we strive to exact upon all of our scholars and send them out again as Christian teachers."[16] Since school administrators considered hands-on training invaluable, they found summer teaching employment for several promising students beginning with the summer of 1874. In addition to the traditional normal program curriculum, the donation of a printing press permitted advanced Emerson Normal students to learn how to operate the machine. Students then employed this skill in the publication of the school's newspaper and materials for the Sabbath schools. William A. Caldwell, Mary Europe, Artemesia Europe, and other students also served on the editorial board for the school's newspaper. The robust curriculum made the initial students qualified for both teaching and administering a student newspaper within their future schools upon graduation. By 1876, Lord reported approximately 100 students attending the normal program.[17]

In the spring of 1876, Emerson Normal held its first graduation exercises with former slaves composing the graduating class. The Europe sisters, Artemesia and Mary, received their entire education from primary to normal solely at Emerson Institute. Both sisters initially received appointments as educators and administrators in the city's private school systems. Mary Europe Jones, the elder sister, eventually left the private school system and devoted her energies to motherhood. She occasionally operated a private school out of her home in order to supplement her family's income. Artemesia Europe eventually received a teaching position in the Mobile County public school system when school commissioners began hiring African American teachers in earnest.[18]

William Aymar (W. Aymar) Caldwell graduated alongside the Europe sisters. Born on September 22, 1859, Caldwell pursued normal training and Congregationalism against the advice of young African American men living in his neighborhood. According to a letter written by his Emerson Normal teacher, Kate A. Lord, they regarded Caldwell's decision as "sinning against the Holy Ghost." Caldwell dismissed this advice and pursued both. As his instructor recounted, Caldwell knew that his reward would "be everlasting life." Caldwell's drive and academic success garnered the praise and support of his instructors. Like the Europe sisters, Caldwell did not receive a teaching position in the Mobile schools upon graduation. Instead, he enrolled and graduated from Talladega College. As a student at Talladega, though, he remained involved in the community, including their challenges to existing hiring practices.[19]

As Emerson Normal held its first graduation, arsonists struck. The resulting fire destroyed Emerson Institute in April 1876. The school's destruction, though, did not result in the effects desired by the arsonists. The relationship between Black Mobilians and the AMA strengthened rather than weakened. African Americans, in particular, evoked the memory of the destroyed building in their activism. "Remember Old Blue" and "Remember Blue College" became their rallying cry. Plans for rebuilding began quickly.[20]

In December 1877 the community participated in the groundbreaking ceremony at the school's new location. At this ceremony, the reverends William H. Ash, Albert F. Owens, and E. D. Taylor delivered addresses. These African American ministers, specifically Owens and Taylor, commended the partnership while stressing a message of racial uplift through education. Owens's address praised the AMA for its continued participation in the city's educational efforts. The *American Missionary* noted that Owens "said that ignorance was our greatest enemy, and that the building which was to be erected might be regarded as a fort, from which guns were to be aimed at this inveterate foe, and exhorted the people to sustain the teachers who were leading them in their intellectual and moral warfare." Taylor's remarks focused on the educational achievement of African Americans while commending the rebuilding efforts. In an anecdotal style, the elder minister commented that "he had been taught that the negro race could not be educated – that his brains lay in his heels, etc.; but he was glad to see proof to the contrary in the speeches that had just been made by Mr. Ash and Mr. Owen[s]." In both addresses,

Owens and Taylor pointed to the mental and intellectual skills achieved through useful education. These skills, according to the men, justified the continued partnership in the "warfare" against White resistance. The partnership and rebuilding efforts affirmed their resolve and activism. Thus, normal and primary classes continued in a rented, ill-suited, old store building in the city while work at the new Holley Garden location proceeded. Construction was completed in late April 1878.[21]

Rev. E. D. Taylor's address featured prominently at the school's dedication ceremony in May 1878. His remarks encapsulated the feelings of many Black Mobilians. "I have cautiously watched the movements of these teachers and their school work, and I am convinced that they are here for the lifting up of my race, and as I go down the steps of life," Taylor told the audience, "I look back upon this school, and these teachers, with a great deal of pleasure knowing that they are leading my people out from a bondage worse than slavery. I thank God that we have these friends to help us." Taylor's comments illustrated the importance of the educational partnership to the community. While the partnership brought frustration at times, Taylor reminded the overwhelmingly African American audience that the partnership also produced fruitful results. Hence Emerson Normal and the partnership between Black Mobilians and the AMA endured instead of falling apart after the fire. Perseverance and overcoming obstacles had defined Black Mobilians' long struggle for African American teachers. The fire was one of many challenges faced. The school's rededication, as Taylor's comments suggest, validated their struggle and enabled their perseverance. Hence the destruction of "Blue College" never deterred them from fulfilling their goal.[22]

Despite its relocation, arson plagued the school again during the winter of 1881–82. This fiery attempt to permanently close the school initially caused sadness. Emerson principal Emma Caughey bemoaned the school's destruction:

Emerson Institute is lying in ruins. For the second time in her history she is smoldering in ashes, and we are in mourning for the destruction of our little church, made dear by so many sacred and hallowed associations, and our beautiful school building in which so many happy hours of toil have been spent and labors of love performed…. The enemy approaches again and applies the torch – this time with marvelous success.[23]

While Caughey mourned, Black Mobilians jumped immediately into action by evoking the memory of "Old Blue College." Rev. Albert F. Owens, pastor of the Third Baptist Church, made his church's basement

available. Other ministers followed Owens's lead. As a result of Black
Mobilians' initiative and resolve, classes resumed within days of the fire.
In an article to the *American Missionary*, Caughey reported that the
school reopened "on Monday, Jan. 30, with three departments, at the
Third Baptist Church, about one mile from the 'Home' and two departments in the basement of the Little Zion Church, about three blocks
distant from the Home." Moreover, the new school was rebuilt more
quickly. Emerson Normal and Institute reopened in October 1882.[24]

In addition to arson, student poverty and a major yellow fever epidemic affected both graduation rates and overall enrollment. To be sure,
the school managed to overcome these obstacles by supplying qualified
African American teachers to the city's schools. Yet progress was slow.
After the initial graduation, the next graduation did not occur until 1880,
in which two students graduated. Two graduated in 1884, nine in 1887,
five in 1889, and two in 1890.

Fortunately, the incidence of arson and other extreme acts of violence
toward the school declined after the second rebuilding. White extremists
were unable to break the resolve of Black Mobilians and their AMA partners; their efforts never permanently shut down the school. Ultimately, the
relationship between the AMA and Black Mobilians proved resilient.[25]

Evoking the memory of "Blue College" also resulted in a shift in Black
Mobilians' struggle for African American public schoolteachers. After
the first normal class graduated, hopes for the employment of African
American teachers and all–African American teaching staffs were quickly
dashed. The Mobile County Board of School Commissioners refused to
hire the graduates from the inaugural class. The board's continued resistance dismayed the African American community. In 1878 Rev. E. D.
Taylor, the pastor of the Good Hope and Mount Moriah Methodist
churches, Rev. Albert F. Owens, and several African American leaders
petitioned the board regarding its hiring practices. Petitioners questioned
the board's decision in not hiring qualified African American teachers.
They demanded transparency by inquiring how the board made its decision before insisting on the hiring of Black teachers in the future. The board
responded to the petition in its September 18, 1878, meeting. Swayed by
the activists and the existence of Emerson Normal, the Mobile County
Board of School Commissioners adopted the following resolution:

The Board of School Commissioners have given our weight to the regard of the
petitioners and agree that other things being equal, it would be reasonable to
prefer Colored teachers for Colored schools. But in the organization of be found
capable of managing them and it is the Established policy of this Board to make

places for others whether white or Colored, when new Schools are Established or vacancies occur in the Colored Schools, The Claims of Colored applicants to fill the same will receive consideration and when equally competent in Scholarship and ability to govern will have the preference in selection.

After this resolution, William A. Caldwell found employment as the principal of the Good Hope School during the 1878–79 academic year and then from 1881 to 1887.[26] Caldwell's hiring made possible the employment of other Emerson Normal graduates.

Black Mobilians deemed Caldwell's hiring as a victory. They resumed their efforts for additional teachers by submitting qualified applicants for the board's consideration, petitioning school commissioners directly, and even threatening a boycott. Community pressure, the success of Caldwell, and the presence of Emerson Normal eventually led to an increase in the number of African American teachers employed by the mid-1880s. Artemesia Europe permanently moved from the private to public school system in 1887 after taking a midyear appointment in 1885. Non–Emerson Normal graduates also received teaching positions, especially those who had attended Emerson Institute as students. For instance, William R. Gleason worked alongside William A. Caldwell as a teacher at the Good Hope School from 1884 to 1887. Other Emerson Institute graduates, including Annie Ewing, Mattie Ewing, and Theresa Page, received teaching positions during the 1880s. Without the presence of these local schools and continued community pressure, the struggle for African American teachers and better conditions may have continued much longer.[27]

Emerson Normal graduates also sought reform to the hiring practices of the AMA. William A. Caldwell and other First Congregational Church congregants began to question the organization's failure to hire African American educators and ministers who had graduated from their higher educational institutions. They initially voiced their concerns in several conversations with J. D. Smith. AMA officials hired this advanced theological student at Talladega College for its religious efforts while the regular ministry vacationed during the summer of 1877. In a letter to AMA administrators, Smith outlined their demands: "I have had men say to me, 'Smith if a colored minister would come here and show to the people that he is *true to his principles; not suffering himself to be led astray* in five or six months, he would soon be the means of leading the more intelligent class without much difficulty.'" He concurred with their reasoning and recommended, on their behalf, the hiring of the "young men … being trained up in our Schools and Colleges." Congregants had valid concerns.

While the organization hired advanced students from Talladega and other AMA colleges during the summer months, the organization relied predominantly on White northern missionaries as educators at the school and church during the academic year. American Missionary Association officials responded by transferring Rev. William H. Ash from Providence, Rhode Island, to Mobile in 1878.[28]

Rev. William Henry Ash was born in Charleston, South Carolina, in 1847. Although little is known about his early years, he graduated from Lincoln University in southern Chester County, Pennsylvania, in 1873. This renowned historical Black college fully prepared Ash for his entry into the theological school of Boston University. Shortly after obtaining his A.B. in sacred theology, Ash was ordained at the Central Church in Providence in 1877. Mobile represented his first major post since being ordained in the Congregational Church.[29]

Caldwell, church members, and community leaders considered the hiring of Ash as a victory, signaling to them a possible change in the organization's hiring practices that had the potential of extending to Emerson Normal and Institute. Appreciative of Ash's hiring, Caldwell drafted a letter to the American Missionary Association on behalf of the congregants. The letter opened, "Dear sir, we the undersigned members of the 1st Congregation Church of Mobile Alabama take this method of showing you our appreciation of our worthy pastor Rev. W. H. Ash, whom you have sent amongst us." Caldwell and the eight other signers felt that Ash exerted "a powerful influence for good in our community." Caldwell and the other petitioners reasoned, "He is just the man the colored people of Mobile need." In detailing their appreciation, church members noted the early results, from increased membership among young people and the educated middle class to the elevation of the public opinion of Congregationalism. Indeed, Ash's transfer sparked much enthusiasm in Mobile.[30]

His establishment of the Aristotle Literary Club justified their enthusiasm. This literary society attracted church members, Emerson Normal graduates, and other "true representatives – or rather, the best representatives – of the colored population in our city." The club organized public programs consisting of literary discussions, musical entertainment, and debates. Like other period literary societies, the Aristotle Literary Club promoted a new literate identity. As a result, the participation of Emerson Normal graduates increased. Ash recognized the success of his efforts resulted from "his peculiar relation and identification with my race [which gave him an] advantage over them [the white Emerson teachers]." Unlike his White predecessors, Ash better integrated himself into the community. Black Mobilians found an ally to combat the racism within the AMA.[31]

Unfortunately, racism within the AMA precipitated Ash's removal. Missionaries purposely excluded Ash from the educational efforts. B. F. Koons justified this exclusion by claiming that Ash lacked the knowledge of properly leading a Sabbath school and a church. She also claimed that the "colored population" had more faith in her, a White northern missionary, than in Ash, an African American. Koons's assessment convinced AMA administrators to contemplate and eventually remove Rev. Ash to Florence, Alabama, where he remained until his death of kidney disease in 1882.[32]

The decision shocked and dismayed Caldwell and other Black Mobilians. They had previously voiced their approval of Ash's hiring to the organization and could not understand his removal. Caldwell actively participated in the special meetings demanding Ash's reinstatement. Drafting one of the numerous petitions sent to the AMA executives, Caldwell argued for retaining Ash based on his position as an educational and moral leader. The AMA regarded the development of African American leadership as a major organizational aim. Missionaries prepared their students for entry into the middle class and for becoming moral leaders in their respective communities. As an Emerson Normal graduate, Caldwell appealed to this fundamental organizational aim. He wrote,

Since he has been here, he has accomplished a great amount of good by his influence and example both for the church and the community. His ability as a scholar and his model deportment as a minister of the gospel has won for him the respect and admiration of both white and colored in our city. He has certainly rendered faithful and efficient service in the cause of education and Christianity.

By citing Ash's personal character and leadership abilities, Caldwell hoped to show that he both lived and instilled the values promoted by organization at Emerson Normal and the church. Through his example, Ash inspired others.[33]

Caldwell even discussed the educational programs implemented under Ash's administration. Since 1865 the AMA had stressed religion and education as the best means to achieve the transition from slavery to freedom and focused their efforts on Black Mobilians' moral and intellectual development. Caldwell's keen awareness of this broader mission guided the concluding section. He felt that Ash instilled these values. "He has especially interested himself in the young people here, and one grand result of his efforts in that direction may be seen in the 'Aristotle Literary Club,' the only successful organization of its kind ever before established among our people here," Caldwell reminded them. Through this literary society, Caldwell contended that a "greater thirst for knowledge and improvement has been created among them than has ever been seen before." After outlining his reasons for reinstating Ash, Caldwell ended the petition with the following demand: "Hence we feel that his removal from here just now would be really detrimental to the cause of religion, morality and education. Impelled by the highest motives and a deep solicitude for the welfare of my people I pen you these few lines." His petition, however, never swayed administrators who were committed to Ash's removal. In this instance, Caldwell's efforts failed.[34]

While Emerson Normal graduates continued to question the organization's practices, they remained devoted to the school. Internal questioning and reform efforts never overshadowed the broader struggle for teacher training and employment of African American teachers in the public schools. Graduates understood the limits of the partnership. Undaunted by failure and frustration, graduates sustained the association. Their Emerson Normal training and their sense of obligation to the African American community drove their activism within and outside the classroom for the benefit of the entire community.

The resiliency of Black Mobilians' educational relationships and determination made the Mobile County Board of School Commissioners reconsider its position regarding African American teacher training. In 1887 Broad Street Academy opened as the first public normal and high school for African Americans in the city. The school drew from an educated African American ministry, Emerson Normal graduates, and Emerson Institute graduates for its all-Black faculty. School commissioners appointed William A. Caldwell for the position of principal. Artemesia Europe was the other Emerson Normal graduate hired. In addition to Europe and Caldwell, the faculty featured William R. Gleason, Miss Mattie Ewing, Rev. Albert F. Owens, and Theresa E. Page as teachers and Kate Parkis and Luella B. Thomas as assistants. The curriculum mirrored Emerson Normal and other normal schools, and featured both classroom and hands-on training in the model school attached to the program.[35] Emerson Normal graduates and other educators refashioned the education received in the training of future African American teachers. Caldwell, Europe, and others instilled racial pride and the rhetoric of racial progress via education in their students through their lessons and continued activism within Mobile. As a former student recalled,

Caldwell "ran the school with discipline and never tolerated any foolish-
ness of any kind on campus. If there was ever any kind of trouble with
a pupil it would be dealt with that day with the parents' involvement."
The school's inaugural graduating class of thirteen students reflected the
school's focus of academic achievement and discipline. Henry Europe
Jones, one of the two male graduates, continued the educational legacy
established by pioneer Emerson Normal students Mary Europe Jones and
Artemesia Europe. Without perseverance and Black Mobilians' activism,
Broad Street Academy would not have been possible.[36]

Broad Street Academy coexisted with Emerson Normal. Both schools
provided choice in normal education and represented major victories for
Black Mobilians and their allies. The schools' respective graduates built up
a corps of African American teachers on which Mobile, Mobile County,
and the surrounding Gulf region could draw for their public schools. Each
school resulted from the continued activism and collective determination
of the African American community to fulfill their communal desire to
become an educated and literate people. Broad Street Academy, though,
permitted the training of future African American teachers by qualified
African American educators using public funds. Thus the school's existence marked a major achievement in racial progress through education.
Until the school's closure due to a suspicious fire in 1947, Broad Street
Academy remained a source of pride among Black Mobilians.[37]

CONCLUSION

Emerson Normal reflected the communal desire and determination for the
training and hiring of African American teachers in Mobile. Relying on
their diverse educational relationships, Black Mobilians achieved success.
By 1890 two normal schools existed, one public and one private. The
corps of teachers established by the schools filled faculties of the African
American public schools. In the public normal school, Emerson Normal
graduates trained future generations of African American teachers. The
long and arduous struggle reinforced in the minds of Black Mobilians the
need for perseverance and alliances. Both proved essential to the future
of African American education in Mobile.

The experiences of Black Mobilians reveal that educational alliances
were essential to the creation of a corps of African American teachers.
They drew on their relationships with proponents of African American
education. Of these relationships, those with government officials proved
critical. Government support provided access to money and other

resources. While not ideal, these relationships aided in legitimizing and realizing the communal desire for African American teachers in the public schools. With the creation of a corps of African American public school-teachers, Black Mobilians had an important ally within the school system. These educators strove for the betterment of the schools and greater access to an education and citizenship in their communities. In many instances, their education and post-graduation expectations revealed that African Americans were as capable as, and perhaps even more capable than, their White counterparts in the instruction and occasionally the administration of the African American public schools. Therefore, relationships forged by urban African Americans proved beneficial.

Second, and most important, this corps of teachers served an important role beyond the classroom in the fight for racial uplift. The educators challenged the racism in their community, from the discriminatory hiring practices in the public schools to the racism within the AMA. Their participation, as evidenced in petitions, publications, and racial uplift organizations, evoked and sustained a particular collective memory of their normal school. By inspiring hope and perseverance, this memory proved essential in the broader civil rights struggle. Thus Emerson Normal represented a major victory by developing a new type of leadership that would be instrumental in the future struggles for African American education.

Notes

INTRODUCTION

1 "Complaint of Emily," February 24, 1868, www.bwwfproject.com; accessed March 20, 2023.
2 Eric Foner, *The Second Founding: How the Civil War and Reconstruction Remade the Constitution* (New York, 2019).
3 Joseph P. Reidy, *Illusions of Emancipation: The Pursuit of Freedom and Equality in the Twilight of Slavery* (Chapel Hill, 2019).
4 Thavolia Glymph, *Out of the House of Bondage: The Transformation of the Plantation Household* (New York, 2008), 97–136.
5 Works that are representative of the ways in which Black women were political actors include Ella Forbes, *African American Women during the Civil War* (New York, 1998); Stephanie M. H. Camp, *Closer to Freedom: Enslaved Women and Everyday Resistance in the Plantation South* (Chapel Hill, 2004); Glymph, *Out of the House of Bondage*; Hannah Rosen, *Terror in the Heart of Freedom: Citizenship, Sexual Violence, and the Meaning of Race in the Postemancipation South* (Chapel Hill, 2009). See also Edward E. Baptist and Stephanie M. H. Camp, eds., *New Studies in the History of American Slavery* (Athens, GA, 2006).
6 Thavolia Glymph, "Roses's War and the Gendered Politics of a Slave Insurgency in the Civil War," *Journal of the Civil War Era* 3, no. 4 (2013), 522.
7 Kidada E. Williams, *I Saw Death Coming: A History of Terror and Survival in the War against Reconstruction* (New York, 2023), xviii.
8 Rosen, *Terror in the Heart of Freedom*, 217–18.
9 Carole Emberton, *To Walk About in Freedom: The Long Emancipation of Priscilla Joyner* (New York, 2022); David Blight and Jim Downs, eds., *Beyond Freedom: Disrupting the History of Emancipation* (Athens, GA, 2017), 5.

1 "THE PROCEEDS OF MY OWN LABOR"

1   Robert Harrison, "Welfare and Employment Policies of the Freedmen's Bureau in the District of Columbia," *Journal of Southern History* 72, no. 1 (2006), 75; Carol Faulkner, *Women's Radical Reconstruction: The Freedmen's Aid Movement* (Philadelphia, 2004).

2   Steven Hahn, *A Nation under Our Feet: Black Political Struggles in the Rural South, from Slavery to the Great Migration* (Cambridge, MA, 2003), 6, 24; Letitia Woods Brown, *Free Negroes in the District of Columbia, 1790–1846* (New York, 1972); Elizabeth Clark Lewis, *First Freed: Washington D.C. in the Emancipation Era* (Washington DC, 2002). For the connections between the pursuit of freedom before and after slavery see particularly Amrita Chakrabarti Myers, *Forging Freedom: Black Women and the Pursuit of Liberty in Antebellum Charleston* (Chapel Hill, 2011).

3   The circumstances of its founding meant that the laws regarding manumission and Black freedoms continued to reflect the liberal attitudes towards emancipation prevalent during the Revolution, even as state governments in Maryland and Virginia tightened restrictions surrounding manumission and sought to force all freed slaves to leave the state immediately. Although the city corporation passed laws to restrict free people of color's freedoms and required them to register with the courts, as the District grew, city officials found it more troublesome to enforce these codes and migrants were often able to evade license and registration requirements. See Constance McLaughlin Green, *The Secret City: A History of Race Relations in the Nation's Capital* (Princeton, 1967), 18, 33–38; Mary Elizabeth Corrigan, "A Social Union of Heart and Effort: The African American Family in the District of Columbia on the Eve of Emancipation," PhD diss., University of Maryland, 1996, 49, 55–56, 66–80; Tamika Nunley, *At the Threshold of Liberty: Women, Slavery, and Shifting Identities in Washington, D.C.* (Chapel Hill, 2021).

4   Although many historians have explained Black women's dominance in southern cities because of their greater ability to gain freedom due to a close or sexual relationship with their employers, in Upper South cities like Washington, Baltimore and Norfolk, migration was more of a factor in creating the sexual difference in the population as free women of color responded to economic opportunities in the city. In Upper South cities, the sex ratio of males to females ranged from 61 males to every 100 females in Norfolk Virginia, to 74 in Baltimore, 82 in Petersburg, Virginia, and 83 in Louisville, Kentucky. Washington fell in the middle with 71 males to every 100 females. Even in Richmond, Virginia, where industrial employment provided a more reliable source of labor for Black men, the sex ratio remained at 86. See Tommy Bogger, *Free Blacks in Norfolk, Virginia, 1790–1860: The Darker Side of Freedom* (Charlottesville, 1997), 53; Wilma King, *The Essence of Liberty: Free Black Women during the Slave Era* (Columbia, MO, 2006), 64–65. For the motivations that led free women of color to prefer the city over the rural counties, see Jennifer Hull Dorsey, *Hirelings: African American Workers and Free Labor in Early Maryland* (Ithaca, 2011).

5 Unlike other Upper South cities like Baltimore or Richmond, there was little industry in the District of Columbia to offer skilled employment to free men of color. Although government work dominated the local economy, the only jobs that were open to free men of color were as messengers between the various departments. Midori Takagi, *Rearing Wolves to Our Own Destruction: Slavery in Richmond, Virginia, 1782–1865* (Charlottesville, 1999); Christopher Phillips, *Freedom's Port: The African American Community of Baltimore, 1790–1860* (Urbana, 1999); Green, *The Secret City*, 37.

6 This study draws on several relational databases, which combined personal information about Black women in the District of Columbia gleaned from various sources including Free Black Registers from the antebellum period, The Board of Emancipation Petitions for Compensation from 1862, and Marriage Registers compiled by the Freedmen's Bureau with the corresponding household information from the 1850, 1860 and 1870 US Census. Using the website Ancestry.com's search functionality, individuals and families were traced to their census entries, and the data combined to analyze how free women of color balanced their domestic economies during the antebellum period and how freedwomen adapted to urban labor conditions. Dorothy S. Provine, *District of Columbia Free Negro Registers, 1821–1861*, 2 vols. (Bowie, MD, 1996); Records of the Board of Commissioners for the Emancipation of Slaves in the District of Columbia, 1862–1863, National Archives, Microfilm M217; Reverend John Kimball, "Register of Marriages," Records of the Field Offices for the District of Columbia, Records of the Bureau of Refugees, Freedmen and Abandoned Lands, 1865–1869, National Archives, Microfilm M1902; Superintendent of Marriages, Register of Marriages, November 1866–July 1867, 1850 US Census, 1860 US Census, 1870 US Census, accessed digitally at http://ancestry.com.

7 Tera Hunter, *To 'Joy My Freedom: Southern Black Women's Lives and Labors after the Civil War* (Cambridge, MA, 1997), 74–97; Petition No. 2161, Petition No. 2275, Provine, *District of Columbia Free Negro Registers*, 416, 489; 1850 US Census; 1860 US Census.

8 Elizabeth Keckley, *Behind the Scenes: Or Thirty Years a Slave and Four Years in the White House* (New York, 1988); Jennifer Fleischner, *Mrs. Lincoln and Mrs. Keckly: The Remarkable Story of the Friendship between the First Lady and a Former Slave* (New York, 2003).

9 Provine, *District of Columbia Free Negro Registers*; US Census 1850, US Census 1860.

10 This sample traced 100 individuals from their personal information contained in the Petitions to the Board of Emancipation Commissioners and the Register of Marriages kept by the Freedmen's Bureau to the 1870 census, recording variables such as pre- and postwar occupations, family structure, and the number of children attending school. As the only program of compensated emancipation in the South, the petitions submitted to the Board of Commissioners established to determine the worth of slave property are a unique and invaluable resource. Owners typically listed the origins of their slave property and

gave information on the slave's skills and even temperament to prove their worth. Records of the Board of Commissioners, 1870 Census.

11 Petition of James Riordan, Records of the Board of Commissioners, 1870 US Census. James Riordan (or Reardon) was not listed in the household in 1870.

12 Petition of Noble Young, Records of the Board of Commissioners, 1870 US Census.

13 Hunter, *To 'Joy My Freedom*, 52–61; Thavolia Glymph, *Out of the House of Bondage: The Transformation of the Plantation Household* (New York, 2008).

14 As the data only records where the individual former slave resided in 1870, it is not clear at what point they left their former owner or how many employers they had worked for between 1862 and 1870. Petition of Ann Bisco, Records of the Board of Commissioners, 1870 US Census.

15 Nunley, *At the Threshold of Liberty*, 128–59.

16 Petition of Margaret Loughborough, Petition of Joseph Fearson, Records of the Board of Commissioners, 1870 US Census.

17 Stephanie McCurry, "War, Gender, and Emancipation in the Civil War South," in *Lincoln's Proclamation: Emancipation Reconsidered*, ed. William A. Blair and Karen Fisher (Chapel Hill, 2009), 120–50; Amy Dru Stanley, "Instead of Waiting for the Thirteenth Amendment: The War Power, Slave Marriage, and Inviolate Human Rights," *American Historical Review* 115, no. 3 (2010), 732–65.

18 John P. Shortman to D. B. Nichols, October 8, 1862, Mobile Units in the Department of Washington, Records of United States Continental Commands, 1821–1890, National Archives, Record Group 393: Part 2, No 12, Ser. 642 Letters Sent, Vol. 98; James E. Montgomery to James L. Ferree, August 15, 1863, Mobile Units in the Department of Washington Ser. 642 Letters Sent, Vol. 99. During the Civil War, women such as Dorothea Dix and the United States Sanitary Commission fought to legitimize women's nursing and to force female nurses into army hospitals. Jane E. Schultz, *Women at the Front: Hospital Workers in Civil War America* (Chapel Hill, 2004).

19 Leslie Schwalm, '*A Hard Fight for We': Women's Transition from Slavery to Freedom in South Carolina* (Urbana and Chicago, 1997), 90.

20 After the war, Elias Greene, the chief officer in charge of the quartermaster department was investigated for improper handling of the department and the Contraband Fund that was also under his administration. It was believed that thousands of laborers went unpaid, and thousands of dollars were unaccounted for from the fund. See Records of the Office of the Quartermaster General, National Archives, Record Group 92, Series 225, Consolidated Correspondence File, "Greene."

21 R. G. C. Patten to Hon. Mr. Joselyn, December 20, 1862, American Missionary Association Archives, (microform) 15910, The Schomberg Center for Research in Black Culture; Dorothy Sterling, *We Are Your Sisters: Black Women in the Nineteenth Century* (New York, 1997), 245.

22 See, for example, Petition of Anna Bradley, Petition of Elizabeth Cissel, Board of Emancipation Records; Mary Beth Corrigan, "'It's A Family Affair':

Buying Freedom in the District of Columbia, 1850–1860," in *Working toward Freedom: Slave Society and Domestic Economy in the American South*, ed. Larry E. Hudson (Rochester, NY, 1995), 171.

23 Adjutant General L. Thomas to Brig. Gen. M. C. Meigs, September 27, 1862, Consolidated Correspondence File, "Contraband Fund."

24 Elias M. Greene to Col. Charles Thomas, December 17, 1863, Consolidated Correspondence File, "Contraband Fund."

25 Capt. J. J. Ferree to Unknown June 22, 1863, Mobile Units in the Department of Washington Ser. 646, Letters Received; George E. H. Day to Colonel Foster, December 6, 1864, Consolidated Correspondence File, "Arlington," George E. H. Day to Hon. E. M. Stanton, December 8, 1864, Ibid.

26 Stephanie Cole, "Servants and Slaves: Domestic Service in the Border Cities, 1800–1850," PhD diss., University of Florida, 1994, 82–86.

27 Schwalm, '*A Hard Fight for We*,' 205–209; Hahn, *A Nation under Our Feet*, 171; Mary Farmer Kaiser, *Freedwomen and the Freedmen's Bureau: Race, Gender, and Public Policy in the Age of Emancipation* (New York, 2010), 64–96.

28 Provine, *District of Columbia Free Negro Registers*; 1860 US Census.

29 Petition of Margaret Loughborough, Board of Emancipation Records; 1870 US Census.

30 Register of Marriages; 1870 US Census.

31 Tera Hunter and Elizabeth Clark Lewis have detailed the struggles of Black domestic servants to negotiate "living out" positions where they could remain in their own homes. Hunter, *To 'Joy My Freedom*, 58–59; Elizabeth Clark Lewis, *Living In, Living Out: African American Domestics in Washington, D.C., 1910–1940* (Washington, DC, 1994), 147–73.

32 Petition of Sally T. Matthews, Board of Emancipation Records; 1870 US Census.

33 Petition of Thomas Donaho, Board of Emancipation Records; 1870 US Census.

34 Carol Faulkner, "The 'Irrepressible' Mrs. Griffing: Josephine Griffing and Freedmen's Aid Work in Reconstruction Washington D.C.," MA diss., State University of New York at Binghamton, 1995; Keith Melder, "Angel of Mercy in Washington: Josephine Griffing and the Freedmen, 1864–72," *Records of the Historical Society for the District of Columbia 63–65* (1966), 243–72.

35 Bvt. Brig. Gen. J. G. Fullerton to Maj. Gen. O. O. Howard, September 6, 1866, Records of the Assistant Commissioner for the District of Columbia, Records of the Bureau of Refugees, Freedmen and Abandoned Lands, 1865–1869, National Archives, Microfilm M1055, Letters Sent; J. V. W. Vandenburgh to Stuart Eldridge, April 8, 1868, Records of the Field Office, Local Supt., Letters Sent.

36 Edward O'Brien to S. N. Clark, October 13, 1865, Records of the Assistant Commissioner, Letters Received.

37 Mrs. J. S. Griffing to Bvt. Brig. Gen C. H. Howard, October 20, 1866, Records of the Assistant Commissioner, Letters Received.

38 Mrs. J. S. Griffing to Col. John Eaton, August 31, 1865, Records of the Assistant Commissioner, Reports of Visiting Agents; Bvt. Brig. Gen. C. H. Howard, to Maj. Gen. O. O. Howard, October 10, 1867, Records of the Assistant Commissioner, Letters Sent.

39 Bvt. Brig. Gen. C. H. Howard to Maj. Gen. O. O. Howard, October 10, 1867, Records of the Assistant Commissioner, Letters Sent; S. N. Clark to Reverend J. L. Roberts, March 27, 1866, Records of the Field Office, Asst. Insp. Gen. Letters Sent; Mrs. Josephine Griffing to Bvt. Brig. Gen. C. H. Howard, October 20, 1866, Records of the Assistant Commissioner, Letters Received.

40 Kaiser, *Freedwomen and the Freedmen's Bureau*, 10.

41 Ibid., 38; Paul Cimbala, *Under the Guardianship of the Nation: The Freedmen's Bureau and the Reconstruction of Georgia* (Athens, GA, 2003), 82–84; Carol Faulkner, *Women's Radical Reconstruction: The Freedmen's Aid Movement* (Philadelphia, 2004), 94.

42 Capt. W. F. Spurgin to S. N. Clark, November 1, 1865, Records of the Assistant Commissioner, Memorandum Received; Bvt. Brig. Gen. J. G. Fullerton, to Maj. Gen. O. O. Howard, September 6, 1866, Records of the Assistant Commissioner, Letters Sent.

43 J. V. W. Vandenburgh to Stuart Eldridge, March 31, 1868, Records of the Assistant Commissioner, Letters Received.

44 Kaiser, *Freedwomen and the Freedmen's Bureau*, 52–53, 151–53. See Laura Edwards, *Gendered Strife and Confusion: The Political Culture of Reconstruction* (Urbana, 1997) especially 145–84, for a discussion of Black women's use of the courts in familial disputes in Granville, North Carolina.

45 Catherine Stevenson to Bvt. Brig. Gen. C. H. Howard, November 6, 1867, Records of the Assistant Commissioner, Letters Received; W. S. Chase to Gen. C. H. Howard, May 3, 1866, Records of the Field Office, Local Supt., Letters Received; Sarah Anne Taylor to Capt. W. F. Spurgin, August 22, 1865, Records of the Assistant Commissioner, Letters Received.

46 J. V. W. Vandenburgh, June 24, 1867, Records of the Field Office, Local Supt., Endorsements Sent.

47 Edwards, *Gendered Strife and Confusion*, 6–8.

48 Mary Lacy to W. W. Rogers, November 17, 1866, Records of the Assistant Commissioner, Letters Received.

49 Mary Lacy to W. W. Rogers, November 17, 1866, Records of the Assistant Commissioner, Letters Received.

2 "PLEASE ATTEND TO IT FOR ME"

1 Ira Berlin and Leslie Rowland, eds., *Freedom: A Documentary History of Emancipation, 1861–1867, series 2: The Black Military Experience* (Cambridge, 1982), 667.

2 Ibid.

3 "The Great Victory," *Daily Dispatch*. July 22, 1861.

4 For a more information on the number of battles in each state, see the National Parks Service in collaboration with American Battlefield Protection Program which collects data on the battles in each state: www.nps.gov/abpp/battles/bystate.htm#ms.

5 For more information on the 1860 census which includes a count of the enslaved population in each household see United States 1860 Federal Census Population, Microfilm publication M653, National Archives and Records Administration (NARA), Washington, DC.

6 For more information on Black Virginians during the Civil War see Robert Engs, *Freedom's First Generation: Black Hampton Virginia 1861–1890* (Philadelphia, 1979); Jeffrey Kerr- Ritchie, *Freedpeople in the Tobacco South 1860–1900* (Chapel Hill, 1999); Lynda J. Morgan, *Emancipation in Virginia's Tobacco Belt 1850–1870* (Atlanta, 1992). Other works that examine Black Virginians' experience during the Reconstruction era include Alrutheus A. Taylor, *The Negro in the Reconstruction of Virginia* (New York, 2017); Daniel B Horp, *Facing Freedom: An African American Community in Virginia from Reconstruction to Jim Crow* (Charlottesville, 2019); Edna G. Medford "The Transition from Slavery to Freedom in a Diversified Economy: Virginia's Lower Peninsula,1860–1900," PhD diss., University of Maryland, 1987. For historiographical essays on African Americans in Virginia see Phillip J Schwartz. " 'A Sense of Their Own Power': Self-Determination in Recent Writings on Black Virginians," *Virginia Magazine of History and Biography* 97, no. 3 (1989).

7 *Compendium of the Seventh Census, Virginia,* 320–31; *Compendium of the Eighth Census, Agriculture, Virginia,* 159. Although Virginia has long been associated with tobacco, agricultural production varied based on region. Many of the Northwestern counties profited from grain and livestock and later coal and iron. Northwestern counties were able to create an economy not solely dependent on enslaved labor. Over time, this dissimilarity between the northwestern counties and eastern counties led to a dissolution. In 1861, when Virginia seceded from the Union, the northwestern counties seceded from Virginia, forming a new territory known as West Virginia and altering the composition of the state forever. For more information on the creation of West Virginia see Scott A. Mackenzie, *The Fifth Border State: Slavery Emancipatiom and the Formation of West Virginia 1829–1872* (Morgantown, WV, 2023).

8 Benjamin F. Butler, *Private and Official Correspondence of Gen. Benjamin F. Butler during the Period of the Civil War* (Norwood, MA, 1917), 116–18; Eric Foner, *Reconstruction: America's Unfinished Revolution 1863–1877* (New York, 1988), 5.

9 Amy Murrell Taylor, *Embattled Freedom: Journeys through the Civil War's Slave Refugee Camps* (Chapel Hill, 2018).

10 Butler, *Private and Official Correspondence of Gen. Benjamin F. Butler,* 30.

11 "Two Hundred Dollars Reward," *Daily Dispatch,* January 10, 1863.

12 "One Hundred Dollars Reward," ibid., April 1, 1863.

13 For an in-depth analysis of Black women's efforts during the Civil War see Thavolia Glymph's *Out of the House of Bondage: The Transformation of*

      the Plantation Household (New York, 2000) and *The Women's Fight: The Civil War's Battles for Home, Freedom, and Nation* (Chapel Hill, 2020).

14   "What Soldiers 'Snacks' Are Made Of," *Richmond Dispatch*, July 27, 1863.

15   Ira Berlin, Barbara J, Fields, and Steven F. Miller, "Testimony by the Superintendent of Contrabands at Fortress Monroe, Virginia before the American Freedmen's Inquiry Commission," featured in *Free at Last: A Documentary History of Slavery, Freedom and the Civil War* (New York, 1993), 107–10.

16   Charles L. Perdue, Thomas E. Barden, and Robert K. Phillips. *Weevils in the Wheat: Interviews with Virginia Ex-slaves* (Bloomington, 1980), 54.

17   Engs, *Freedom's First* Generation, 38.

18   Arlisha R. Norwood, "Women without Men: Single African American Women in Post–Civil War Virginia," PhD diss., Howard University, 2019.

19   Ibid.

20   Berlin et al., "Testimony by the Superintendent of Contrabands," 107.

21   Virginia, Freedmen's Bureau Field Office Records, 1865–1872, Fort Monroe (Department of Negro Affairs, 1863–1865; Departments of Virginia and North Carolina), Roll 115, Letters.

22   Virginia, Freedmen's Bureau Field Office Records, 1865–1872, Fort Monroe (Department of Negro Affairs, 1863–1865; Departments of Virginia and North Carolina), Roll 115, Letters, orders, and telegrams, Oct–Dec 1864, NARA microfilm publication RG M1913 (Washington, DC).

23   Virginia, Freedmen's Bureau Field Office Records, Accomack County Jan–Sep 1866, Reports Received (Subassistant Commissioner, 5th district), Roll 125, M1913.

24   Michelle Krowl, "Dixie's Other Daughters: African American Women in Virginia, 1861–1868," PhD diss., University of California Berkeley, 1998, 185.

25   Henry Lee Swint, *Dear Ones at Home; Letters from Contraband Camp* (Nashville, 1966), 120.

26   Case file 00-654, Private Charles Clark, Co. D, 20th New York Cavalry, Records of the Judge Advocate General, RG 153, NARA; Casefile 00886, Private Thomas Mitchell CO E 1st New York, Records of the Judge Advocate General, RG 153, NARA.

27   Virginia, Freedmen's Bureau Field Office Records, 1864–1872, Fort Monroe (Department of Negro Affairs, 1863–1865; Departments of Virginia and North Carolina) Letters, orders, and telegrams, Oct–Dec 1864.

28   Adjutant General Lorenzo Thomas to General Montgomery Meigs, September 27, 1865, in official records Meigs to Edwin Stanton, November 6, 1862, 740–41.

29   "General orders No. 46 concerning the recruitment of non-white troops," The Gilder Lehrman Collection, The Gilder Lehrman Institute of American History, New York, accessed May 29, 2019.

30   Case Files of Approved Pension Applications of Widows and Other Dependents of Civil War Veterans, ca. 1861–ca. 1910, WC148009, Jane Fitchett, December 19, 1863, Widow of Andrew Fitchett, Co. C, 10th United States Colored Infantry, USCT, NARA.

31   The Freedmen's Bureau has been studied widely by scholars. See William S. Mcfeely, *Yankee Stepfather: General O.O. Howard and the Freedmen*

(New York, 1994); Paul A. Cimbala and Hans L. Trefousse, eds., *The Freedmen's Bureau: Reconstructing the American South after the Civil War* (Huntington, WV, 2005); Richard Loew, "The Freedman's Bureau and Local Black Leadership," *Journal of American History* (1993), 80.

32 Virginia, Freedmen's Bureau Field Office Records, W. Tidball to J. A Bates, July 31, 1866, Monthly Narrative Reports of Operations and Conditions. M1045 Roll#45.

33 Paul Cimbala and Randall Miller, eds., *The Freedmen's Bureau and Reconstruction: Reconsiderations* (New York, 1999), 187.

34 Virginia, Freedmen's Bureau Field Office Records, Reverend James Ferree to General O. O Howard, January 24, 1866, M1045, Roll#45.

35 Howard Rabinowitz, "From Exclusion to Segregation: Health and Welfare Services for Southern Blacks, 1865–1890," *Social Service Review* 48, no. 3 (1974), 327–54.

36 Ibid., 40.

37 Mary Farmer Kaiser, *Freedwomen and the Freedmen's Bureau: Race, Gender, and Public Policy in the Age of Emancipation* (New York, 2010), 48.

38 Virginia, Freedmen's Bureau Field Office Records, Fort Monroe, Jan–Sep 1866, Reports Received (Subassistant Commissioner, 5th district), Roll 125, M1913.

39 Ibid.

40 Ibid., September 1866–December 1867.

41 The Freedmen's Bureau court structure varied from state to state. Additionally, in many states the court also operated concurrently with the local court system. As a result, the court systems in post–Civil War Virginia were unorganized. Unfortunately, no scholarly work covers the Freedmen's Bureau court system in depth. However, Bureau administrators did leave behind detailed notes on inner workings of the system: see Virginia, Freedmen's Bureau Field Office Records, Nov 1865–Aug 1866, Albemarle County (Assistant Sub-assistant Commissioner), Proceedings of freedmen's court, Roll 67, M1913.

42 Virginia, Freedmen's Bureau Field Office Records, 1865–1872, Drummondtown (Assistant Subassistant commissioner), Proceedings of Freedmen's Court, May 1865–May 1867, M1913, NARA.

43 Virginia, Freedmen's Bureau Field Office Records, 1865–1872, Subordinate Field Offices, Charlottesville (Albemarle County, Assistant Subassistant Commissioner), Register of Complaints, Volume 131, M1913, NARA.

44 Virginia, Freedmen's Bureau Field Office Records, May 1865–May 1867, Drummondtown (Assistant Subassistant Commissioner), Proceedings of freedmen's court, Roll 73, M1913; Virginia, Freedmen's Bureau Field Office Records, Albemarle County (Assistant Subassistant commissioner), Register of complaints Roll 67, M1913; Virginia, Freedmen's Bureau Field Office Records, 1866–1867, Fort Monroe (Assistant Subassistant commissioner), Proceedings of cases before freedmen's court, Roll 130, M1913.

45 Virginia, Freedmen's Bureau Field Office Records, May 1865–May 1867, Drummondtown (Assistant Subassistant Commissioner), Proceedings of freedmen's court, Roll 73, M1913.

46 Perdue, Barden, and Phillips, *Weevils in the Wheat*, 161.

47 Virginia, Freedmen's Bureau Field Office Record, Fort Monroe, Dec 1865–Jul 1867 (Assistant Subassistant commissioner), Register of proceedings of freedmen's court for Elizabeth City County, Roll 130, M1913.
48 Ibid., Roll 45.
49 Virginia, Henrico County, Overseer of the Poor Minute Books 1869–1891, Library of Virginia Reel 214; Kidada E. Williams, *I Saw Death Coming: A History of Terror and Survival in the War against Reconstruction* (New York, 2023).
50 For more information on Black women in post–Reconstruction era Virginia, see Jane Dailey *Before Jim Crow: The Politics of Race in Postemancipation Virginia* (Chapel Hill, 2000); Gertrude Marlowe, *A Right Worthy Grand Mission: Maggie Lena Walker and the Quest for Black Economic Empowerment* (Washington, DC, 2003).
51 W. E. B. Du Bois, "The Negro in Farmville Virginia: A Social Study," in *Bulletin of the Department of Labor No 14 January 1898*, ed. Caroll D. Wright, Department of Labor (Washington, DC, 1898), 2.
52 Ibid., 11.

3 "I HAD TIME FOR MYSELF"

This chapter is an outgrowth of a 2018 paper presented at the Rutgers Center for Historical Analysis, a seminar directed by Marisa Fuentes and Kali Gross. Seminar members provided me with invaluable comments and suggestions, which especially helped me articulate and theorize the "politics of acquisition." Also, I would like to thank Maria Ximena Abello Hurtado for her significant feedback on early drafts of this chapter.
1 Francis Brown, Southern Claims Commission Records (hereafter SCC), Case Number 20638, National Archives and Records Administration (NARA), Washington, DC.
2 Tera Hunter discusses the significance of clothing for freedwomen who lived in Atlanta during the postbellum period, in *To 'Joy My Freedom: Southern Black Women's Lives and Labors after the Civil War* (Cambridge, MA, 1998).
3 In her Southern Claims Commission claim, Francis Brown listed 8 hogs, 12 bushels of corn, 15 bushels of rice, fowls and clothes that were taken by the Union Army during the Civil War. Francis Brown, SCC No. 20638.
4 The words and experiences of freedpeople demonstrate that while enslaved, they regularly purchased, sold, and inherited goods, and passed them on to their kin with little interference from their enslavers during the antebellum period. As such, this chapter refers to enslaved people as "property owners" to reflect the manner in which they acted and viewed themselves.
5 Philip Morgan, "Work and Culture: The Task System and the World of Lowcountry Blacks, 1700 to 1880," *The William and Mary Quarterly* 39, no. 4 (1982), 598.

6 Dylan Penningroth, *The Claims of Kinfolk: African American Property and Community in the 19th Century South* (Chapel Hill, 2003), 47. For Penningroth's doctoral work that also analyzes the experiences of bondpeople who owned property in Liberty County, Georgia, see Dylan Penningroth, "Slavery, Freedom, and Social Claims to Property among African Americans in Liberty County, Georgia, 1850–1990," *Journal of American History* 84, no. 2 (1997), 405–35.

7 Deborah Gray White, *Ar'n't I a Woman?: The Female Slave in the Plantation South* (New York, 1999), 89.

8 Jennifer Morgan, *Laboring Women: Reproduction and Gender in New World Slavery* (Philadelphia, 2011).

9 Leslie Schwalm, '*A Hard Fight for We': Women's Transition from Slavery to Freedom in South Carolina* (Urbana and Chicago, 1997); Judith Carney, *Black Rice: The African Origins of Rice Cultivation in the Americas* (Cambridge, MA), 2001.

10 Stephanie M. H. Camp, "The Pleasures of Resistance: Enslaved Women and Body Politics in the Plantation South, 1830–1861," in *New Studies in the History of American Slavery*, ed. Edward E. Baptist and Stephanie M. H. Camp (Athens, GA, and London, 2006), 88.

11 The Southern Claims Commission was created in 1871 by the United States government to allow southerners an avenue to file claims for property loss during the Civil War. In order to receive reimbursements from the organization, claimants had to prove that they had been loyal to the Union during the war and that the property had been destroyed by the Union Army. The process involved interviews with the claimant and his or her witnesses. Many African Americans filed claims and received reimbursements from the Southern Claims Commission.

12 Eighteen of the claims were filed by women originally. There were an additional two cases in which widows continued the claim for their deceased husbands. The Southern Claims Commission awarded the claims of ten women in Liberty County. SCC, NARA; Penningroth, *The Claims of Kinfolk*, 73–74.

13 Ibid.

14 Patsey Campbell, SCC No. 21475.

15 Penningroth, *The Claims of Kinfolk*, 51.

16 Gray White, *Ar'n't I A Woman?*, 129.

17 Rachel Norman, SCC No. 21416.

18 Susan Bennett, SCC No. 21473; US 1870 Population Census.

19 Susan Bennett, SCC No. 21473. Thompson was a midlevel plantation owner who owned forty-eight slaves. United States Census Bureau, 1860, Schedule 2: Slave Inhabitants in the 15th District in the County of Liberty State of Georgia. NARA.

20 Susan Bennett, SCC No. 21473.

21 Ibid.

22 Silvy Baker, SCC No. 21451; United States Census Bureau, 1870, Schedule 1: Inhabitants in the County of Liberty State of Georgia. NARA.

23 Peggy Jones, SCC No. 20664.

24 Leslie M. Harris and Daina Ramey Berry, eds., *Slavery and Freedom in Savannah*, (Athens, GA, 2014), 54. See Alsiha M. Cromwell's essay, "Enslaved Women in the Savannah Marketplace." in that volume.

25 Linda and Caesar Jones, SSC No. 20662. The mother and son filed the claim jointly.

26 Susie King Taylor, *Reminiscences of My Life in Camp with the 33rd United States Colored Troops* (Self-published, 1902), 15.

27 Adrienne Davis, "Don't Let Nobody Bother Yo' Principle," in *Sister Circle: Black Women and Work* (New Brunswick, NJ, 2002), 107. Also see Morgan, *Laboring Women*.

28 Legally, enslaved people were civilly dead except in the case of either committing or being victims of a crime. Enslaved people were purchased and sold, deeded, and listed alongside livestock in plantation ledgers. Jeannine Marie DeLombard, "The Very Idea of a Slave Is a Human Being in Bondage," in *The Routledge Research Companion to Law and Humanities in Nineteenth-Century America* (New York, 2017), 24. Also see Row W. Copeland, "The Nomenclature of Enslaved Africans as Real Property or Chattels Personal: Legal Fiction, Judicial Interpretation, Legislative Designation, or Was a Slave a Slave by Any Other Name?," *Journal of Black Studies* 40, no. 5 (2010), 946–59; Edward F. Sweat, "Social Status of the Free Negro in Antebellum Georgia." *Negro History Bulletin* 21, no. 6 (March 1958), 129–31.

29 Dainey Ramey Berry, *The Price for Their Pound of Flesh: The Price of the Enslaved from the Womb to the Grave in the Building of a Nation* (Boston, 2017), 2. Jennifer Morgan writes, "Whether laboring among sugar cane, coffee bushes, or rice swamps, the cost–benefit calculations of colonial slaveowners included the speculative value of a reproducing labor force." Morgan, *Laboring Women*, 3.

30 Jane Holmes, SCC No. 20656.

31 This chapter uses the term property interchangeably with goods. It does so with the understanding that the legal definition of property differed greatly than the manner in which enslaved people acquired goods in the antebellum and Civil War periods. Legally, property could only be owned by citizens and was protected by a number of laws. However, the experiences of bondpeople who owned, inherited, and passed on goods are in direct conflict with the legal parameters of property ownership. For more about enslavers and property rights see James L. Huston, *Calculating the Value of the Union: Slavery, Property Rights, and the Economic Origins of the Civil War* (Chapel Hill, 2003).

32 Karen B. Bell, "Rice, Resistance, and Forced Transatlantic Communities: (Re)Visioning the African Diaspora in Low Country Georgia 1750–1800," *Journal of African American History* 95, no. 2 (Spring 2010), 169.

33 Saidiya V. Hartman, *Scenes of Subjection: Terror, Slavery, and Self-Making in Nineteenth-Century America* (Oxford, 1997), 42.

34 Ibid., 36.

35 An 1801 state law prohibited enslavers from manumitting bondpeople. Harris and Berry, eds., *Slavery and Freedom in Savannah*, 96.

36 US Population Census, 1860.

37 "Enrollment of Free Persons 1852–1861, Liberty Co., GA," Liberty County Court House. Hinesville, Georgia; Amrita Chakrabarti Myers, *Forging Freedom: Black Women and the Pursuit of Liberty in Antebellum Charleston*. (Chapel Hill, 2011), 40. In her study of emancipated Black women in Charleston, South Carolina, Myers articulates that enslaved African American women were less likely to purchase their freedom due to their "limited job opportunities and the low wages that Black women commanded in the labor market."

38 Silvy Baker, SCC No. 21451.

39 Erskine Clarke, *Dwelling Place: A Plantation Epic* (New Haven, 2005), 414–15.

40 In 1860, there were 6,083 bondpeople in Liberty County, with women making up a slight majority of 3,086. US Population Census, 1860.

41 Eliza James, SCC No. 21427.

42 Jane Holmes, SCC No. 20656.

43 Lucy McIver, SCC No. 21418.

44 Silvy Baker, SCC No. 21451.

45 Clarinda Porter, SCC No. 18544.

46 Ira Berlin et al., *Slaves No More: Three Essays on Emancipation and the Civil War* (New York, 1992), 163–67.

47 Susan and Scipio Bennett, SCC No. 21473.

48 Berlin et al., *Slaves No More*, 68.

49 Clarinda Porter, SCC. NARA.

50 Eliza James, SCC No. 18544.

51 Matilda McIntosh, SCC No. 18121. Disallowed and Barred Claims.

52 Lydia Baker, SCC No 21415.

53 Edward Thomas, *Memoirs of a Southerner, 1840–1923: Documenting the American South* (Chapel Hill, 1923), 9–10. In his memoir R. Q. Mallard explains how bondpeople were given more food depending on their number of children enslaved. They were also given more food during the part of the year when the workload was heavier. R. Q. Mallard, *Plantation Life before Emancipation* (New Orleans, 1892), 32. For a general overview of bondpeople's rations during slavery see Herbert C. Covey and Dwight Eisnach, *What the Slaves Ate: Recollections of African American Foods and Foodways from the Slave Narratives* (Santa Barbara, 2009), 20–30.

54 Nancy Bacon, SCC No. 21406.

55 Thomas, *Memoirs of a Southerner*, 9–10; Mallard, *Plantation Life before Emancipation*, 32.

56 Linda Brent, *Incidents in the Life of a Slave Girl* (Boston, 1861), 20.

57 Charles Joyner, *Remember Me: Slave Life in Coastal Georgia* (Athens, GA, 2011), 33–34. Clarke, *Dwelling Place*, 329; Penningroth, "Slavery, Freedom, and Social Claims to Property," 420.

58 Stephanie M. H. Camp, *Closer to Freedom: Enslaved Women and Everyday Resistance in the Plantation South* (Chapel Hill, 2004), 68.

59 Patsey Campbell. SCC No. 21475.

60 Ibid.

61 Ibid.

62 Matilda McIntosh. SCC No. 18121. Disallowed and Barred Claims.

63 Glymph, *Out of the House of Bondage*, 206.
64 Lydia Baker, SCC No. 21415.
65 Ibid. Lydia valued her claim at $100 and was awarded $55 by the commission.
66 Silvia Walthour, SCC No. 18127. Disallowed and Barred Claims.
67 Ibid. In her claim, Silvia mentioned five adult children who were married. Their names were Pattie, Lydia, Charles, James, and Simon. Raymond Cay, Jr., the son of Silvia's former enslaver, also testified that she "had lots of children and grandchildren around."
68 Francis Brown. SCC No. 20638; Silvy Baker. SCC No. 21451.
69 Joseph James, SCC No. 20664.
70 Clarinda Porter, SCC No. 18544.
71 Sandy Austin, SCC No. 20636.
72 Pulaski Baker, SCC No. 21446.
73 Rachel Norman, SCC No. 21416.
74 Patsey Campbell, SCC No. 21475.
75 Joseph Bacon, SCC No. 21447.
76 Susan and Scipio Bennett, SCC No. 21473.
77 Silvy Baker, SCC No. 21451.
78 Linda and Caesar Jones, SCC No. 20662.
79 Silvy Baker, SCC No. 21451.
80 The Tax Digest Records of Liberty County, 1871 and 1880, Georgia Archives. Morrow, Georgia.
81 This information is from a current work in progress in which I analyze Black women's accumulation of property from the 1830s until the early 1900s. The project is tentatively titled, *Reconstructing Freedom: Black Women and Property Ownership in the Rural South.*
82 Susan Bennett. SCC No. 21473.
83 Jane Holmes, SCC No. 20656.
84 Francis Brown stated this information while testifying in the SCC case of Linda and Caesar Jones. Linda and Caesar Jones, SCC No. 20662. Francis Brown's land had once belonged to Charles Colcock Jones. In 1872, after several years of receiving low yields from sharecroppers and unsuccessfully trying to sell their Arcadia estate to White buyers, the Jones family divided their 2,000-acre estate into small plots and began to sell them to freedpeople. "For the Love of Place: Paternalism and Patronage in the Georgia Lowcountry, 1865–1898," *Journal of Southern History* 70, no. 4 (Nov. 2004), 838–39 and 834.
85 Susan and Scipio Bennett valued their property at $215 and Susan was awarded $120. Jane valued her goods at $492.50 and was awarded $120. Francis Brown valued her goods at $145 and was later awarded $77. Susan Bennett, SCC No. 21473; Jane Holmes. SCC No. 20656; Francis Brown, SCC No. 20638.

4 BLACK WOMEN, WAR, AND FREEDOM IN SOUTHERN LOUISIANA AND LOW COUNTRY GEORGIA

Thank you to the *Journal of African American History* for allowing the republication of this article, which appeared as "Self-Emancipating Women, Civil War, and the Union Army in Southern Louisiana and LowCountry Georgia," in the Winter–Spring 2016 issue.

1 Testimony of Corporal Octave Johnson before the American Freedmen's Inquiry Commission, (February 1864), filed with O-328 1863, Letters Received, ser. 12, Record Group 94, Records of the Adjutant General's Office, 1780s–1917, [K-219] cited in Ira Berlin ed., *Freedom: A Documentary History of Emancipation 1861–1867*, series 1, vol. 1: *The Destruction of Slavery* (New York, 1985), 217.

2 Ibid.

3 "Louis Manigault Civil War Diary," Dec. 3, 1863; Manigault Family Papers, Reel 2; "List of Negroes at Gowrie," "Hermitage," "East Hermitage," Manigault Family Papers (#484), Southern Historical Collection (SHC), The Wilson Library, University of North Carolina, Chapel Hill; hereinafter cited as SHC.

4 "List of Negroes at Gowrie," Manigault Family Papers (#484), SHC.

5 Robert E. Birt, ed., *The Quest for Community and Identity: Critical Essays in Africana Social Philosophy* (New York, 2002), 2, 4.

6 Leslie A. Schwalm, *'A Hard Fight for We': Women's Transition from Slavery to Freedom in South Carolina* (Urbana, 1997); Ella Forbes, *African American Women during the Civil War* (New York, 1998); Stephanie M. H. Camp, *Closer to Freedom: Enslaved Women and Everyday Resistance in the Plantation South* (Chapel Hill, 2004); Hannah Rosen, *Terror in the Heart of Freedom: Citizenship, Sexual Violence, and the Meaning of Race in the Postemancipation South* (Chapel Hill, 2008); and Thavolia Glymn, *The Women's Fight: The Civil War's Battles for Home, Freedom, and Nation* (Chapel Hill, 2020).

7 Schwalm, *'A Hard Fight for We,'* 75.

8 Forbes, *African American Women*, 8.

9 John Hope Franklin and Loren Schweninger, *Runaway Slaves: Rebels on the Plantation* (New York, 1999).

10 David Williams, *I Freed Myself: African American Self-Emancipation during the Civil War Era* (New York, 2014), 17.

11 Ibid., 9.

12 Ibid.

13 Evelyn Nakano Glenn, *Unequal Freedom: How Race and Gender Shaped American Citizenship and Labor* (Cambridge, MA, 2002), 6–8.

14 Mary Hawkesworth, *Political Worlds of Women: Activism, Advocacy, and Governance in the Twenty-first Century* (New Brunswick, NJ, 2012), 138; see also Williams, *I Freed Myself*.

15 Ira Berlin et al., eds., *Freedom: A Documentary History of Emancipation 1861–1867*, series 1, vol. I: *The Destruction of Slavery* (New York, 1985), 190. Slaves produced rice in Louisiana prior to the Civil War for domestic purposes; however, surpluses were marketed. Plaquemines Parish produced 985,000 pounds of rice and St. Charles 800,000. Thirteen parishes reported producing some rice in 1839. W. N. Ginn, "A New History of Rice Industry in America," Louisiana Sugar and Rice Trade Collection, 1884–1936, Mss. 784, LSU Libraries, Baton Rouge, Louisiana.

16 Karen B. Bell, "'The Ogeechee Troubles': Federal Land Restoration and the 'Lived Realities' of Temporary Proprietors, 1865–1868," *Georgia Historical Quarterly* (Fall 2001), 381.

17 *U.S. Statutes at Large, Treaties, and Proclamations*, vol. 12 (Boston, 1863), 319.

18 *Official Records of Union and Confederate Navies* (hereafter cited as *ORUCN*), series I vol. 6, 242–43; James McPherson, *Ordeal by Fire: The Civil War and Reconstruction*, (New York, 2001), 195–99; Clarence Mohr, *On the Frontline of Freedom: Masters and Slaves in Civil War Georgia* (Athens, GA, 1986); Thomas Wentworth Higginson, *Army Life in a Black Regiment* (New York, 2002), 40–61. See also Benjamin Quarles, *The Negro in the Civil War* (Boston, 1953).

19 US Census Bureau, Chatham, Liberty, McIntosh, Camden, Georgia, 1860.

20 *ORUCN*, series I, vol. 13, pp. 21, 159.

21 James McPherson, *Ordeal by Fire* (New York, 2009), 253–54.

22 Ibid., 253–55; Works Project Administration, *Louisiana: Past and Present* (New York, 1971), 47.

23 Ibid.

24 Letter to Mrs. Henrietta Matthews, Bayou Sara, December 5, 1864; "List of Slaves Killed in Red River Uprising," Charles L. Matthews Family Papers, Mss. 910; Louisiana and Lower Mississippi Valley Collections; Special Collections, Louisiana State University (LSU), LSU Libraries, Baton Rouge, LA. The Matthews family owned Greenwood Plantation, Georgia Plantation, Coco Bend, and Chaseland Plantations located on the Red River in Rapides Parish. See also Auguste Le Blanc Family Papers, Mss. 214; Special Collections, LSU Libraries. See C. Peter Ripley, *Slaves and Freedmen in Civil War Louisiana* (Baton Rouge, 1973), 7.

25 *Opelousas Courier*, 23 January 1864, p. 1; John D. Winters, *The Civil War in Louisiana*, (Baton Rouge, 1963), 332–35. See *Louisiana Democrat*, 15 November 1865, p. 3 for discussion of the economic significance of the Red River for Confederate forces.

26 Winters, *The Civil War in Louisiana*, 333. See Junius P. Rodriguez, "'We'll Hang Jeff Davis on the Sour Apple Tree': Civil War Era Slave Resistance in Louisiana," *Gulf Coast Historical Review* 10, no. 2 (Spring 1995), 7–23, for a discussion of other areas in Louisiana where uprisings occurred.

27 *U.S. Statutes at Large*, vol. 12, 589–600.

28 James Schmidt, *Free to Work: Labor Law, Emancipation and Reconstruction, 1815–1880* (Athens, GA, 1999), 95; George Bentley, *A History of the Freedmen's Bureau* (New York, 1970), 14; *United States Statutes at Large, Volume XII*, 590–92, 599. See also Theda Skocpol, *Protecting Soldiers and Mothers: The Political Origins of Social Policy in the U.S.* (Cambridge, MA, 1992).

29 *U.S. Statutes at Large*, vol. 12, 599; Ira Berlin, Joseph P. Reidy, and Leslie Rowland, *Freedom's Soldiers: The Black Military Experience in the Civil War* (New York, 1988), 21, note 39.

30 *U.S. Statutes at Large*, vol. 13 (Washington, DC), 571; Ira Berlin et al., *Freedom's Soldiers*, 21, note 39.

31 Captain George G. Davis to Brig. Gen. James Bowen, August 21, 1863, Letter Received, ser. 1845, Provost Marshal, Department of the Gulf, Record Group 393, Pt. 1 [C-768]; Provost Marshal of St. Bernard Parish to the Provost General of the Dept. of the Gulf, St. Bernard [Parish, La.],

August 21, 1863, in Ira Berlin et. al., *Freedom: A Documentary History of Emancipation, 1861–1867*, series 2: *The Black Military Experience*, 157. See also James G. Hollandsworth, *The Louisiana Native Guards: The Black Military Experience during the Civil War* (Baton Rouge, 1998); Mary Frances Berry, "Negro Troops in Blue and Gray: The Louisiana Native Guards, 1861–1863," *Louisiana History* 8, no. 4 (Autumn 1967), 165–90.

32 Affidavit of Mary Wilson, 17 June 1865, filed with H-8 1865, Registered Letters Received, ser. 3379, TN Asst. Comr., Record Group 105 Bureau of Refugees, Freedmen and Abandoned Lands, [A-6148] cited in Ira Berlin et al., *Freedom: A Documentary History of Emancipation, 1861–1867*, series 1, *vol. I: The Destruction of Slavery* (New York, 1986), 623–24.

33 John W. Blassingame, *Black New Orleans, 1860–1880* (Chicago, 1973), 53; Howard A. White, *The Freedmen's Bureau in Louisiana* (Baton Rouge, 1970), 101–102; Bentley, *A History of the Freedmen's Bureau*, 23–24.

34 Registers and Payrolls of Freedmen Employed on Plantations, Terre-Bonne-West Feliciana, Louisiana, Records of the Field Offices of the State of Louisiana, M1905, Roll 39, BRFAL, RG 105, NAB.

35 Julie Saville, *The Work of Reconstruction: From Slave Labor to Wage Labor in South Carolina, 1860–1870* (New York, 1996), 68.

36 Amy Dru Stanley, *From Bondage to Contract: Wage Labor, Marriage, and the Market in the Age of Slave Emancipation* (Cambridge, MA, 1998), 29.

37 Registers and Payrolls of Freedmen Employed on Plantations, Terre Bonne, Louisiana, M1905, Roll 39, BRFAL, RG 105, NAB; Schmidt, *Free to Work*, 2.

38 Schmidt, *Free to Work*, 5. See also William E. Nelson, *The Roots of American Bureaucracy, 1830–1900* (Cambridge, MA, 1982), 1–8. Nelson argues that the origins of the modern state lie in the "tension between the idea of majority self-rule and the concern for protecting minority and individual rights." The contract system developed by the Freedmen's Bureau sought to strike a balance between these two ideas, but ultimately protecting the interests of the majority prevailed.

39 US Census Bureau, New Orleans, Louisiana, 1860. The slave population in the state of Louisiana in 1860 consisted of 326,726 men and women compared with a total White population of 351,556. The free colored population consisted of 18,547.

40 Record of Complaints, November 19, 1864, New Orleans, Records of the Field Offices of the State of Louisiana, M1905, Vol. 1, Roll 7, BRFAL, RG 105, NAB.

41 Record of Complaints, November 19, 1864, New Orleans, Records of the Field Offices of the State of Louisiana, M1905, Vol. 1, Roll 7, BRFAL, RG 105, NAB.

42 Registers and Payrolls of Freedmen Employed on Plantations, Terre-Bonne-West Feliciana, Louisiana, 1864–68, M1905, Roll 39, BRFAL, RG 105, NAB.

43 Frankel, *Freedom's Women*, 2; see also Mary J. Farmer, "'Because They Are Women': Gender and the Virginia Freedmen's Bureau's 'War on Dependency'," in *The Freedmen's Bureau and Reconstruction: Reconsiderations*,

ed. Paul A. Cimbala and Randall M. Miller (New York, 1999), which argues that government officials waged a "war on dependency."

44 Jacqueline Jones, *Labor of Sorrow: Black Women, Work, and the Family, from Slavery to the Present* (New York, 1985), ch. 2.

45 Farmer, 'Because They Are Women,' 163.

46 Register of Proceedings in the Freedmen's Court, June 20, 1865, Sarah Moore, Mary DeLisle, Lorina Jones, Cecilia Jones, Records of the Field Offices of the State of Louisiana, M1905, Vol. 1, Roll 7, BRFAL, RG 105, NAB. For the cultural value of resistance forged in slave communities, see V. P. Franklin, *Black Self-Determination: A Cultural History of African American Resistance* (Brooklyn, NY, 1992), 69–102.

47 Record of Complaints, August 1, 1865, New Orleans, Elizabeth White, Amelie Candole, Caroline Starks, Charlotte Ann Hall, Henrietta Henderson, Records of the Field Offices of the State of Louisiana, M1905, Vol. 1, Roll 7, BRFAL, RG 105, NAB; Register of Proceedings in the Freedmen's Court, 20 June 1865, New Orleans, Sarah Moore, Mary DeLisle, Lorina Jones, Cecilia Jones, Records of the Field Offices of the State of Louisiana, M1905, Vol. 1, Roll 7, BRFAL, RG 105, NAB. See Farmer, "'Because They Are Women'," 163; Darlene Clark Hine, *Hine Sight: Black Women and the Reconstruction of American History* (Indianapolis, 1994), 3–4. For a discussion of the experiences of women in Civil War Mississippi, see Nora Lee Frankel, *Freedom's Women: Black Women and Families in Civil War Era Mississippi* (Bloomington, 1999).

48 Record of Complaints, August 1, 1865, New Orleans, Elizabeth White, Amelie Candole, Caroline Starks, Charlotte Ann Hall, Henrietta Henderson, Records of the Field Offices of the State of Louisiana, M1905, Vol. 1, Roll 7, BRFAL, RG 105, NAB.

49 Record of Complaints, August 1, 1865, New Orleans, Amelie Candole, Records of the Field Offices of the State of Louisiana, M1905, Vol. 1, Roll 7, BRFAL, RG 105, NAB.

50 Record of Complaints, November 18, 1864, New Orleans, Edith Williams, Records of the Field Offices of the State of Louisiana, M1905, Vol. 1, Roll 7, BRFAL, RG 105, NAB.

51 Record of Complaints, December 12, 1864, New Orleans, Lucy Coleman, Records of the Field Offices of the State of Louisiana, M1905, Vol. 1, Roll 7, BRFAL, RG 105, NAB. See also Record of Complaints, November 18, 1864, New Orleans, Matilda James who worked for two and a half weeks for .30 cents per day for Mrs. Burch without recompense.

52 Record of Complaints, February 8, 1865, New Orleans, Esther, Records of the Field Offices of the State of Louisiana, M1905, Vol. 1, Roll 7, BRFAL, RG 105, NAB.

53 Letters Sent, St. Mary's (Agent); National Archives Microfilm Publication M1903, roll 52; Records of the Field Offices for the State of Georgia, BRFAL, RG 105, NAB.

54 Schmidt, *Free to Work*, 94–95. Schmidt argues that emancipation was a "legal event that destroyed a legal apparatus that had been instituted and perpetuated in the South."

55 See David R. Roediger, *The Wages of Whiteness: Race and the Making of the American Working Class* (New York, 1991), 85. According to Roediger, northern workers became angry when called white slaves by southerners. The term white slavery was used analogously to compare the plight of white workers who were not paid the value of their labor: Winthrop D. Jordan, *The White Man's Burden: Historical Origins of Racism in the United States* (New York, 1974); Gerald Horne, *The Deepest South: The United States, Brazil, and the African Slave Trade,* (New York, 2007) chs. 3 and 8; Paul Cimbala, *Under the Guardianship of the Nation: The Freedmen's Bureau and the Reconstruction of Georgia, 1865–1870* (Athens, GA, 1997) 7.

56 Camp, *Closer to Freedom,* 119; Rev. C.C. Jones to Lt. Charles C. Jones, Jr., July 10, 1862, July 21, 1862, in *The Children of Pride: A True Story of Georgia and the Civil War,* ed. Robert Myers (New Haven, 1972). 929, 935; Higginson, *Army Life,* 162–63; Malcolm Bell, *Major Butler's Legacy: Five Generations of a Slaveholding Family* (Athens, GA, 1986), 360.

57 Higginson, *Army Life,* 163; Ella Forbes, *African American Women during the Civil War* (New York, 1998), 46.

58 *U.S. Statutes at Large,* vol. 12, 589–600.

59 *Official Records of the War of the Rebellion,* Series I, Vol. XLIV (Washington, DC, 1893), 159, 787.

60 Berlin et. al., *Freedom: A Documentary History of Emancipation,* series 1, vol. I, 123.

61 Higginson, *Army Life,* 162; Lt. Charles C. Jones, Jr. to Rev. C. C. Jones, July 19, 1862, in *The Children of Pride,* ed. Myers, 934; Forbes, *African American Women during the Civil War,* 46.

62 Ibid.

63 George L. Hendricks, "Union Army Occupation of the Southern Seaboard, 1861–1865," (PhD diss., Columbia University, 1954, 80–89; Dudley T. Cornish, *The Sable Arm: Negro Troops in the Union Army, 1861–1865* (New York, 1966), 138.

64 Ibid.

65 Ibid. See also Phillis M. Cousins, "A History of the 33rd United States Colored Troops," MA thesis, Howard University, 1961, 35–51, 61–64. The activities of Colonel James Montgomery's 2nd South Carolina Volunteers (34th United States Colored Troops) are discussed in Willie Lee Rose, *Rehearsal for Reconstruction: The Port Royal Experiment* (Oxford, 1976), 244–53; Cornish, *Sable Arm,* 138–42, 148–50, 244.

66 Bell, *Major Butler's Legacy,* 365.

67 *Savannah Daily Morning News,* June 16, 1863.

68 ORUCN, series I, vol. 13, pp. 21, 159; Rev. C. C. Jones to Lt. Charles C. Jones, Jr., 14 March 1862, in *The Children of Pride,* ed. Myers, 858.

69 See for instance Ira Berlin et al., *Freedom: A Documentary History of Emancipation, 1861–1867, series 2: The Black Military Experience* (New York, 1982), 142.

70 Hawkesworth, *Political Worlds of Women,* 9.

71 Clarence Mohr, "Before Sherman: Georgia Blacks and the Union War Effort, 1861–1864," *Journal of Southern History* 45 (August 1979), 331–52.

72 Ibid. Elinor Barnes and James A. Barnes, eds., *Naval Surgeon: Blockading the South, 1862–1866: The Diary of Samuel Pellman Boyer* (Bloomington, 1963), 247, 254–55; cited hereinafter as Barnes and Barnes, eds., *Boyer Diary*.

73 Clarence Mohr, "Before Sherman," 331–52; "Commander of the U.S.S. Mohican to the Commander of the South Atlantic Squadron," March 30, 1862, in Berlin et al., *Freedom*, series1, vol. I, 118–19.

74 Ibid.

75 Commander of the U.S.S. Mohican to the Commander of the South Atlantic Squadron, March 30, 1862, in Berlin et. al., *Freedom*, series 1, vol. I, 118–19; Susie King Taylor, *A Black Woman's Civil War Memoirs: Reminiscences of My Life in Camp with the 33rd U.S. Colored Troops, Late 1st South Carolina Volunteers*, ed. Patricia Romero (New York, 1988). See also John Blassingame, "The Union Army As an Educational Institution for Negroes, 1862–1865," *Journal of Negro Education* 34 (Summer 1965), 152–59.

76 Cimbala, *Under the Guardianship of the Nation*, 109, 118; John W. Alvord, *Tenth Semi-Annual Report on Schools for Freedmen, July 1, 1869* (Washington, DC, 1869), 22. See also Jacqueline Jones, *Soldiers of Light and Love: Northern Teachers and Georgia Blacks, 1865–1873* (Athens, GA, 2004), 63; Heather A. Williams, *Self-taught: African American Education in Slavery and Freedom* (Chapel Hill, NC, 2005), 100–101.

77 Ripley, *Slaves and Freedmen*, 136–38, 144; Ronald E. Butchart, *Schooling the Freedpeople: Teaching, Learning, and the Struggle for Black Freedom, 1861–1876* (Chapel Hill, 2010), 45–46.

78 "Rev. C.C. Jones to Lt. Charles C. Jones, Jr.," July 21, 1862 in *The Children of Pride*, ed. Myers, 935; "Commander of the U.S.S. Dale to the Commander of the South Atlantic Squadron," June 13, 1862, in Berlin et. al. *Freedom*, series 1, vol. I, 125–26; Saville, *The Work of Reconstruction*, 39.

79 "Commander of a Confederate Cavalry Battalion to the Headquarters of the 3rd Military District of the Confederate Department of South Carolina, Georgia, and Florida," June 14, 1862, in Berlin et al., eds., *Freedom*, series 1, vol. I, 128.

80 "List of Negroes at Gowrie," "East Hermitage," April 21, 1861, Manigault Family Papers (#484), SHC.

81 "Louis Maniguilt Civil War Diary," September 3, 1863, Manigault Family Papers, Reel 2, SHC; "List of Negroes at Gowrie," "Hermitage," April 22, 1860, Manigault Family Papers (#484), SHC; *New York Daily Tribune*, August 10, 1854, p. 6. For a discussion of illnesses among African Americans during the Civil War and Reconstruction see Jim Downs, *Sick from Freedom: African American Illness and Suffering during the Civil War* (New York, 2012). From June 1, 1865 to November 1, 1865, 13 percent of the 45,848 freedmen and women treated by the Freedmen's Bureau died of illnesses. See Paul Skeels Peirce, *The Freedmen's Bureau: A Chapter in the History of Reconstruction* (New York, 1971), 91.

82 James M. Clifton, ed., *Life and Labor on Argyle Island: Letters and Documents of a Savannah River Rice Plantation, 1833–1867* (Savannah, GA, 1978), 184.

83 "Louis Manigault Civil War Diary," September 3, 1863, Manigault Family Papers, Reel 2, SHC; Higginson, *Army Life*, 74; John Duffy, "The Impact of Malaria on the South," in *Disease and Distinctiveness in the American South*, ed. Todd L. Savitt and James Harvey Young (Knoxville, 1988), 40–41.

84 William Tecumseh Sherman, *Memoirs of General William T. Sherman*, vol. II (New York, 1990), 1104–1105.

85 *The War of the Rebellion: A Compilation of the Official Records of the Union and Confederate Armies* (Washington, DC, 1880–1902) (hereinafter cited as *ORUCA*), series I, vol. 44, pp. 75, 159, 410.

86 Bell, *Major Butler's Legacy*, 380.

87 Sherman, *Memoirs*, vol. II, 652–53.

88 Ibid., 651; Benjamin Quarles, *The Negro in the Civil War*, (Boston, 1969), 317; "Report of Major General Slocum," January 9, 1865, *ORUCA*, series I, vol. 44, pp. 159, 836. Statistics of slaves set free in northern and central Georgia by the Army of Tennessee also reference the figure 3,000 from October 4 to December 31, 1864; see ibid., 75.

89 "Report of Major General Slocum," January 9, 1865, ibid., 159.

90 Jacob D. Cox, *March to the Sea* (New York, 1882), 37–38.

91 Sherman, *Memoirs*, vol. II, 1106.

92 "Report to General Joseph Wheeler, CSA," *ORUCA*, series I, vol. 44, p. 410; W. C. Dodson, ed., *Campaigns of Wheeler and His Calvary*, (Atlanta, 1899), 301; Bell, *Major Butler's Legacy*, 383.

93 Bell, *Major Butler's Legacy*, 383.

94 Works Progress Administration, *Annals of Savannah 1850–1937: A Digest and Index of the Newspaper Record of Events and Opinions in Eighty-seven Volumes*, vol. XVI (Savannah, GA, 1937), 5; "The March to the Sea," *Western Reserve Chronicle*, December 28, 1864; "From Rebel Papers," *Cleveland Morning Leader*, December 5, 1864; "From Sherman," *Raftsman Journal*, January 21,. 1865; "Review of Sherman's Grand Campaign," *The Caledonian*, December 30, 1864.

95 Sherman, *Memoirs*, vol. II, 1105–1106; List of Possessory Titles Issued to Freedpeople, Register of Land Titles Issued to Freedpeople; Records of A. P. Ketchum, Savannah, Ga., BRFAL, RG 105, NAB.

96 US Census Bureau, Chatham County, Seventh Militia District, 1860.

97 *Savannah Daily Herald*, December 6, 1865; Bell, "The Ogeechee Troubles," 376–97.

98 Kidada E. Williams, *They Left Great Marks on Me: African American Testimonies of Racial Violence from Emancipation to World War I* (New York, 2012), ch. 1.

99 Chatham County Tax Digest, 1876, Chatham County Courthouse, Savannah, Ga.; Loren Schweninger, *Black Property Owners in the South, 1790–1915* (Urbana, 1992), 149. Schweninger purports that the vast majority of the Lower South's landowners were ex-slaves. See also John Simpson, "A Reflection of Black Enterprise in the Old South," *Lincoln Review* 10 (Spring 1990), 35–38, which examines "virtually free slaves" in Savannah who participated in the free market system.

5 RAPE AND MUTINY AT FORT JACKSON

"Rape and Mutiny at Fort Jackson: Black Laundresses Testify in Civil War Louisiana," appeared in *Labor* 19, no. 1 (2022), 11–31. The author thanks Duke University Press for allowing republication.

1 Trial of Corporal William W. Chinock, 26 Massachusetts Regiment, R.G. 153, Records of the Judge Advocate General's Office (US Army), National Archives and Records Administration, Washington, DC. Hereafter, cases from these records will be cited as R.G. 153, NARA.

2 Adrienne Davis, "Don't Let Nobody Bother Yo' Principle," in *Sister Circle: Black Women and Work* (New Brunswick, 2002), 107.

3 Homer Sprague, *History of the 13th Infantry Regiment of Connecticut Volunteers, during the Great Rebellion* (Hartford, CT, 1867), 51.

4 Ibid., 52–53.

5 Ibid., 53.

6 Ibid.

7 John Gaines, "Westward Expansion: Laundresses," in *Encyclopedia of Prostitution and Sex Work*, vol. II, ed. Melissa Hope Ditmore (Santa Barbara, 2006), 537–39; Virginia Mescher, "Tubs and Suds: Civil War Laundresses in the Field, Camp and Hospital," *Camp Chase Gazette* (August–September 2003), 1–15; John R. Sibbald, "Camp Followers All: Army Women of the West," *American West* 3 (Spring 1966), 56–67; Patricia Y. Stallard, *Glittering Misery: Dependents of the Indian Fighting Army* (New York, 1978); Miller J. Stewart, "Army Laundresses: Ladies of the 'Soap Suds Row'," *Nebraska History* 61, no. 4 (1980), 424; Kellie Wilson Buford, "Troublesome Hellions and Belligerent Viragoes: Enlisted Wives, Laundresses and the Politics of Gender on Nineteenth Century Army Posts," *Military History of the West* 41 (2011), 13–26; C. A. Wood, "Army Laundresses and Civilization on the Western Frontier," *Journal of the West* 41, no. 3 (June 2002), 26–34; Thavolia Glymph, "Noncombant Military Labor in the Civil War," *OAH Magazine of History* 26, no. 2 (March 2012), 25–29; Thavolia Glymph, "I'm a Radical Black Girl," *Journal of the Civil War Era* 8, no. 3 (2018), 359–87; Lisa Y. King, "In Search of Women of African Descent Who Served in the Civil War Union Navy," *Journal of Negro History* 83, no. 4 (1998), 302–309; Susan Barber and Charles F. Ritter, "Dangerous Liaisons: Working Women and Sexual Justice in the American Civil War"; Jane E. Schultz, "Race, Gender, and Bureaucracy: Civil War Army Nurses and the Pension Bureau," *Journal of Women's History* 6, No. 2 (Summer 1994), 45–69; Jane E. Schultz, *Women at the Front: Hospital Workers in Civil War America* (Chapel Hill, 2004).

8 John F. Callan, *Military Laws of the United States* (Philadelphia, 1863).

9 US War Department, *General Regulations for the Army* (Washington, DC, 1841), 48.

10 Ibid., 94.

11 Ibid., 37.

12 Schultz, "Race, Gender, and Bureaucracy," 45–69; Stewart, "Army Laundresses," 424; and US War Department, *Revised United States Army*

Regulations of 1861, with an Appendix Containing the Changes and Laws Affecting Army Regulations and Articles of War to June 25, 1863 (Washington, DC, 1863).

13 Unfiled Papers and Slips Belonging in Confederate Compiled Service Records, in database with images Fold3 (www.fold3.com//title/656/civil-war-service-records-cmsr-confederate-miscellaneous).

14 Ibid.

15 Ibid.

16 For discussions of Black women in contraband camps, see Thavolia Glymph, *The Women's Fight: The Civil War's Battles for Home, Freedom, and Nation* (Chapel Hill, 2020); Jim Downs, *Sick from Freedom: African-American Illness and Suffering during the Civil War and Reconstruction* (Oxford, 2012); Leslie Schwalm, *'A Hard Fight for We': Women's Transition from Slavery to Freedom in South Carolina* (Urbana, 1997); Chandra Manning, *Troubled Refuge: Struggling for Freedom in the Civil War* (New York, 2016); and Amy Murrell Taylor, *Embattled Freedom: Journeys through the Civil War's Slave Refugee Camps* (Chapel Hill, 2018).

17 Sprague, *History of the 13th Infantry Regiment of Connecticut Volunteers*, 60.

18 *New London Daily Chronicle*, June 17, 1862; *Minnesota Pioneer*, June 27, 1862; and *New York Times*, July 3, 1862.

19 Sprague, *History of the 13th Infantry Regiment of Connecticut Volunteers*, 341–47.

20 Special Orders, No. 44 New Orleans, May 26, 1862, in *The War of the Rebellion: A Compilation of the Official Records of the Union and the Confederate Army* (hereafter cited as *OR*), Series 1, Vol. 15 (Washington, DC, 1880–1902), 444; Sprague, *History of the 13th Infantry Regiment of Connecticut Volunteers*, 60; and *New York Times*, July 3, 1862.

21 Sprague, *History of the 13th Infantry Regiment of Connecticut Volunteers*, 345.

22 US War Department, *Revised United States Army Regulations of 1861*, 24, 12, 160, 162, and 246.

23 *New York Times*, July 3, 1862.

24 Sprague, *History of the 13th Infantry Regiment of Connecticut Volunteers*, 341.

25 Ibid., 342.

26 Ibid.

27 Ibid.

28 Ibid.

29 Sprague, *History of the 13th Infantry Regiment of Connecticut Volunteers*, 345–46.

30 James Parton, *General Butler in New Orleans* (Boston, 1864), 557.

31 *Daily Delta*, July 4, July 31, and August 5, 1862; and *Boston Traveler*, July 26, 1862.

32 *Louisville Daily Journal*, July 11, 1862.

33 *New York Times*, July 3, 1862.

34 Special Order, No. 99, June 14, 1862 in *P & O*, vol. 1, 591–92; *New York Times*, June 23, 1862; and *National Anti-Slavery Standard*, June 28, 1862.

35 Berlin et al., *Freedom: A Documentary History of Emancipation Freedom*, series 1 vol. III, 445.

36 William Dwight to Elizabeth Dwight, Fort Jackson December 15, 1863, Dwight Family Papers in Massachusetts Historical Society (henceforth cited as MHS).
37 *Tri-weekly Mercury*, December 29, 1863.
38 William Dwight to Elizabeth Dwight, Fort Jackson, December 15, 1863, MHS.
39 *OR*, Ser. 1 Vol. XXVI, Pt. I, 457–59.
40 *OR*, Ser. 1 Vol. XXVI, Pt. I, 473.
41 This took place August 7 in Baton Rouge – they would repeat this punishment at Fort St. Philip on August 25. See *OR*, Ser. 1 Vol. XXVI, Pt. I, 468 and 471.
42 *OR*, Ser. 1 Vol. XXVI, Pt. I, 473.
43 *OR*, Ser. 1 Vol. XXVI, Pt. I, 471.
44 John Fabian Witt, *Lincoln's Code: The Laws of War in American History* (New York, 2013).
45 *OR*, Ser. 1 Vol. XXVI, Pt. I, 456; Foner, *The Fiery Trail*, 251; and *Washington Daily Morning Chronicle*, April 20, 1863.
46 *OR*, Ser. 1 Vol. XXVI, Pt. I, 460.
47 William Dwight to Mother, Fort Jackson, December 15, 1863, MHS.
48 *OR*, Ser. 1 Vol. XXVI, Pt. I, 476–77.
49 Ibid., 476–79.
50 Ibid., 457, 476–79.
51 For further discussion of the mutiny see Fred Harvey Harrington, "The Fort Jackson Mutiny," *Journal of Negro History* 27, no. 4 (1942), 420–31; William A. Dobak, *Freedom by the Sword: The U.S. Colored Troops, 1862–1867* (New York, 2013), 96–97 and 112–13; Keith P. Wilson, *Campfires of Freedom: The Camp Life of Black Soldiers during the Civil War* (Kent, OH, 2002), 204–205; William F. Messner, *Freedom and the Ideology of Free Labor: Louisiana 1862–1865* (Southwest Louisiana, 1978), 157–63; and C. Peter Ripley, *Slaves and Freedmen in Civil War Louisiana* (Baton Rouge, 1973), 115–16.
52 William Dwight, Jr. to Chief of Staff General Charles P. Stone, January 27, 1864, MHS. All quotations that follow are from this same document, unless otherwise noted.
53 William Dwight to Charles P. Stone, January 31, 1864, MHS.
54 Ibid.
55 Ibid.
56 Ibid.
57 Ibid.
58 Ibid.
59 C. P. Stone to William Dwight, January 31, 1864, RG 393, Part 1, Vol. 6 Entry 1738, National Archives.
60 Report of Military Commission, February 3, 1864, RG 153 NN 1332, National Archives.
61 Military Commission Convened at Fort Jackson, February 1, 1864, NN1332, RG 153 National Archives.
62 Report of Military Commission.
63 Ibid.
64 Ibid.
65 Military Commission Convened at Fort Jackson.

66 Ibid.
67 Ibid.
68 Ibid.
69 Ibid.
70 Ibid.
71 *The Weekly Times-Democrat*, March 26, 1864.
72 William Dwight to Chief of Staff Charles P. Stone, February 4, 1864, MHS.
73 Ibid.
74 Ibid.
75 *The Weekly Times-Democrat*, March 26, 1864.
76 Trials of G. E. Wentworth, C. A. Goff, W. H. Knapp, H. F. Blakeslee, and W. H. O'Dell, 4th Corps d'Afrique, NN1332 and LL2744, R. G. 153, NARA.

6 "I TOLD HIM TO LET ME ALONE, THAT HE HURT ME"

"'I Told Him to Let Me Alone, that He Hurt Me': Black Women and Girls and the Battle over Labor and Sexual Consent in Union-Occupied Territory," appeared in *Labor* 19, no. 1 (2022), 32–51. The author thanks Duke University Press for allowing republication.

1 Susan's testimony names George "Larley" as the owner of the plantation where she lived. This is likely a misspelling. The 1860 US Federal Census – Slave Schedule identifies a person called George Lyiely (more commonly spelled as "Lyerly" or "Lyrely") who owned a plantation in Salisbury, Rowan County, NC. See Records of the Judge Advocate General's Office (Army), Entry 15, Court Martial Case File, file MM2407, Record Group 153, National Archives and Records Administration (hereafter cited as RG 153, NARA); US Federal Census, George Lyrely, 1860, Salisbury, Rowan, NC, p. 529, Family History Library Film 803912; George Lyrely, 1870; Providence, Rowan, NC, Roll M593_1158, p. 548A.

2 In the wake of emancipation, formerly enslaved families confronted new systems of oppression, such as forced apprenticeships, that undermined parental authority. See Karin L. Zipf, *Labor of Innocents: Forced Apprenticeship in North Carolina, 1715–1919* (Baton Rouge, 2005).

3 MM2407, NARA, RG 153.

4 Ibid.

5 Ibid.

6 Ibid.

7 Early American historian Sharon Block makes the excellent point that "social and economic power relations underwrote sexual power, not only in the ability to evade legal punishment but also through the very commission of sexual coercion…. In other words, men could commit rape not just as an act of power – they could use their power to define the act." Block, *Rape and Sexual Power in Early America* (Chapel Hill, 2006), 54.

8 MM2407, NARA, RG 153.

9 Ibid.

10 Ibid.

11 Bork was also on trial for "assault with intent to kill" another soldier. In a broader military court culture that repeatedly failed to recognize the humanity of Black female victims, the severity of the initial sentence was most certainly due to this second charge. Ibid.

12 As a concept in Western liberalism, the idea of consent has traditionally affirmed notions of individual proprietary rights as part of the social contract. Feminist critiques of contract theory have underscored how consent has historically served as a mechanism of white patriarchal supremacy. With such rights demarcated within the parameters of the law, consent thus must be understood as an instrument of subjectivity and its attendant freedoms, as well as an aide of imperial conquest, Indigenous dispossession, colonialism, slavery, and capitalist exploitation. See Carole Pateman, *The Sexual Contract* (Cambridge, 1988); Pamela Haag, *Consent: Sexual Rights and the Transformation of American Liberalism* (Ithaca, 1999).

13 Haag, *Consent*, xviii.

14 Ben Fuller Fordney, *George Stoneman: A Biography of the Union General* (Jefferson, NC, 2008), 113.

15 Black feminist scholar Adrienne Davis offers the crucial language of the "sexual economy of American slavery" to describe enslaved women's systemic sexual exploitation within the institution. See Adrienne D. Davis, "'Don't Let Nobody Bother Yo' Principle: The Sexual Economy of American Slavery," in *Black Sexual Economies: Race and Sex in a Culture of Capital*, ed. Davis and the BSE Collective (Champaign, 2019), 15–38.

16 Saidiya V. Hartman, *Scenes of Subjection: Terror, Slavery, and Self-Making in Nineteenth-Century America* (Oxford, 1997), 105.

17 For example, see Thomas D. Morris, *Southern Slavery and the Law, 1619–1860* (Chapel Hill, 1996); Laura F. Edwards, "Status without Rights: African Americans and the Tangled History of Law and Governance in the Nineteenth-Century U.S. South," *American History Review* 112, no. 2 (2007), 365–93," 369; Peter W. Bardaglio, "Rape and the Law in the Old South: 'Calculated to Excite Indignation in Every Heart'," *Journal of Southern History* 60, no. 4 (1994), 749–72. at 760.

18 See Crystal Feimster, "Rape and Justice in the Civil War," *New York Times*, April 26, 2013,Opinionator: https://opinionator.blogs.nytimes.com/2013/04/25/rape-and-justice-in-the-civil-war/.

19 See Estelle B. Freedman, *Redefining Rape: Sexual Violence in the Era of Suffrage and Segregation* (Cambridge, MA, 2013).

20 In a meeting with Secretary of War and Major-General William T. Sherman on January 12, 1865, twenty African American ministers and church officers expressed their understanding of slavery. They stated, "Slavery is, receiving by *irresistible power* the work of another man, and not by his *consent.*" Invoking the language of consent, these figures demonstrated that African Americans held their own meanings of consent. It bears highlighting that the voices in this interview represent an African American male perspective. The systemic intimate abuses that marked Black women's experiences in slavery demonstrated the gendered nature of the institution. As such, meanings of slavery and freedom should be analyzed along gendered lines. See Ira Berlin

et al., eds., *Freedom: A Documentary History of Emancipation 1861–1867*, series 1, vol. III: *The Wartime Genesis of Free Labour in the Lower South*, (New York, 1991); and for an excellent discussion of gendered meanings of liberation, see Shatema Threadcraft, *Intimate Justice: The Black Female Body and the Body Politic* (New York, 2016).

21 Thavolia Glymph, *The Women's Fight: The Civil War's Battles for Home, Freedom, and Nation* (Chapel Hill, 2020)., 247.

22 Thomas P. Lowry estimates around 250 prosecuted cases, whereas an ongoing project by scholars E. Susan Barber and Charles F. Ritter has measured at least 450 cases. Lowry, *Sexual Misbehavior in the Civil War: A Compendium* (Bloomington, 2006); Barber and Ritter, "Physical Abuse … and Rough Handling: Race, Gender and Sexual Justice in the Occupied South," in *Occupied Women: Gender, Military Occupation and the American Civil War*, ed. LeeAnn Whites and Alecia P. Long (Baton Rouge, 2009), 49–64, at 51.

23 Many of these cases involved Black female victims. Acknowledging this point, Barber and Ritter also emphasize that "no woman was safe from wartime sexual predation. The female victims came from all economic and social strata of Southern society." Barber and Ritter, "Physical Abuse … and Rough Handling," 57–58.

24 Feimster, "Rape and Justice in the Civil War."

25 Rebecca Epstein, Jamilia J. Blake, and Thalia González, *Girlhood Interrupted: The Erasure of Black Girls' Childhood* (Washington, DC, 2017), 6.

26 Stephanie McCurry, *Women's War: Fighting and Surviving the American Civil War* (Cambridge, MA, 2019), 7.

27 Thavolia Glymph, "Noncombatant Military Laborers in the Civil War," *OAH Magazine of History* 26, no. 2, special issue (2012), 25–29, at 25.

28 Ibid.

29 Barber and Ritter, "Physical Abuse … and Rough Handling," 56.

30 Francis Lieber, "Instructions for the Government of Armies of the United States in the Field," repared by Francis Lieber, LLD, originally issued as General Order No. 100, Adjutant General's Office, 1863 (Washington, DC, 1898), The Avalon Project, Yale Law School: https://avalon.law.yale.edu/19th_century/lieber.asp.

31 Ibid.

32 Feimster, "Rape and Justice in the Civil War."

33 McCurry, *Women's War*, 7.

34 Drew Gilpin Faust, *Confederate Women and Yankee Men*, a UNC Press Civil War Short, excerpted from *Mothers of Invention: Women of the Slaveholding South in the American Civil War* (Chapel Hill, 2012), 199.

35 Ibid., 200.

36 Susie King Taylor, *Reminiscences of My Life in Camp with the 33rd United States Colored Troops* (Self-published, 1902), 16.

37 "Letter from Charles Francis Adams, Jr., to Henry Adams, Milne Plantation, Port Royal Island, Monday, April 6, 1862," in *A Cycle of Adams Letters, 1861–1865*, vol. I, ed. Worthington Chauncey Ford (Boston, 1920), 128.

38 US Department of the Treasury and Edward Lillie Pierce, *The Negroes at Port Royal: Report of E. L. Pierce, Government Agent, to the Hon. Salmon P. Chase, Secretary of the Treasury* (Boston, 1862), 7.

39 Ibid., 13.

40 Ibid., 13.

41 NN624, NARA, RG 153, as quoted in Lowry, *Sexual Misbehavior in the Civil War*, 138–39.

42 See Barber and Ritter, "Dangerous Liaisons," 8.

43 As quoted in Kellie J. Hedger, "Broken Promises: Rape, Race, and the Union Army," Master's thesis, Central Washington University, 2015, 8; and Lowry, *Sexual Misbehavior in the Civil War*.

44 NN624, NARA, RG 153, as quoted in Lowry, *Sexual Misbehavior in the Civil War*, 138–39.

45 Ibid.

46 Ibid.

47 Ibid.

48 Ibid.

49 Ibid.

50 MM746, NARA, RG 153.

51 Ibid.

52 Kaisha Esty, "A Crusade against the Despoiler of Virtue: Black Women, Sexual Purity and the Gendered Politics of the Negro Problem, 1839–1920," PhD diss., Rutgers University, 2019.

53 MM746, NARA, RG 153.

54 Ibid.

55 Ibid.

56 For more on slavery and discourses of pain see Elizabeth B. Clark, "'The Sacred Rights of the Weak': Pain, Sympathy, and the Culture of Individual Rights in Antebellum America," *Journal of American History* 82, no. 2 (1995): 463–93.

57 Epstein, Blake, and Gonzalez, "Girlhood Interrupted."

58 Ibid.

59 Wilma King, "'Prematurely Knowing of Evil Things': The Sexual Abuse of African American Girls and Young Women in Slavery and Freedom," *Journal of African American History* 99, no. 3 (2014), 173–96, at 174.

60 Lowry, *Sexual Misbehavior in the Civil War*, 131.

61 NN2099, NARA, RG 153.

62 Ibid.

63 Ibid.

64 Ibid.

65 Ibid.

66 OO1056, NARA, RG 153.

67 Ibid.

68 See Amy Dru Stanley, *From Bondage to Contract: Wage Labor, Marriage, and the Market in the Age of Slave Emancipation* (Cambridge, 1998).

69 Lowry, *Sexual Misbehavior in the Civil War*, 126.

70 Ibid.

71 Feimster, "Rape and Justice in the Civil War."
72 MM2774, NARA, RG 153.
73 Ibid.
74 Ibid.
75 Ibid.
76 Ibid.
77 Ibid.
78 Freedman, *Redefining Rape*, 21–22.
79 MM2774, NARA, RG 153, RG 153.
80 Ibid.
81 Between 1863 and 1865, the town of Chattanooga, Tennessee, was under military occupation by the Union Army. Ideally located near the Tennessee River and railroad connections, Chattanooga "retained the appearance of an armed camp" with an "important supply base." This attracted a number of freedpeople who set up residence within the vicinity of the town. Gilbert E. Govan and James W. Livingood, "Chattanooga under Military Occupation, 1863–1865," *Journal of Southern History* 17, no. 1 (1951), 23–47.
82 MM2774, NARA, RG 153. African American soldiers generally received harsher sentences for the same crime committed by White soldiers. Private John Lewis's conviction was the result of three charges. The first charge was "Disobedience of Orders"; the second charge was "Pillaging"; and the third charge was "Assault and Attempt to Commit Rape." Private Lewis was sentenced to one year of hard labor in a military prison, and the loss of pay and allowances for the duration of that time.
83 Ibid.
84 Mrs. Sarah Beuford's status is not explicitly referenced in the court-martial record. It is possible that she was a free or freedperson. I draw the distinction on the basis of her legal status prior to Andrew Johnson's emancipation notice in Tennessee, delivered in October 1864.
85 OO654, NARA, RG 153.
86 MM2774, NARA, RG 153.
87 NN854, NARA, RG 153. See also Lowry, *Story the Soldiers Wouldn't Tell*, 124. Mrs. Farnan's race is not listed in the military record.
88 OO857, NARA, RG 153.
89 Ibid.
90 Ibid.
91 Evelyn Brooks Higginbotham, *Righteous Discontent: The Women's Movement in the Black Baptist Church, 1880–1920*, (Cambridge, MA, 1994).

7 MAKING THEIR PLACE ON THE SOUTH'S RAGGED EDGE

1 Lt. Jefferson Robinson to Miss Mary Burrell, July 5, 1866, Jeff and Mary Burnell Robinson Collection, box 1, folder 19, Butler Center for Arkansas Studies, Central Arkansas Library System, Little Rock; *Arkansas Gazette* (Little Rock), July 6, 1866, p. 3.

2 *Arkansas Gazette* (Little Rock), July 4, 1866, p. 3.

3 The USCTs who spent time in Little Rock included the 54th, 57th, and the 11th, 112th, and 113th, which, never having comprised complete regiments, were merged to form the 113th (New) in April 1865. Steven L. Warren, "Black Union Troops," *Encyclopedia of Arkansas*, Central Arkansas Library System, encyclopedia.net (accessed November 1, 2022).

4 Anthony Kaye, *Joining Places: Slave Neighborhoods in the Old South* (Chapel Hill, 2007); Stephanie M. H. Camp, *Closer to Freedom: Enslaved Women and Everyday Resistance in the Plantation South* (Chapel Hill, 2004); Chandra Manning, *What This Cruel War Was Over: Soldiers, Slavery, and the Civil War* (New York, 2007); Chandra Manning, "Working for Citizenship in Civil War Contraband Camps," *Journal of the Civil War Era* 4 (June 2014), 172–204; Chandra Manning, *Troubled Refuge: Struggling for Freedom in the Civil War* (New York, 2016); Dylan W. Penningroth, *The Claims of Kinfolk: African American Property and Community in the Nineteenth-Century South* (Chapel Hill, 2003); Amy Murrell Taylor, *Embattled Freedom: Journeys through the Civil War's Slave Refugee Camps* (Chapel Hill, 2018); Thavolia Glymph, *The Women's Fight: The Civil War's Battles for Home, Freedom, and Nation* (Chapel Hill, 2020).

5 Gregory P. Downs, *After Appomattox: Military Occupation and the Ends of War* (Cambridge, MA, 2015); Andrew F. Lang, *In the Wake of War: Military Occupation, Emancipation, and Civil War America* (Baton Rouge, 2017).

6 Leslie A. Schalm, *'A Hard Fight For We': Women's Transition from Slavery to Freedom in South Carolina* (Urbana, 1997); Tera W. Hunter, *To 'Joy My Freedom: Southern Black Women's Lives and Labors after the Civil War* (Cambridge, MA, 1997).

7 Brandi Clay Brimmer, *Claiming Union Widowhood: Race, Respectability, and Poverty in the Post-Emancipation South* (Durham, NC, 2020), 1–3. Other relevant works include Michelle A. Krowl, "'Her Just Dues': Civil War Pensions of African American Women in Virginia," in *Negotiating Boundaries of Southern Womanhood: Dealing with the Powers That Be*, ed. Janet L. Coryell et al. (Columbia, 2000), 48–70; Elizabeth Regosin, *Freedom's Promise: Ex-slave Families and Citizenship in the Age of Emancipation* (Charlottesville, 2002).

8 Anthony E. Kaye, "The Second Slavery: Modernity in the Nineteenth-Century South and the Atlantic World," *Journal of Southern History* 75 (August 2009), 627–50; Kelly Houston Jones, *A Weary Land: Slavery on the Ground in Arkansas* (Athens, GA, 2021), 21, 84–88; Kaye, *Joining Places*; Camp, *Closer to Freedom*.

9 George E. Lankford, ed., *Bearing Witness: Memories of Arkansas Slavery, Narratives from the 1930s WPA Collections*, 2nd ed. (Fayetteville, 2006), 344; Paul D. Lack, "An Urban Slave Community: Little Rock, 1831–1862," *Arkansas Historical Quarterly* 41 (Autumn 1982), 263, 258–59.

10 Lankford, *Bearing Witness*, 314–15, 344–45.

11 Thomas A. DeBlack, *With Fire and Sword: Arkansas, 1861–1874* (Fayetteville, 2003), 96; Lankford, *Bearing Witness*, 344.

12 Donald Lewis, "Second Arkansas Infantry," *Encyclopedia of Arkansas*, Central Arkansas Library System, encyclopediaofarkansas.net (accessed October 15, 2022).

13 Glymph, *Women's Fight*, 6.

14 Taylor, *Embattled Freedom*, 118; Brimmer, *Claiming Union Widowhood*, 39; Jane Clay testimony, Washington Campbell testimony, Jane Clay widow app, George Clay, 54th USCT.

15 Jane Clay testimony, Washington Campbell testimony, Jane Clay widow app, George Clay, 54th USCT; Taylor, *Embattled Freedom*, 108.

16 Randy Finley, *From Slavery to Uncertain Freedom: The Freedmen's Bureau in Arkansas, 1865–1869* (Fayetteville, 1996); Jim Downs, *Sick from Freedom: African-American Illness and Suffering during the Civil War and Reconstruction* (Oxford, 2012).

17 Carl H. Moneyhon, "The Little Rock Freedmen's Home Farm, 1863–1865," *Pulaski County Historical Review* 42 (Summer 1994), 32–34. There were also some plantations leased to Unionists in the county, but the number declined near the end of the war – down to twelve by 1865. Carl H. Moneyhon, "From Slave to Free Labor: The Federal Plantation Experiment in Arkansas," *Arkansas Historical Quarterly* 53 (Summer 1994), 144, 154–55, 157; Finley, *From Slavery to Uncertain Freedom*, 4; E. S. Peake to superiors, June 30, 1865; July 31, 1865.

18 E. S. Peake to C. L. Thomas, February 28, 1865, and March 31, 1865. Pub number M619 Letters Received by the Adjutant General, 1861–1870 Rec Group 94, Roll 0395 Fold3.com.

19 Glymph, *Women's Fight*, 103.

20 She married soldier Henry Smith in Argenta in spring 1866. Sarah Smith deposition in own claim, soldier Henry Smith, 54th USCT.

21 Freedmen's Bureau Claims Little Rock Office.

22 Adolphine Fletcher Terry, *Charlotte Stephens: Little Rock's First Black Teacher* (Little Rock, 1973), 108–109; "Our History," Wesley Chapel United Methodist Church, wesleychapelumclr.org/our-history/ (accessed October 15, 2022).

23 E. S. Peake to Thomas, June 30, July 31, 1865; Taylor, *Embattled Freedom*.

24 E. S. Peake to Thomas, July 31, 1865; "Arkansas, Freedmen's Bureau Field Office Records, 1864–1872," Little Rock (Pulaski County) Roll 14, Register of complaints, April 1866–May 1868. Images. FamilySearch. http://FamilySearch.org: 18 July 2022. NARA microfilm publication M1901. National Archives and Records Administration, Washington, DC.

25 Lankford, *Bearing Witness*, 344; Glymph, *Women's Fight*, 230; US Army Map, 1864, Butler Center for Arkansas Studies, Little Rock.

26 "Blissville, Arkansas," *Harper's Weekly*, June 2, 1866, p. 346.

27 Glymph, *Women's Fight*, 232; Freedmen's Bureau Claims, Little Rock Office.

28 Edward G. Longacre, "Letters from Little Rock of Captain James M. Bowler, 112th United States Colored Troops," *Arkansas Historical Quarterly* 40 (Autumn 1981), 239, 245.

29 Mary Kyles testimony, Isaac Gillam testimony, Mary Robinson testimony, Kyles app; Henry Kiles testimony for Lucas claim; Freedmen's Bureau claims, Little Rock office.

30 Discussions of Black women asserting themselves publicly can also be found in Elsa Barkley Brown, "Negotiating and Transforming the Public Sphere: African American Political Life in the Transition from Slavery to Freedom," *Public Culture* 7 (Winter 1994), 107–46.

31 William H. Grey, "The Present Condition and Future Prospects of the Colored People in the South," *Proceedings of the Convention of Colored Citizens of the State of Arkansas, Held in Little Rock, Thursday, Friday, and Saturday, Nov. 30, Dec. 1 and 2, 1865*. See, for example, Tera Hunter, *Bound in Wedlock: Slave and Free Black Marriage in the Nineteenth Century* (Cambridge, MA, 2017).

32 Manning, "Working for Citizenship in Civil War Contraband Camps," 184–85 (first quotation), 191 (second quotation); Glymph, *Women's Fight*, 230–32. See classic works like Schwalm, *'A Hard Fight For We'* and recent scholarship like Taylor, *Embattled Freedom*.

33 DeBlack, *With Fire and Sword*, 201.

34 Katherine McKittrick, *Demonic Grounds: Black Women and the Cartographies of Struggle* (Minneapolis, 2006), xix.

35 Eliza Hudson deposition, widow certificate 504875, Albert Hudson 54th USCT. Because their marriage occurred in November 1865, when the 54th would have been on the north side of the Arkansas River, I situate the wedding in Argenta.

36 Charity Love testimony, Sophia Cornelia Jackson testimony, Charity Love widow application, Allen Love 54th USCT.

37 Hahn, *Nation under Our Feet*, 166.

38 Fannie Garrett testimony, Delia Burks testimony, Laura Caldwell claim.

39 Sarah Smith testimony, Frank Govan testimony, Sarah Smith widow app, Henry Smith.

40 Glymph, *Women's Fight*, 115; Freedmen's Bureau Claims, Little Rock Office.

41 Lang, *In the Wake of War*; Glymph, *Women's Fight*, 116.

42 Jane Clay testimony, Washington Campbell testimony, Jane Clay widow app, George Clay, 54th USCT.

43 Glymph, *Women's Fight*, 116. For former slaves independently caretaking the land see Willie Lee Rose, *Rehearsal for Reconstruction: The Port Royal Experiment* (Oxford, 1976); Taylor, *Embattled Freedom*; and Ira Berlin et al., eds., *Freedom: A Documentary History of Emancipation*, series 3, vol. I: *Land and Labor, 1865* (Chapel Hill, 2008).

44 Edward G. Longacre, "Letters from Little Rock of Captain James M. Bowler, 112th United States Colored Troops" *Arkansas Historical Quarterly* 40 (Autumn 1981), 248.

45 Margaret Storey, "War's Domestic Corollary: Union Occupation Households in the Civil War South," in *Household War: How Americans Lived and Fought the Civil War*, ed. Lisa Tendrich Frank and Leeann Whites, (Athens, GA, 2020), 168–69.

46 *Harper's Weekly*, June 2, 1866.

47 "Mustered Out," *Harper's Weekly*, May 19, 1866, p. 308.

48 Ibid., p. 318; US Army map, 1864.

49 Taylor, *Embattled Freedom*, 220; Glymph, *Women's Fight*, 232. See Joseph P. Reidy, "Coming from the Shadow of the Past: The Transition from Slavery

to Freedom at Freedmen's Village, 1863–1869," *The Virginia Magazine of History and Biography* 95 (October 1987), 403–28.

50 Finley, *From Slavery to Uncertain Freedom*, 77, 103.

51 US Bureau of the Census, Manuscript Census returns, 1870, Second and Third Wards of Little Rock, Pulaski County, AR; Little Rock City Directory, 1871.

52 Freedmen's Bureau claims, 1866, Little Rock office; US Bureau of the Census, Manuscript Census returns, 1870, Second and Third Wards of Little Rock, Pulaski County, AR; Little Rock City Directory, 1871.

53 Claims, Freedmen's Bureau Little Rock Office, 1866; US Bureau of the Census, manuscript census returns, 1870, Pulaski County, AR; US Bureau of the Census, manuscript census returns, 1860, Pulaski County, AR; Freedmen's Bureau marriage record; Glymph, *Women's Fight*, 230–232; US Army map, 1864; 1871 Little Rock city directory.

54 George Champ testimony, his claim for disability, George Champ disability claim; Aaron Williams and Warner McCray testimonies, Lou Holmes application.

55 John Phillips testimony, Calvin Davis testimony, Aaron Williams testimony, Lou Holmes widow app.

56 Sarah Smith testimony, Write Allen testimony, widow app, Henry Smith.

57 Moneyhon, "The Federal Plantation Experiment in Arkansas," 159–160.

58 Civil War Service Records (CMSR) – Union – Colored Troops 56th-138th Infantry, Compiled Military Service Records of Volunteer Union Soldiers Who Served the United States Colored Troops: 56th-138th USCT Infantry, 1864–1866. Fold 3; US Census, 1870, Pulaski County AR.

59 Isaac Gillam testimony, Lou Holmes widow application, Alfred alias Albert Holmes, widow app #739427.

60 Civil War Service Records (CMSR) – Union – Colored Troops 56th-138th Infantry, Compiled Military Service Records of Volunteer Union Soldiers Who Served the United States Colored Troops: 56th-138th USCT Infantry, 1864–1866. Fold 3; 1870 Census Pulaski County.

61 Willis Gray deposition for Brooks app; compiled service records, fold 3; 1870 census.

62 Blake J. Wintory, "African-American Legislators in the Arkansas General Assembly, 1868–1893," *Arkansas Historical Quarterly* 65 (Winter 2006), 387, 388.

63 US Bureau of the Census, manuscript census returns, 1870, Pulaski County, AR; 1871 Little Rock City Directory.

64 Adolphine Fletcher Terry, *Charlotte Stephens: Little Rock's First Black Teacher* (Little Rock, 1973), 108–109; "Our History," Wesley Chapel United Methodist Church, https://wesleychapelumclr.org/our-history (accessed July 1, 2020); Tera W. Hunter, *To 'Joy My Freedom: Southern Black Women's Lives and Labors after the Civil War* (Cambridge, MA, 1997), 130–31, 135, 143 (quotation), 149–51, 161.

65 "Mrs. Cora Gillam," in *The American Slave: A Composite Autobiography*, ed. George P. Rawick (Westport, CT, 1972); Tom W. Dillard, "Isaac Taylor Gillam," *Encyclopedia of Arkansas*, Central Arkansas Library System; Isaac Gillam testimony, Charity Love widow application.

66 DeBlack, *With Fire and Sword*, 219.

67 Moneyhon, *Reconstruction*, 260–61; DeBlack, *With Fire and Sword*, 218–19.

68 "Arkansas," Buffalo *Weekly Courier*, May 13, 1874; "The Arkansas War," New York *Daily Herald*, May 12, 1874, p. 7; DeBlack, *With Fire and Sword*, 223; Downs, *After Appomattox*.

69 Joseph Harris testimony, Jane Allen pension application, Austin Allen 54th USCT.

70 Moneyhon, *Reconstruction*, 262–63; Blake J. Wintory, "African-American Legislators in the Arkansas General Assembly, 1868–1893," *Arkansas Historical Quarterly* 65 (Winter 2006), 387, 388.

71 Tom W. Dillard, "The Gilliam [*sic*] Family, Four Generations of Black Arkansas Educators." *Journal of Arkansas Education* 45 (1973), 19, 22; *American Slave*, ed. Rawick, 30–33.

72 Albert Anderson testimony, Fannie Garrett testimony, Laura Caldwell minor claim, James Buckner (alias Lucas), certificate 261271.

8 BLACK WOMEN'S LIVES AND LABORS IN POST-EMANCIPATION NORTH CAROLINA

1 Deposition of Martha Fulford, February 13, 1901, Pension file of Fanny Whitney (WC 1304030).

2 This study draws on the category of widowhood in an effort to add a new dimension to the study of freedwomen's transition to freedom. I am blending and building on the collective works of Thomas Holt, Thavolia Glymph, Elsa Barkley Brown, and Abigail Cooper, "'Away I Goin' to Find My Mama': Self-Emancipation, Migration, and Kinship in Refugee Camps in the Civil War Era," *Journal of African American History* 107, 44–67.

3 Diverse scholarship on the experiences of Black women during the Civil War and Emancipation, their contribution to the destruction of slavery, and the impact the relationships they had with enlisted soldiers had on the state informed much of my thinking in this essay: Thavolia Glymph, *The Women's Fight: The Civil War's Battle for Home, Freedom, and Nation* (Chapel Hill, 2020); Stephanie McCurry, *Women's War: Fighting and Surviving the American Civil War* (Cambridge, MA, 2019); Janice L. Reiff, Michel R. Dahlin, and Daniel Scott Smith, "Rural Push and Urban Pull: Work and Family of Older Black Women in Southern Cities, 1880–1900," *Journal of Social History*, 16, no. 4, 39–48; Jacqueline Jones, *Labor of Love, Labor of Sorrow: Black Women, Work and Family from Slavery to the Present* (New York, 1985), 44–78; Michelle A. Krowl, "African American Women and the United States Military in Civil War Virginia," in *Afro-Virginian History and Culture*, ed., John Saillant (New York, 1999), 173–210.

4 Glymph, *Women's Fight*; Brandi Clay Brimmer, *Claiming Union Widowhood* (Durham, NC, 2020).

5 Cooper, "'Away I Goin' to Find My Mama'," and Thulani Davis, *The Emancipation Circuit: Black Activism Forging a Culture of Freedom* (Durham, NC, 2022).

6 Walt Wolfram and Erik Thomas estimated that 220 slaves resided on Judge
   Donnell's Hyde plantation in 1850; the next largest had only 45. Walt
   Wolfram and Erik Thomas, *The Development of African American English*
   (Hoboken, NJ, 2002), 57–59. Sandra S. Carawan, "Hyde County's Largest
   Plantation Owner of 1850 and 1860: John R. Donnell," *High Tides: Hyde
   County Historical Society Journal, North Carolina* (Spring 2000), 36–41.
   So far, I have identified the following pension files of men, women, and chil-
   dren enslaved by the Donnell family: Pension file of Fanny Whitney, 37th
   United States Colored Troops (USCT), Widow's Certificate (WC) 130403,
   Pension Application Files Based Upon Service in the Civil War and Spanish-
   American War, Pension Bureau Records. All pension files for Union veterans
   and their dependents from the records that are cited in this article will be
   documented as Pension file of [the applicant], [dependent of the veteran,
   with military details], type of pension certificate, and certificate number.
   The files are indexed by military unit Organization Index to Pension Files of
   Veterans Who Served Between 1861 and 1900, National Archives Microfilm
   Series (NAMS) T-289 (765 reels 541–79), accessed through the subscrip-
   tion database Ancestry.com. Gatsey Donald, widow of Moses Donald,
   37th USCT (WC 159349); Dilsey (aka Delacy) Donnells, widow of George
   Donnells, 35th USCT (WC 137101); and Freedmen's Bureau Bank Record,
   New Bern, # 1493; Mardecia Whitney widow of Nathan Whitney, 37th
   USCI (WC 745221); Abram Blount (Affidavit of Abram Blount), February
   18, 1899, Pension file of Phillis Blount, widow of Abram Blount, 37th USCT
   (WC 793022); Pension file of Mary E. Bell, widow of Adam Bell (Alias
   Adam J. C. Walker), 35th USCT (WC 586827). Clarissa Silver, widow of
   Thomas Silver, 37th USCT (WC 300188), Julia Merrick and Riley Merrick
   identified in Clarissa Silver to the Commissioner of Pensions, December 6,
   1916, Pension file of Clarissa Silver (WC: 300188); Caroline Butler said
   that she had been married to Charles Peterson a "Slave of Judge Donald of
   New Bern" Judge Donnells (Deposition of Caroline Jack), June 29, 1900,
   Pension file of Caroline Butler (now Jack) widow of Godfrey Butler and
   John Jackson (WC 134795). See also the joint affidavit of Francis Holloway
   and Nelson Green August 23, 1867, Pension file of Fanny Whitney (WC
   130 403); Francis Holloway lived in Hyde County and she was enslaved
   by T. H. Smith of Hyde County. "Widow's Claim for Pension," July 14,
   1868, Francis Holloway Pension file of Francis Halloway widow of Edwin
   Halloway, 35th USCT (WC 147 997); and the Pension file of Brazilla
   Benson widow of Nelson Green, 37th USCT (WC 969 102; MC 683 675).
   I also traced individual families using records from the US Freedman's Bank
   Records, 1865–1874, Register of Signatures of Depositors in Branches of
   the Freedman's Savings and Trust Company, microfilm ser. M816. National
   Archives, Washington, DC accessed via Ancestry.com. Dilsey Donnells
   (#1498; 1870), Gatsey Donnells (1872; #3159), Frances Holloway (both
   records are blank 1604, 1870; and 2166, 1871), Adam Whitney (1871;
   #2328), Harry Whitney (1870; #2076), and Emanuel Merrick (1872;
   #3097) opened accounts at the Freedmen's Bank, which Congress chartered
   in 1865 especially for freedpeople.

7 The 1860 Federal Census showed that John R. Donnell enslaved thirteen people (men, women, and children) in New Bern. US Bureau of Census. Eighth Census of the US 1860, Series M653, Record Group (hereinafter RG) 29; New Bern, North Carolina, Craven. The same census indicates the Donnell family enslaved another 229 persons, ranging in age from three months to eighty years, in Hyde County. The 1850 Federal Census reveals the Donnell Speight family enslaved eighty-four men, women, and children in Craven County. Seventh Census of the United States, 1850. National Archives and Records Administration, Washington, DC, 1850. M432; I have not been able to determine if these people constituted the group of people (including Fanny Fonville) transported to Hyde County. David S. Cecelski, *The Waterman's Song: Slavery and Freedom in Maritime North Carolina*, (Chapel Hill, 2001), 179–201, 159; William K. Scarborough, *Masters of the Big House: Elite Slaveholders of the Mid-Nineteenth-Century South* (Baton Rouge, 2003), 365–66.

8 Rebecca J. Fraser, *Courtship and Love among the Enslaved in North Carolina* (Jackson, MI, 2007); Heather A. Williams, *Help Me to Find My People: The African American Search for Family Lost in Slavery* (Chapel Hill 2010), esp. 48–88. Brenda E. Stevenson, "Distress and Discord in Virginia Slave Families, 1830–1860," in *In Joy and in Sorrow: Women, Family, and Marriage in the Victorian South, 1830–1900* (New York, 1991), 103–24.

9 Affidavit of Alexander Williams, April 7, 1869, Pension file of Fanny Whitney (WC 130403).

10 Identification of Overseer William Simmons from Deposition of Fanny Whitney, June 20, 1900; identification of Alexander Williams from Affidavit of Alexander Williams, April 7, 1869; quote from Affidavit of Nelson Green, August 22, 1867, Pension file of Fanny Whitney (WC 130403). On enslaved marriages see Tyler Parry, *Jumping the Broom: The Surprising Multicultural Origins of a Black Wedding Ritual* (Chapel Hill, 2020).

11 Affidavit of Dilsey Donals [Donnells], November 8, 1869, Pension file of Dilsey Donald widow of George, 35th USCT (WC 137101). Various documents spell this name Dilsey Donnels, Dilsey Donnalls, and Delacy. I refer to the claimant as Dilcy Donnell but I have retained various spellings in quotations. As with many of the descendants enslaved, the Donnell surname appears as Donnels, Donnells, Donals, and Donald throughout the documents.

12 Brenda E. Stevenson, "'Us never had no big funerals or weddins on de place': Ritualizing Black Marriage in the Wake of Freedom," in *Beyond Freedom: Disrupting the History of Emancipation* (Athens, GA, 2018): 39–59.

13 Deposition of Emanuel Merrick, October 11, 1892 (reexamined), Pension file of Moses Longest (MC 137141).

14 I am drawing on the term coined by Willie Lee Rose in *Rehearsal for Reconstruction: The Port Royal Experiment* (Athens, GA, 1964).

15 Richard Reid, "Government Policy, Prejudice, and the Experience of Black Civil War Soldiers and their Families," *Journal of Family History* 27 (2002), 374–98 (esp. 384).

16 Deposition of Martha Fulford, February 13, 1901, Pension file of Fanny Whitney (WC 1304030).

17 Patricia C. Click, *Time Full of Trial: The Roanoke Island Freedmen's Colony, 1862–1867* (Chapel Hill, 2001); Reid, "Government Policy, Prejudice, and the Experience of Black Civil War Soldiers and their Families"; and the group of documents reprinted in Ira Berlin, Thavolia Glymph, Steven F. Miller, Joseph P. Reidy, Leslie S. Rowland, and Julie Saville, eds., *Freedom: A Documentary History of Emancipation, 1861–1867*, series 1, vol. II: *The Wartime Genesis of Free Labor: The Upper South* (New York, 1990), 20, 135–37, are foundational to understanding the experiences of Black refugees on the Ronoake Colony.

18 Ira Berlin and Leslie Rowland, eds., *Families and Freedom: A Documentary History of African American Kinship in the Civil War Era* (New York, 1997), 122. Click, *Time Full of Trial*, and Gregory P. Downs, "Lost, Again," *New York Times online*, accessed February 9, 2022.

19 Horace James, *Annual Report of the Superintendent of Negro Affairs in North Carolina, 1864* (Boston, 1865 [Biblio Life Reprint]), 20–34; Ira Berlin, Joseph P. Reidy, and Leslie Rowland, eds., *Freedom: A Documentary History of Emancipation, 1861–1867*, series 2: *The Black Military Experience* (New York, 1982), 12, 113–15, 127–28, 132–34; Ira Berlin, Thavolia Glymph, Steven F. Miller, Joseph P. Reidy, Leslie S. Rowland, and Julie Saville, eds., *Freedom: A Documentary History of Emancipation, 1861–1867, series 1, vol. II: The Wartime Genesis of Free Labor: The Upper South* (New York, 1990), 20, 135–37.

20 The Second Confiscation Act on July 17, 1862, freed Blacks entering Union-occupied zones. US, *Statutes at Large, Treaties, and Proclamations of the United States of America*, vol. 12 (Boston, 1863), 589–600, esp. 597–600 (accessed through www.freedmen.umd.edu) Also See Karen Cook Bell, "Self-Emancipating Women, Civil War, and the Union Army, in Southern Louisiana and Low Country Georgia, 1861–1865," *Journal of African American History* 101, nos. 1–2 (2016), 1–22, esp. 5;

US, *Statutes at Large*, pp. 589–92. Jim Downs points to the gendered dimensions of the term "able-bodied," which is used to describe the status of fugitive slaves in the Second Confiscation Act. See Downs, *Sick from Freedom: African American Illness and Suffering during the Civil War* (New York, 2012), 126; and "The Other Side of Freedom: Destitution, Disease, and Dependency among Freedwomen and Their Children during and after the Civil War," in *Battle Scars: Gender and Sexuality in the American Civil War*, ed. Nina Silber and Catherine Clinton (New York, 2006), 80. Though this policy deployed gender-neutral language that favored men, scholars such as Karen Cook Bell, Louis Gerteis, and others have documented important examples of women who garnered pay from the military in southern Louisiana and Low Country Georgia. Cook Bell documents freedwomen on St. Simons Island selling foodstuffs and earning wages for such as laundering to Union men. See Cook Bell, "Self-Emancipating Women, Civil War, and the Union Army," 10–11, Louis Gerteis, *From Contraband to Freedman: Federal Policy toward Southern Blacks, 1861–1865* (Westport, CT, 1973), 72–73.

21 Heather A. Williams, *Help Me To Find My People: The African American Search for Family Lost in Slavery* (Chapel Hill, 2012), 142.

22 Elizabeth Dempsey's attempt to secure benefits under the 1892 Nurses Pension Act is evidenced in the Civil War Pension Index: General Index to Pension Files, 1861–1934.

23 On the impact of military mobilization on Black family life see, Jones, *Labor of Love, Labor of Sorrow*, 48, Reid, "Government Policy, Prejudice, and the Experience of Black Civil War Soldiers and Their Families," 374–98.

24 Reference to the eight men appears in the Deposition of Martha Fulford, February 13, 1901, Pension file of Fanny Whitney (WC 130403). They included: Green Cradle, Ira Holwell, Nathan Whitney, George Spencer, Moses Long, Washington Whitfield, Frank Brimmage, and Harry Whitney. Date and place of enlistment and, in some instances, dates of death determined by their military service records (accessed on ancestry.com) for Harry Whitney, Nathan Whitney, George Spencer, Washington Whitfield, Green Cradell, and Ira Howell. The records for Nathan Long and Frank Brimmage have not been located in the military service records accessed through ancestry.

25 Deposition of Fanny Whitney, February 9, 1901, Pension file of Fanny Whitney (WC 130403).

26 Elijah Marrs, *Life and History of Elijah P. Marrs, First Pastor of Beargrass Baptist Church, and Author* (Louisville, KY, 1885), quote from 19, in Documenting the American South, https://docsouth.unc.edu, accessed on February 18, 2022.

27 Deposition of Martha Fulford, February 13, 1901, Pension file of Fanny Whitney (WC 130403).

28 In addition to Harry Whitney's death on July 30, 1865, several other men who enlisted in the USCT from Donnells's plantation died around the same time. See for example the service records of Ira Howell (aka Holliway; Holloway), who enlisted in the USCT at Plymouth, North Carolina, on December 10, 1863, and died on September 26, 1865; Washington Whitfield enlisted at Roanoke on December 13, 1863, and died on October 5, 1865; and Green Cradell enlisted on December 1, 1863, and died on August 29, 1865.

29 Stevenson, "Distress and Discord in Virginia Slave Families," 109.

30 Deposition of Nathan Whitney, February 14, 1901, Pension file of Fanny Whitney (WC130403).

31 Deposition of Emmauel Merrick, October 7, 1892, Pension file of Moses Longest (MC137141).

32 Deposition of Eliza J. Tooley, October 7, 1892, Pension file of Moses Longest (MC 137141).

33 See Karin Zipf, *Labor of Innocents: Forced Apprenticeship in North Carolina, 1715–1919* (Baton Rouge, 2005), 71; On the significance of Black women's networks see Deborah Gray White, *Arn't I a Woman?: The Female Slave in the Plantation South* (New York, 1985), 119–41; Katheleen Berkeley, "Colored Ladies Also Contributed: Black Women's Activities from Benevolence to Society Welfare, 1866–1896," in, *The Web of Southern Social Relations: Women, Family and Education*, ed. Walter J. Fraser, Jr., R. Frank Saunders, Jr., and Jon Wakelyn (Athens, GA, 1985), 181–203.

34 Steven Hahn, *A Nation under Our Feet: Black Political Struggles in the Rural South from Slavery to the Great Migration* (Cambridge, MA, 2003), 163–215, esp. 166. On the conceptual value of analyzing Black women's lives and labors in the context of their communities, see Leslie Alexander, "The Challenge of Race: Rethinking the Position of Black Women in the Field of Women's History," *Journal of Women's History* 16, no. 4, 50–60.

35 Jones, *Labor of Love, Labor of Sorrow*, 44–78, quote on 50.

36 Deposition of Harriet Boyd, March 23, 1897, Pension file of Matilda Wells widow of Toney Wells, Co I, Thirty-seventh USCT (WC 455 514).

37 Deposition of Matilda Wells, July 2, 1904, Pension file of Charlotte Banks (aka Capehart) widow of Caesar Banks, Co. D, Thirty-fifth regiment USCT (WC 157 383). [(Lucinda Stamps (housekeeper)), Jacob Pool (laborer), Ann Stamps (midwife), William F. Bell (Corn Weigher).]

38 "The figure for tidewater North Carolina is derived from a census conducted in January 1865, which counted 17,307 Black people (evidently excluding soldiers) in the territory under Union control." Horace *James, Annual Report of the Superintendent of Negro Affairs in North Carolina, 1864. With Appendix* (Boston, 1865), 4. According to the editors at the Freedmen and Southern Society Project Documentary series, adding the 5,035 Black soldiers credited to the state brings the total Black population to 22,342. Ira Berlin, Steven F. Miller, Joseph P. Reidy, and Leslie S. Rowland, *Freedom: A Documentary History of Emancipation, 1861–1867*, series 1, vol. II: *The Wartime Genesis of Free Labor in the Upper South* (Cambridge, 1993), 78, n. 193.

39 Glymph, *Women's Fight*, 218–20; Angela Davis, "Reflections on the Black Woman's Role in the Community of Slaves," *The Black Scholar* 12 (1981), 2–15, esp. 7; McCurry, *Women's War*, 63–124.

40 Deposition of Elizabeth Howard, November 22, 1899, Pension file of Peggie Slade.

41 Glymph, *Women's Fight*, 222. Janette Thomas Greenwood recounts the story of Nicholas Bray, who re-enslaved to Black sisters with permission from Union military administrators in New Bern, in *First Fruits of Freedom: The Migration of Former Slaves and Their Search for Equality in Worchester, Massachusetts, 1862–1900* (Chapel Hill), 44–46.

42 Katherine Franke, "Becoming a Citizen: Reconstruction Era Regulation of African American Marriages," *Yale Journal of Law and Humanities* 11 (Summer 1999), 252. See also Stephanie McCurry, "Enemy Women and the Laws of War in the American Civil War," *Law and History Review* 35 (2017), 669–710; and Amy Dru Stanley, "Instead of Waiting for the Thirteenth Amendment: The War Power, Slave Marriage, and Inviolate Human Rights," *American Historical Review* (2010), 732–65.

43 Deposition of Harriet Barlow, February 6, 1894, Pension file of Harriet Barlow widow of Phillip Barlow, 37th USCT (WC 393620). See also Deposition of Jane Williams, March 22, 1893, Pension file of Jane Williams widow of Aleck Williams, 37th USCI (WC 370 646).

44 November 18, 1899, Deposition of Peggy Slade, in New Bern, I. C. Stockton, Pension file of Peggy Slade widow of Miles Slade 35th Regt. (WC 486995).

45 Cecelski, *The Waterman's Song*, 179–201.
46 Free Black and slave wives and mothers and Children of Union Soldiers generated a good deal of correspondence in response to the loss of male support at the height of the Civil War. See especially Ira Berlin, Joseph Reidy, and Leslie Rowland, eds., *Freedom: A Documentary History of Emancipation 1861–1867, series 2: The Black Military Experience* (New York, 1982), esp. Jane Welcome the mother of a Pennsylvania Black Soldier to President Abraham Lincoln, November 12, 1864 (#227), 664; Soloman Sanders North Carolina Black Soldier to his wife Mrs. Merina Sanders and Mrs. Sanders' affidavit (#284), 670; and also Rossana Henson the Wife of a New Jersey Black Soldier to President Abraham Lincoln, July 11, 1864 (#290), 680.
47 Ira Berlin and Leslie Rowland's documentary history of African American kinship in the Civil War era depicts the issues that Black women raised in their correspondence with federal officials. *Black Military Experience*, "Missouri Slave Woman to Her Soldier Husband," 686.
48 Deposition of Martha A. Boyd, April 6, 1892, Pension file of Judy Lavenhouse Mother of George Lavenhouse, Co F, Second USCV(MC 332 918).
49 Deposition of Angeline Williams, April 6, 1892, Pension file of Judy Lavenhouse Mother of George Lavenhouse, 2nd USCV (MC 332918).
50 Claim for Mother's Pensions, Pension file of Maria Biggs mother of York Biggs, 14th USCHA (MC 130 543).
51 Proof of Dependence, Susan Murphy, Moses Murphy, Blunt Murphy, February 28, 1888, Pension file of Julia Foy mother of William Foy, 35th USCT (MC 156180).
52 Roanoke Island, NC to Mr. President, March 9, 1865, *Wartime Genesis of Free Labor*, 233. Only fragments of the petitions (or single petition) exist. Written in the same handwriting, the editors believe that the letter was probably written by Richard Boyle, a Black schoolteacher on the Island.
53 Ibid.
54 Quote from Capt. Horace James to Col. J. S. Fullerton, July 10, 1865, *Genesis of Free Labor*, 235–236 (Doc: 47B).
55 Ibid.
56 On Etheredge's wartime experiences and vocal protest, see David Wright and David Zoby, *Fire on the Beach: Recovering the Lost Story of Richard Etheridge and the Pea Island Life Savers* (New York, 2000). See also Deborah Willis, *The Black Civil War Soldier: A Visual History of Conflict and Citizenship* (New York, 2021), 2.
57 *The Black Military Experience*, 727–28 (quote on p. 728). Sent from Chaplain William A. Green et al. to Maj. O. O. Howard, *Wartime Genesis of Free Labor*, 235–36.
58 Circular 2, issued on July 15, 1865, by Col. Eliphalet Whittlesey, Assistant Commissioner's Report to Commissioner Howard, 1–8 (Circular, p 3), 39th Congress, 1st Sess., Ex Doc. No. 70, Vol. 1866; quotes from Reid, "Government Policy, Prejudice, and the Experience of Black Civil War Soldiers," 379 and 380.
59 Testimony of Colonel Epliphalet Whittlesey, February 3, 1866, Testimony before the Joint Committee on Reconstruction, in *Report of the Joint*

Committee on Reconstruction, At the First Session Thirty-Nine Congress (New York, 1969), 182.

60 On the suspension of rations in October 1866, see Click, *Time Full of Trial,* 182; Berlin and Rowland, eds., *Families and Freedom,* 122–23.

61 See especially Leslie Schwalm, '*A Hard Fight for We*': *Women's Transition from Slavery to Freedom in South Carolina* (Urbana, 1997).

62 James Mobley, *James City: A Black Community in North Carolina, 1863–1900* (Raleigh, NC, 1981), 43–65.

63 Quote from James A. Emmerton, *A Record of the Twenty-third Regiment Mass. Vol. Infantry in the War of the Rebellion, 1861–1865* ... (Boston, 1886), 95.

64 Tera W. Hunter, *To 'Joy My Freedom: Southern Black Women's Lives and Labors after the Civil War* (Cambridge, MA, 1997), 44–73; esp. 53. Roberta Sue Alexander estimates females earned six dollars per month, including board. See Alexander, *North Carolina Faces the Freedmen* (Durham, NC, 1985), 106. Talithia LeFlouria, *Chained in Silence: Black Women and Convict Labor in the New South* (Chapel Hill, 2015), ch. 1, esp. 23–31.

65 Susan O'Donnovan's rendering of an agricultural wage-labor economy composed of families appears in *Becoming Free in the Cotton South,* ch. 5. Among other issues, O'Donnovan's example of Rachel, a single mother with child, is illustrative of the challenges some Black women had to face. O'Donnovan, *Becoming Free in the Cotton South* (Cambridge, MA, 2010), 180–83.

66 Jones, *Labor of Love, Labor of Sorrow,* 112; Reiff, Dahlin, and Smith, "Rural Push and Urban Pull," O'Donnovan, *Becoming Free in the Cotton South,* 162–207, esp. 163. It is worth noting that the casual, low-paying, physically demanding occupations soldiers and wives war widows say they performed in their testimony reflect the experiences of women with children who lived in their own households in urban areas, both North and South, in late nineteenth-century America. See especially the work of Kali Gross, *Colored Amazons: Crime, Violence, and Black Women in the City of Brotherly Love, 1880–1910* (Durham, NC, 2006), 1–2.

67 Affidavit of Dilcy Jarmon, March 14, 1887, Pension file of Dilcey Jarmon widow of George Jarmon, 35th USCT (WC 154826).

68 Deposition of Fanny Wiggins, January 14, 1909, Pension file of Gordon Wiggins, 14th USCHA (SC 460093)/(WC 679867).

69 Reif, Dahlin and Smith, "Rural Push and Urban Pull," 40.

70 1870 US Federal Census (Ancestry.Com). Adam's occupation, see 1870 Census and #2328, Freedmen's Bureau Bank Records; Identification of Harry Whitney's instructor on Harry Whitney's bank record, # 2076, Freedmen's Bureau Bank records, accessed through ancestry.com.

71 Linda Gordon, *The Great Arizona Orphan Abduction* (Cambridge, MA, 1999), 118–48.

72 The provisions of North Carolina's marriage act, passed by the General Assembly in March 1866 appear in section 5 of "An Act Concerning Negroes and Persons of Color of Mixed Blood," in *Public Laws of the State of North Carolina,* Passed by the General Assembly at the Session of 1866 (Raleigh, NC, 1866),. 99–105.

73 Schwalm, *'A Hard Fight for We,'* ch. 7, esp. 263.

74 The experiences endured by Black Union widows when they entered the pension application process have been well documented in works such as Brimmer, *Claiming Union Widowhood*; Donald Shaffer, Elizabeth Regosin, and Linda Williams Elizabeth Ann Regosin, *Freedom's Promise: Ex-slave Families and Citizenship in the Age of Emancipation* (Charlottesville, 2002); Linda Faye Williams, *Constraint of Race: Legacies of White Skin Privilege in America* (University Park, 2004); Donald Shaffer, *After the Glory: The Struggles of Black Civil War Veterans* (Lawrence, 2004); Donald Shaffer, "'I Do Not Suppose That Uncle Sam Looks as the Skin': African Americans and, the Civil War Pension System, 1865–1934." *Civil War History* 46, no. 2 (2000), 132–47; Megan McClintock, "Binding up the Nation's Wounds: Civil War Pensions and the Reconstruction of Union Families," *Journal of American History* 83 (September 1996), 456–80; and Jane E. Schultz, "Race, Gender, and Bureaucracy: Civil War Army Nurses and the Pension Bureau," *Journal of Women's History* 6 (Summer 1994), 45–69.

75 Deposition of Fanny Whitney, June 21, 1900, Pension file of Fanny Whitney (WC 130 403).

76 Dow McClain to the Commissioner of Pensions, March 13, 1901, Pension file of Eda Coleman widow of Isaac Coleman, 35th USCT (WC 154770).

77 Pension file of Gatsey Donald [Donnell] widow of Moses Donald, 37th USCT (WC159349). Gatsey Donald [Donnell] Freedmen's Bank Account, (October 21, 1872, #3159).

78 For an example of Emanuel Merrick acting as a claims agent see the pension file of Moses Longest (MC 137141); examples of Nathan Whitney's assisting war widows appear in Pension file of Matilda Wells.

79 Alexander, *North Carolina Faces the Freedmen*, 45.

80 Mary Farmer Kaiser, *Freedwomen and the Freedmen's Bureau: Race, Gender, and Public Policy in the Age of Emancipation* (New York, 2010), pp. 97–118. Farmer Kaiser shows how white southerners, the courts, and even Freedmen's Bureau officers interpreted "orphan" to mean fatherless (rather than parentless).

81 Ibid, 112.

82 Karin L. Zipf, "Promises of Opportunity: The Freedmen's Savings and Trust Company Bank in New Bern, North Carolina," Master's thesis, University of Georgia, 1994; Fanny Whitney established an account for each son, Harry and Adam, but not one for herself or her daughter Malissa. Harry Whitney, entry 2076 and Adam Whitney, entry 2328, New Bern, NC, Freedmen's Bank (accessed through ancestry.com).

83 Zipf, *Labor of Innocents*, 72.

84 Deposition of Dilsey Donnells, June 21, 1875, Pension file of Fanny Whitney (WC 130403).

85 North Carolina, US Wills and Probate Records, 1665–1998 for Dilsey Donnells, Craven County, 1665–1998. Ancestry.com. *North Carolina, U.S., Wills and Probate Records, 1665–1998* [database on-line]. Provo, UT, USA: Ancestry.com Operations, Inc., 2015.

86 Hunter, *To 'Joy My Freedom,* 169; Thavolia Glymph, *Out of the House of Bondage: The Transformation of the Plantation Household* (New York, 2008), 216.
87 Deposition of Julia Benson, October 11, 1892, Pension file of Moses Longest, (MC 137141).
88 Henry Jones to Fannie Whitney, June 8, 1877, Pension file of Fannie Whitney (WC 130403) and Deposition of Julia Benson, October 11, 1892, Pension file of Moses Longest (MC 137141).
89 Affidavit of William Green, April 14, 1877, Pension file of Fanny Whitney (WC 130403).
90 Affidavit of Fanny Whitney, June 26, 1877, Pension file of Fanny Whitney (WC 130403).
91 Affidavit of Fanny Whitney, July 26 187[7], [William H. Green appears on 1870, 1880 census; and NC Death Index; Clarissa Silver to Hon]. Commissioner of Pensions, December 6, 1916, (WC 300188).
92 M. E. Jenks to H. M. Atkinson, Commissioner of Pensions, June 21, 1875, Pension file of Fanny Whitney (WC 130403).
93 Kimberly Welch, "Black Litigiousness and White Accountability: Free Blacks and the Rhetoric of Reputation in the Antebellum Natchez District," *Journal of the Civil War Era* (September 2015), 372–98, esp. 374.
94 Brandi C. Brimmer, "Black Women's Politics, Narratives of Sexual Immorality, and the Pension Bureaucracy in Mary Lee's North Carolina Neighborhood," *Journal of Southern History* 80, no. 4 (November 2014), 827–58, esp. 830.
95 The 1880 Federal Census shows Malissa attending school.
96 The Chief of the Law Division determined that Malissa's "birth out of wedlock" did not bring Fanny's case into violation of the Pension Bureau's cohabitation policy. Chief of Law Division to Chief of S. E. Division, July 14, 1900, Pension file of Fanny Whitney (WC 130403).
97 Deposition of Fanny Whitney, June 21, 1900 (WC 130403); Malissa's father's life history has been culled from his daughter's pension file. Clarissa Silver (daughter of William H. Green, who remained in Swans Quarter, Hyde County, North Carolina and Susan Green). Clarissa Silver widow of Thomas Silver, 37th USCT (WC 300188).
98 North Carolina, US Wills and Probate Records, 1665–1998 for Frances Halloway, Craven County, 1665–1998. Ancestry.com. *North Carolina, U.S., Wills and Probate Records, 1665–1998* [database on-line]. Provo, UT, USA: Ancestry.com Operations, Inc., 2015. Accessed on February 5, 2022.

9 REMAKING OLD BLUE COLLEGE

This chapter is an excerpt from Hilary Green, *Educational Reconstruction: African American Schools in the Urban South, 1865–1890* (New York, 2016).
1 L. B. Moore, "Address of Mr. L. B. Moore, of Alabama, on Negro Work," *American Missionary* 48 (December 1894), 459–60.
2 Ibid.

3 C. W. Buckley, "Draft Report Made to Major General Swayne Relative to Colored Schools, March 30, 1866," reel 1, AL-BRFAL-ED.

4 R. D. Harper, "Report to O. O. Howard, April 15, 1868," reel 1, AL-BRFAL-ED.

5 Horace Mann Bond, *Negro Education in Alabama: A Study in Cotton and Steel* (New York, 1969), 96–97; George Sisk, "Negro Education in the Alabama Black Belt, 1875–1900," *Journal of Negro Education* 22 (Spring 1953), 126–28; John Alvord, *Tenth Semi-annual Report on Schools for Freedmen, July 1, 1870* (Washington, DC, 1870), 5–7, in *Freedmen's Schools and Textbooks*, ed. Robert C. Morris (New York, 1980); Joe M. Richardson, *Christian Reconstruction: The American Missionary Association and Southern Blacks, 1861–1890* (Tuscaloosa, AL, 2009), 118.

6 "Riotous," *Mobile Daily Advertiser and Register*, September 8, 1865; "Southern Education," ibid., February 18, 1866, 2; "A Lecture," ibid., July 1, 1871, 2; "Poisonous Doctrines," ibid., May 5, 1867, 2.

7 Richardson, *Christian Reconstruction*, 112–13; Mobile City Directories, 1871–74, Mobile Municipal Archives, Mobile, Alabama.

8 Richardson, *Christian Reconstruction*, 112–13; Mobile City Directories, 1871–87, Mobile Municipal Archives, Mobile, Alabama. For confusion over Sara Stanley's racial status and her experiences, see Ellen NicKenizie Lawson and Marlene D. Merrill, *The Three Sarahs: Documents of Antebellum Black College Women* (New York, 1994), 48–50, 54–63.

9 M. H. Leatherman to E. M. Cravath, October 15, 1872, reel 3, AMA Archives, Alabama, ACT.

10 Mobile City Directories, 1870–90, Mobile Municipal Archives, Mobile, Alabama.

11 Bond, *Negro Education in Alabama*, 84; "Colored Mass Convention of the State of Alabama," *Mobile Daily Advertiser and Register*, May 4, 1867, 2; "Poisonous Doctrines," ibid., May 5, 1867, 2; C. S. Bradford to C. W. Buckley, August 7, 1867, reel 1, AL-BRFAL-ED.

12 Records of the Board of School Commissioners for Mobile County, Minutes, 1871–87, MCPSS. For defense of its practices, see "Public Schools," *Mobile Daily Advertiser and Register*, July 4, 1871, 3; and September 18, 1878, Meeting Minutes, Records of the Board of School Commissioners for Mobile County, Minutes, 1871–87, MCPSS; Mobile County City Directory, 1878, Mobile Municipal Archives, Mobile, Alabama.

13 Maria Waterbury to E. M. Cravath, November 6, 1871, reel 2; Maria Waterbury to E. M. Cravath, November 21, 1818, reel 2; M. H. Leatherman to E. M. Cravath, October 15, 1872, reel 3; E. P. Lord to E. M. Cravath, June 13, 1873, reel 3, all in AMA Archives, Alabama, ARC. For examples of efforts to regain local confidence, see W. J. Squire to E. M. Cravath, July 31, 1872, reel 2; E. P. Lord to E. M. Cravath, January 11, 1873, reel 3; E. P. Lord to E. M. Cravath, May 28, 1873, reel 3, all in AMA Archives, Alabama, ARC.

14 Maria Waterbury to E. M. Cravath, November 6, 1871, reel 2; Maria Waterbury to E. M. Cravath, November 20, 1871, reel 2; Maria Waterbury to E. M. Cravath, February 17, 1872, reel 2; and E. P. Lord to E. M. Cravath, January 22, 1873, reel 3, all in AMA Archives, Alabama, ARC.

15 Willis G. Clark, *History of Education in Alabama, 1702–1889* (Washington, DC, 1889), 280; Richardson, *Christian Reconstruction*, 119.
16 "Announcement: Opening of Emerson Institute," enclosed in E. P. Lord to E. M. Cravath, September 29, 1873, reel 3; D. L. Hickok to M. E. Strieby, December 10, 1878, reel 7, both in AMA Archives, Alabama, ARC.
17 E. P. Lord to E. M. Cravath, April 10, 1874, reel 3; E. P. Lord to M. E. Strieby, January 11, 1876, reel 5; E. P. Lord to M. E. Strieby, February 14, 1876, reel 5; E. P. Lord to M. E. Strieby, May 11, 1876, reel 5; E. P. Lord to M. E. Strieby, January 11, 1876, reel 5, all in AMA Archives, Alabama, ARC.
18 E. P. Lord to M. E. Strieby, January 11, 1876, reel 5, AMA Archives, Alabama, ARC; American Missionary Association, *Catalog of the Teachers and Student, Course of Study, Etc., of Emerson Normal Institute, Mobile, Alabama, 1900–1901* (Mobile, AL, 1901), 6–9; "Population Schedule for City of Mobile, Alabama," in United States Census Bureau, *Population Schedules of the Ninth Census of the United States, 1870*, National Archives Microfilm Publication M593 (Washington, DC: National Archives, National Archives and Records Service, General Services Administration, 196–), reel 31.
19 Paulette Davis-Horton, *The Avenue: The Place, the People, the Memories, 1799–1986* (Mobile, 1991), 24; Kate A. Lord to E. M. Cravath, July 2, 1874, reel 4, AMA Archives, Alabama, ARC. William A. Caldwell and W. Aymar Caldwell appear interchangeably in the historical record.
20 Davis-Horton, *The Avenue*, 24.
21 Professor T. N. Chase, "Alabama: Breaking Ground for New Emerson Institute," *American Missionary* 32 (March 1878), 78; B. F. Koons, "Alabama: Dedication of Emerson Institute," *American Missionary* 32 (July 1878), 212, both in VF: Emerson Institute, University of South Alabama, Mobile, Alabama.
22 Koons, "Alabama," 212.
23 Emma Caughey, "Emerson Institute, Mobile, Ala., Burned," *American Missionary* 36 (March 1882): 80–81, VF: Emerson Institute, University of South Alabama, Mobile, Alabama.
24 Emma Caughey, "Emerson Institute," *American Missionary* 37 (June 1883), 172, VF: Emerson Institute, University of South Alabama, Mobile, Alabama; Clark, *History of Education in Alabama*, 280; American Missionary Association, *Catalog of the Teachers*, 7–8.
25 For the role of poverty on enrollment, see "Opening of Schools: Emerson Institute, Mobile, Ala.," *American Missionary* 35 (November 1881), 332–33, VF: Emerson Institute, University of South Alabama, Mobile, Alabama; American Missionary Association, *Catalog of the Teachers*, 7–8.
26 September 18, 1878, Meeting Minutes; Mobile County City Directories, 1878–90, Mobile Municipal Archives, Mobile, Alabama.
27 Records of the Board of School Commissioners for Mobile County, Minutes, 1871–87, MCPSS; Mobile City Directories, 1879–90, Mobile Municipal Archives, Mobile, Alabama; Michael Fitzgerald, *Urban Emancipation: Popular Politics in Reconstruction Mobile, 1860–1890* (Baton Rouge, 2002), 264–65; American Missionary Association, *Catalog of the Teachers*, 6–9, 24–28; Davis-Horton, *The Avenue*, 235.

28 J. D. Smith to M. E. Strieby, September 18, 1877, reel 6, AMA Archives-Alabama, ACT.
29 National Council of the Congregational Churches of the United States, *The Congregational Yearbook, 1884* (Boston, 1884), 17; Boston University, *Historical Register of Boston University, Fifth Decennial Issue, 1869–1911* (Boston, 1911), 68.
30 W. Aymar Caldwell to M. E. Strieby, May 31, 1878, reel 6, AMA Archives-Alabama, ARC.
31 William H. Ash, "The Church and the Literary Club," *American Missionary* 32 (July 1878): 213, VF: Emerson Institute, University of South Alabama, Mobile, Alabama; Elizabeth McHenry, *Forgotten Readers: Recovering the Lost History of African American Literary Societies* (Durham, NC, 2002), 141–42; William H. Ash to M. E. Strieby, February 26, 1878; and William H. Ash to M. E. Strieby, March 13, 1878, both in reel 6, AMA Archives, Alabama, ARC.
32 William H. Ash to C. L. Woodward, June 10, 1878; and B. F. Koons to M. E. Strieby, April 13, 1878, both in reel 6, AMA Archives, Alabama; National Council of the Congregational Churches of the United States, *Congregational Yearbook, 1884*, 17.
33 W. Aymar Caldwell et al. to George Harris, June 18, 1878, reel 6, AMA Archives-Alabama, ARC. For other petitions, see Isaac Goddard et al. to M. E. Strieby, June 18, 1878; R. W. Jammitte to Pastor, June 25, 1878; Congregational Church to M. E. Strieby, June 1878; Marten Gladen et al. to M. E. Strieby, July 15, 1878; and A. F. Owens et al. to M. E. Strieby, July 17, 1878, all in reel 6, AMA Archives, Alabama.
34 Caldwell et al. to Harris, June 18, 1878; W. Aymar Caldwell to M. E. Strieby, July 10, 1878, reel 6, AMA Archives, Alabama, ARC.
35 Mobile City Directories, 1888–90, Mobile Municipal Archives, Mobile, Alabama; Davis-Horton, *The Avenue*, 24–25.
36 Davis-Horton, *The Avenue*, 39.
37 Ibid.

Index

Printed by Printforce, United Kingdom